Understanding the SAP Logistics Information System

SAP PRESS

SAP PRESS is issued by
Bernhard Hochlehnert, SAP AG

SAP PRESS is a joint initiative of SAP and Galileo Press. The know-how offered by SAP specialists combined with the expertise of the publishing house Galileo Press offers the reader expert books in the field. SAP PRESS features first-hand information and expert advice, and provides useful skills for professional decision-making.

SAP PRESS offers a variety of books on technical and business related topics for the SAP user. For further information, please visit our website: *www.sap-press.com*.

Martin Murray

Understanding the SAP Logistics Information System

Galileo Press

Bonn • Boston

ISBN 1-59229-108-2
ISBN 13 978-1-59229-108-3

1st edition 2007

Editor Jawahara Saidullah
Copy Editor Nancy Etscovitz, UCG, Inc., Boston, MA
Cover Design Silke Braun
Layout Design Vera Brauner
Production Steffi Ehrentraut
Typesetting SatzPro, Krefeld
Printed and bound in Germany

Contents at a Glance

Contents

The Logistics Information System (LIS) is a flexible tool within the SAP R/3 system, which facilitates the collection, consolidation, and utilization of supply chain data. The LIS functionality lets companies examine the information from the supply chain and act accordingly.

1 Introduction to the Logistics Information System

This book will describe the importance and functionality of the Logistics Information System as it relates to the SAP R/3 software and a company's supply chain. This book was written using ECC 5.0, but it is applicable to all previous R/3 versions supported by SAP.

The Logistics Information (LIS) System comprises information systems for Purchasing, Inventory Controlling, Sales, Plant Maintenance (PM), Quality Management (QM), and the Shop Floor. In addition, the Logistics Information System incorporates information for Planning and Forecasting, the Early Warning System, and the Logistics Information Library.

This book is intended for readers who work within the supply chain and are involved in the retrieval of data or decision-making based on that data. These areas will include:

- SAP consultants who specialize in one or more of the supply chain modules (MM, PP, SD, PM, etc).
- Internal client SAP modular experts whose job function includes the identification, development and support of supply chain data retrieval.
- Supply chain personnel who work with SAP and whose job function requires data to be retrieved and analyzed from supply chain functionality in SAP, i. e., a data analyst.
- Supply chain managers who require data from SAP which then forms the basis for decision making.

The aim of this book is for you, the reader to gain more knowledge and understanding of the LIS and to be able to use that in your day to day tasks.

1.1 Logistics Information System Overview

When an SAP transaction is executed, the data from each action is recorded. This transaction information is written to the database and is available for retrieval for reporting purposes. When a user wants to view the information in the system, a report can be executed. The LIS provides the user with a selection of standard logistics reports that the user can modify by using user variables. In addition, the LIS offers statistical functions to deliver the supply chain information in the required format.

1.1.1 Definition of Logistics and the Supply Chain

Logistics is the management of business operations, including the acquisition, storage, transportation, and delivery of goods along the supply chain. The *supply chain* is a network of retailers, distributors, transporters, storage facilities, and suppliers that participate in the sale, delivery, and production of a product.

1.1.2 LIS and the Supply Chain

Within the supply chain, there are three distinct flows: the material flow, the information flow, and the financial flow. These are described below:

- **Material Flow**
  This describes the movement of materials from the vendor to the company and then to the customer
- **Information Flow**
  This includes the flow of the information within the logistics functionality
- **Financial Flow**
  This includes the flow of financial information that is recorded in the logistics functionality

You can use the Logistics Information System to analyze and report on the data from the supply chain transactions. Companies are working with their customers and suppliers and sharing information in order to give a complete picture of their supply chains. This is because they realize that the greater the improvement in supply chain visibility they can achieve, the greater a competitive advantage they can secure.

1.1.3 Benefits of Supply Chain Visibility

Before the widespread implementation of Enterprise Resource Planning (ERP) systems in the 1990s, companies didn't invest in supply chain software because it was generally expensive and the results did not justify the expenditure. Since then, the adoption of Enterprise Resource Planning (ERP) systems has allowed companies to actively monitor aspects of their supply chains that were previously unavailable.

For companies today, the ability to provide customers with goods at the right time and at the right price is critical. To achieve this, a company must be able to monitor goods through each step of the supply chain—from raw material at the vendor to finished goods delivered to the customer.

Companies concerned about the supply chain, such as retail companies, are focused on reducing inventory in the warehouse, increasing the number of inventory turns, minimizing delivery times to the customer, reducing costs, and ultimately improving profit.

Wal-Mart is a great example of a company that has been proactive in managing its supply chain. It uses the information it gathers from its logistics transactions to plan additional distribution centers, as well as shares the information with its vendors to ensure that finished goods are in stock when stores need to pull on that inventory. Mike Troy, reporting in *DSN Retailing Today*, says, "The heart of Wal-Mart's efforts to gain market share across a broad range of categories continues to be its attitude toward supply chain management ... shorter lead times mean less safety stock has to be kept on hand, and if out-of-stock situations do arise, they can be resolved more quickly."

Companies like Wal-Mart can forecast demand and supply more accurately using supply chain information that is reported using a tool like the SAP LIS. This information allows a company to plan production around its customer demands, rather than around the company's production capabilities.

The main benefits from using supply chain information to make business decisions are improved performance in delivering on time and in full, lower inventory levels, and a better responsiveness to unforeseen events. These unforeseen events can include machine failures, staff absences, delivery delays, receipt of wrong or faulty goods, missing goods, urgent customer orders, and human error. The other benefits include the following:

- **Improved Customer Service**
  This leads to increased responsiveness to order tracking for customers.

- **Improved Planning**
  This includes improved scheduling capabilities.
- **Improved Cost Reduction**
  Electronic Data Interchange (EDI) and electronically sent orders reduce costs.
- **Improved Decision-Making**
  There is visibility to real-time information via LIS.

1.1.4 Best Practices in Supply Chain Visibility

In his 2001 paper entitled *Business Benefits of Supply Chain Connectivity*, Geoffrey E. Bock states that there are three best practices for the supply chain, "mandating complete connectivity, creating a comprehensive plan, and managing by metrics."

Mandating complete connectivity can be achieved only when the company has good working relationships with its vendors based on trust. Vendors should be encouraged to participate in a buying company's plans for visibility across the supply chain. Selling the benefits to vendors where the relationship is good usually produces favorable results; however, there is always the case where the vendors are willing to do whatever a buying company requires in order to remain as a vendor to that company. This occurs most frequently with large global retailers, who impose compliance rather than encourage it, for instance, Wal-Mart in the USA, Carrefour SA in France, Metro AG in Germany, and Tesco in the UK.

Comprehensive plans for the supply chain must include how a company is to achieve the visibility it requires. To ensure total visibility, a company must make plans that include how to bring their vendors up to the satisfactory technological level to provide relevant real-time information. In addition, the company must plan for what level of organization is required to maintain the information links to the vendors and to maintain the information within the SAP system.

Supply chain data is the result of the transactions within the supply chain. The data from these transactions provides those who control the supply chain with the information necessary to plan production against customer demands. It is best practice to develop a set of flexible reports within the LIS system in order to display the information in the format required that would allow decisions to be made.

1.2 Components of the Logistics Information System

As described in this chapter's introduction, the LIS comprises individual information systems for Sales, Purchasing, Inventory Controlling, PM, QM, and the Shop Floor. There is one additional information system that can be included as part of the LIS if the client implements the related components—the Retail Information System (RIS) for clients who have implemented SAP Retail. In the following sections, we will briefly describe the individual information systems of the main components of the LIS.

1.2.1 Sales Information System

The Sales Information System (SIS) is made up of six information structures, which will be described in more detail in later chapters. Briefly, the structures include the following:

- **Customer (S001)**
  Analysis performed directly using customer information
- **Sales Office (S002)**
  Allows analysis at the sales office level
- **Sales Organization (S003)**
  Allows analysis at the sales organization level
- **Material (S004)**
  Analysis can be performed directly for a material
- **Shipping Point (S005)**
  Analysis can be performed directly for a shipping point
- **Sales Employee (S006)**
  Used for data required for employees, e.g., commission

1.2.2 Purchasing Information System (PURCHIS)

The Purchasing Information System consists of four information structures, which will be described in more detail in later chapters. The information structures include the following:

- **Purchasing Group (S011)**
  Allows analysis at the purchasing group level
- **Purchasing (S012)**
  Contains analysis for the vendor, material, and material group

- **Vendor Evaluation (S013)**
  Triggered by purchase orders and goods receipt
- **Subsequent Settlement (S015)**
  Triggered by an invoice receipt or a subsequent settlement

1.2.3 Inventory Controlling Infomation System

The Inventory Controlling Information System (INVCO) comprises seven information structures for Inventory Management (IM) and two information structures for SAP Warehouse Management (WM). All of these structures will be described in more detail in later chapters. The information structures include the following:

- **Movements (S031)**
  Includes material movement data involving current valuated stock and vendor consignment stock, and is updated monthly
- **Stocks (S032)**
  For each goods movement, the current valuated and vendor consignment stocks are updated
- **Individual Movement Records (S033)**
  Based on the S031, but updated daily
- **Batch Movements (S034)**
  Includes all movements recorded at the batch level
- **Stocks, as Related to Batches (S035)**
  Similar to the S032 information, but includes information on batches
- **Planning (S039)**
  Used for flexible planning and contains no data unless the RMCBS039 report is run
- **Stock/Requirements Analysis (S094)**
  Includes all data for the current stock and requirements
- **WM Stock Putaway/Removal (S090)**
  Contains data for the movements of stock putaway and removal
- **WM Quantity Flow (S091)**
  Contains data for the material flow between locations

1.2.4 Plant Maintenance Information System

The Plant Maintenance Information System (PM-IS) uses eight information structures, which are:

- **Location and Planning Group (S061)**
  Includes key figures for processing days, activities, damage, and downtime
- **Object Class and Manufacturer (S062)**
  Includes key figures for processing days, activities, and breakdown
- **Single Object-Damage Analysis (S063)**
  Includes damage and causes of damage
- **Object Statistics (S065)**
  Includes costing information
- **Breakdown Analysis (S070)**
  Includes time to repair and time between repairs
- **Vehicle Consumption (S114)**
  Includes vehicle consumption data, costs per route, operating hours, and costs per hour
- **Cost Analysis (S115)**
  Includes planned and unplanned costs
- **Customer Analysis (S116)**
  Includes processing days, damage, and causes of damages

1.2.5 Quality Management Information System

The Quality Management Information System (QM-IS) has three information structures for Inspection Lots, three for Quality Notifications, and three for QM Problems and Errors. Let's examine them below:

Inspection Lot Information Structures

The structures are briefly looked at below:

- **Vendor (S068)**
  Contains aggregated data from inspection lot and usage decision
- **Material (S069)**
  Based on S068, also contains aggregated data from inspection lot and usage decisions
- **Customer (S104)**
  Based on S068, also contains aggregated data from inspection lot and usage decisions

Quality Notification Information Structures

Let's take a look at these structures now:

- **Vendor (S098)**
  Contains the aggregated data from the quality notifications
- **Material (S097)**
  Based on the S098 structure, also contains the aggregated data from the quality notifications
- **Customer (S099)**
  Based on S098 structure, also contains the aggregated data from the quality notifications

QM Problems/Errors Information Structures

Let's take a quick look at these below:

- **Vendor (S102)**
  Contains the aggregated data from the quality notifications at the problem level
- **Material (S100)**
  Based on S102 structure, also contains the aggregated data from the quality notifications at the problem level
- **Customer (S103)**
  Based on S102 structure, also contains the aggregated data from the quality notifications at the problem level

1.2.6 Shop Floor Information System

In the Shop Floor Information System, there are a number of information structures. There are four information structures for Production Orders, one information structure for Kanban, two for all Orders (Process and Production), and two for Run Schedule Headers (used in Repetitive Manufacturing). Now let's take a closer look:

Production Order Information Structures

Let's take a quick look at these below:

- **Production Order (S021)**
  Contains the material data for the line item on an order

- **Operation (S022)**
  Contains the operation data from a production order
- **Material (S023)**
  Contains the aggregated data for materials at the order level
- **Work Center (S024)**
  Contains the total records for work center for the order level

Kanban Information Structure

The Kanban Information Structure (S029) contains the data for Kanban transactions.

Order Information Structures

Let's take a look at these information structures below:

- **Material Usage (S026)**
  Contains the data for the material usage of orders
- **Product Cost (S027)**
  Contains the data for production and process orders, SAP updates (both planned and actual), and costs for the product costs

Run Schedule Header Information Structures

Here is a brief look at these information structures:

- **Run Schedule Header (S025)**
  Contains the goods receipt statistics for repetitive manufacturing
- **Reporting Point Statistics (S028)**
  Provides the reporting point statistics from the Run Schedule Header

1.3 Summary

This chapter described the importance of the supply chain for companies competing in today's global market. Large numbers of companies have implemented SAP to integrate the various aspects of their enterprises. The fully integrated system gives these companies the ability to use the Logistics Information System to provide relevant data on their supply chain. With this newfound ability, companies can focus on reducing inventory in the warehouse and minimizing delivery times to the customer, thereby improving customer satisfaction, reducing costs, and ultimately increasing profit.

In your position as an SAP consultant, whether you are internal or external, you might be asked to advise the client on information retrieval. From my experience as a consultant on many supply chain projects, I have been asked about the reporting capabilities of the LIS. This book will help you to clearly counsel your client about the LIS as well, as to develop custom LIS evaluations, rather than on costly and static ABAP programs.

In the upcoming chapters, this book will focus on the functionality and configuration of the various aspects of the LIS and its integration with other SAP modules.

Information structures in the LIS comprises groups of key fields used for collecting data from the various logistics transactions. These structures are either standard or user-defined and form the basis of the standard analyses and planning functions.

2 Information Structures

The information structure is defined to allow the SAP modules to deposit information in a format that lets the user extract relevant data in a way that is useful for analysis and reporting. There are two types of information structures in the LIS: the standard information structures that are predefined in SAP and the user-defined structures that can be created by the user.

2.1 Standard Information Structures

Information structures in the LIS are files that contain specific data from the relevant logistics transactions, that is, a purchasing information structure will contain information from the purchase order transactions.

Chapter 1 gave you a list of the standard information structures, with a brief description of the structure and the information structure name. The standard information structures defined in SAP are indicated by a four-character name, which lies in the range between S000 and S500. For instance, the Purchasing Group information structure has the name S011. The information structure is defined as three distinct elements, which are listed below:

- Characteristics
- Key figures
- Period definition

These elements are described in more detail in the following sections.

2.1.1 Characteristics

The information structure is defined by *characteristics*. A characteristic associated with an information structure is an item for which information is collected. An information structure can have up to nine characteristics defined. For example, in Purchasing Group (S011), the characteristics are defined as follows:

- Purchasing Organization
- Purchasing Group
- Vendor

The characteristics for the Purchasing Group information structure are shown in Figure 2.1.

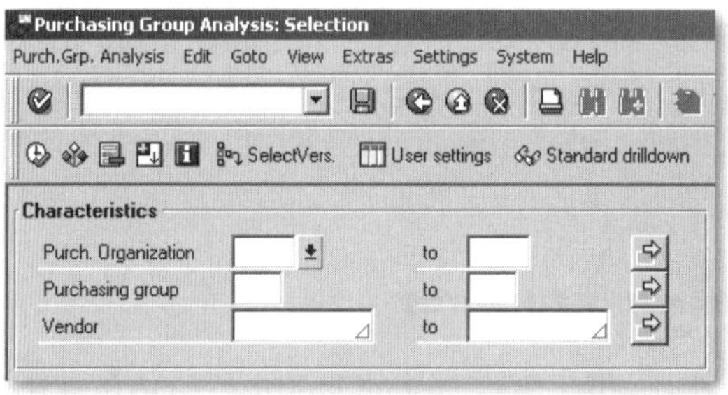

Figure 2.1 Characteristics for Purchasing Group Information Structure (S011)

The characteristics that are defined for an information structure act as the key fields for the collection data table. They are also used to extract data from the structure based on user requirements. For instance, in Figure 2.1, for the Purchasing Group information structure (S011), users can select a Purchasing Organization range, a Purchasing Group range, and a Vendor range to retrieve data from the information structure.

2.1.2 Key Figures

The *key figures* refer to the values that are associated with the characteristics. For example, for the Purchasing Group information structure (S011), the key figures refer to the data collected for the three characteristics: Purchase Organization, Purchase Group, and Vendor. The key figures would include invoice amounts, number of purchase orders, purchase order values, etc.

To show the key figures for the Purchasing Group information structure (S011), the Transaction MCE1 can be executed as shown in Figure 2.2. With the SAP ERP Central Component (ECC) 5.0 system, this transaction can also be reached by using the navigation path: **SAP Menu • Logistics • Logistics Controlling • LIS • Standard Analyses • Purchasing • Purchasing Group**.

If your client or company is not using SAP ECC 5.0, but are using a different version of SAP, please note that the transaction paths and screen displays on your system may vary slightly from the screenshots displayed in this book.

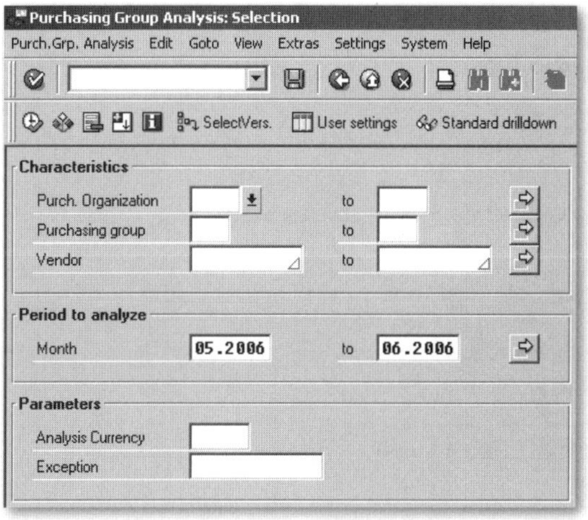

Figure 2.2 Selection Screen for Standard Analysis of Purchasing Group Information Structure (S011)

When the transaction is executed, the data is retrieved from the information structure for the Purchasing Group and for the period range selected. The report shows the information for the characteristics defined in the selection.

In Figure 2.3, the information retrieved for the selection made in Transaction MCE1 shows values for key figures defined in the Purchasing Group information structure, that is, Purchase Order Value, Invoice Amount, and Number of Purchase Orders.

To display all of the key fields for the information structure, the analyst can select this option when the report display is at the characteristics/total line only. At this level, the user can opt to select all key figures from the menu path as shown in Figure 2.3: **Extras • All Key Figures**. Once this option is selected from the top menu, all of the key figures that are associated with the information structure are displayed in Figure 2.4.

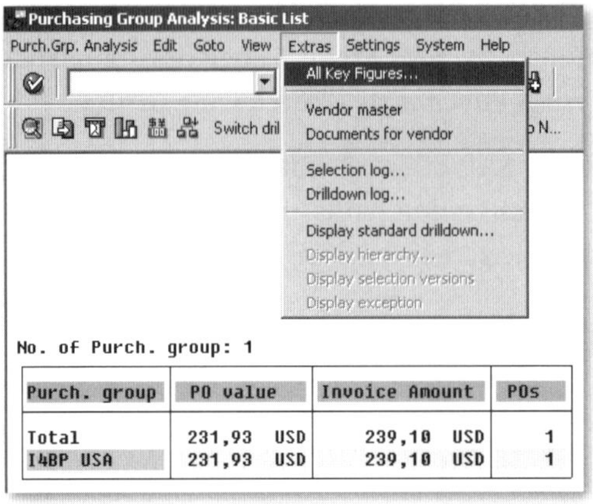

Figure 2.3 Key Figures for Purchasing Group Information Structure (S011)

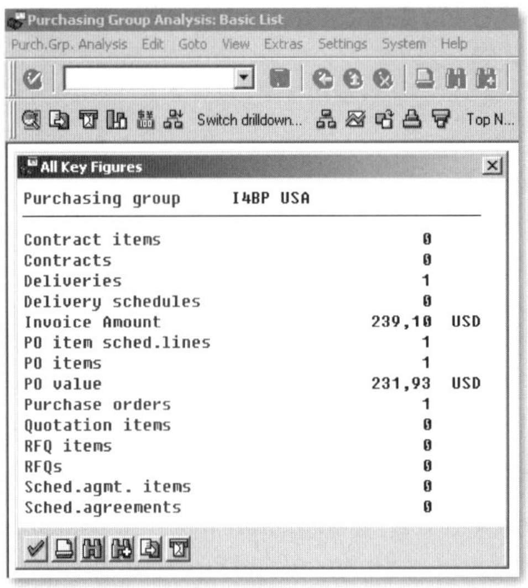

Figure 2.4 Key Figures Associated with Purchasing Group Information Structure (S011)

2.1.3 Period Definition

Data is collected and displayed for a number of specific periodic ranges. The information structure determines that the key figure data is accumulated on either a daily, weekly, monthly, or fiscal yearly basis.

For instance, as we saw in Figure 2.2, the period identified for the Purchasing Group information structure (S011) is a month, whereas the period identified for the Kanban information structure (S029) is daily, which is shown in Figure 2.5.

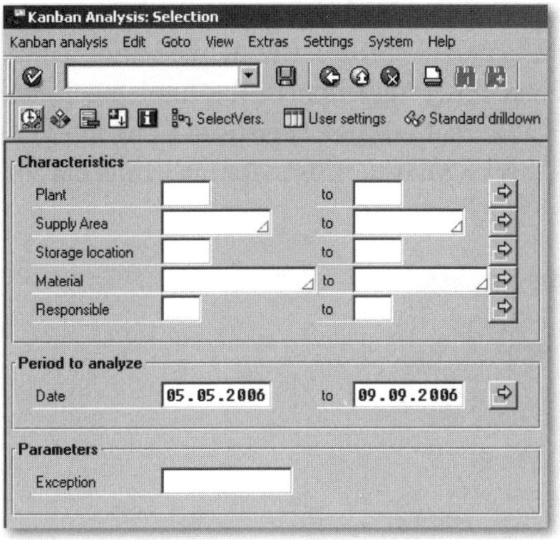

Figure 2.5 Daily Period Definition for Kanban Information Structure (S029)

This section explained the standard information structures supplied by SAP. Now you can see how you can design information structures in such a way as to enable you to customize how data is recorded and reported.

2.2 User-Defined Information Structures

In addition to the standard information structures, users can define their own structures to allow for a collection of specific characteristic data. This flexibility allows users who require specific data, which is not collected by the standard information structures, to design their own information structures without resorting to custom ABAP programming.

2.2.1 Create a User-Defined Information Structure

In preparing to create an information structure, complete analysis should be performed to identify the fields that are suitable for data collection and the areas where those fields are located. Creating user-defined information structures can be time-consuming and requires significant testing.

Once the design of the information structure has been decided and agreed upon, the structure can be created. User-defined information structures should be given a name within the range S500-S999.

User-defined information structures are created and maintained in the SAP IMG configuration area. The transaction to create a user-defined information structure is MC21. You can access this transaction in the Implementation Guide (IMG) by using the navigation path: **IMG • Logistics—General • LIS • Data Basis • Information Structures • Maintain User-Defined Information Structures**.

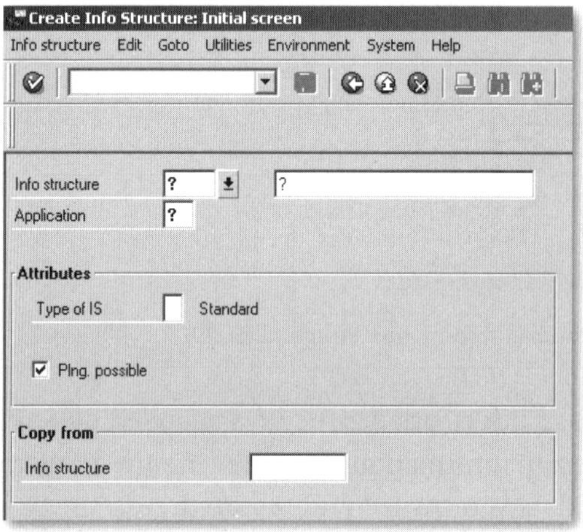

Figure 2.6 Initial Screen for Entering User-Defined Information Structure, Transaction MC21

Figure 2.6 shows the initial screen of MC21 where the name and description of the information structure should be entered. These fields will be discussed now:

- **Information Structure Name**
  On this **Info structure** initial screen, you can enter the name for the user-defined information structure, which, as mentioned previously, should be within the S500–S999 range.
- **Information Structure Description**
  The description for the user-defined information structure, seen to the right of **Info structure**, can be up to 30 characters in length.
- **Application**
  The **Application** field refers to the area of the LIS within which the information structure lies. This field determines what characteristics are available further into the transaction. The user configuring this information structure has a number of application areas to select from. Choosing the **F4** key or the selection arrow displays a list of the available application areas, as shown in Figure 2.7.

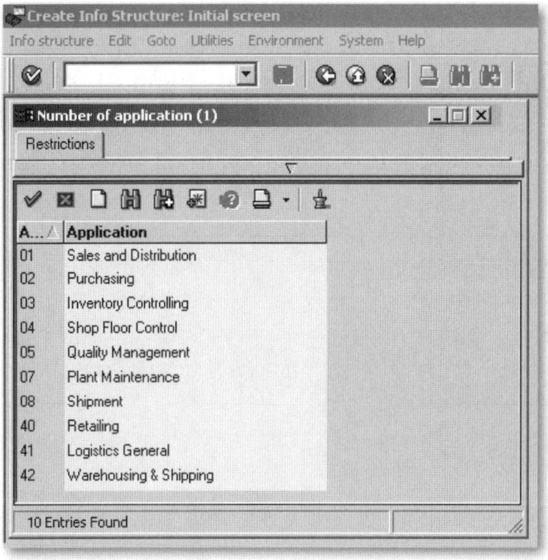

Figure 2.7 Available Application Areas for User-Defined Information Structures

The analyst who designs the new user-defined information structure may feel that the standard applications do not allow access to all of the fields that the new information structure requires. Viewing data from various areas of the supply chain is often required, for example, information for sales management will often consist of production or inventory data. Therefore, the analyst can take this opportunity to define a new application, using configuration that is cross application, i.e., that includes data from two or more modular areas, PM and MM for instance.

The Transaction OMOA allows the analyst to define additional new applications, as shown in Figure 2.8. The transaction can be accessed using the navigation path: **IMG • Logistics—General • LIS • Data Basis • Applications • Maintain User-Defined Applications.**

The designer can select any number of standard application areas from which to create the new application. In Figure 2.8, the new application has been created using the **Inventory, Purchasing,** and **Production** attributes. Therefore, any new information structures created with the new application will be able to access fields from these application areas.

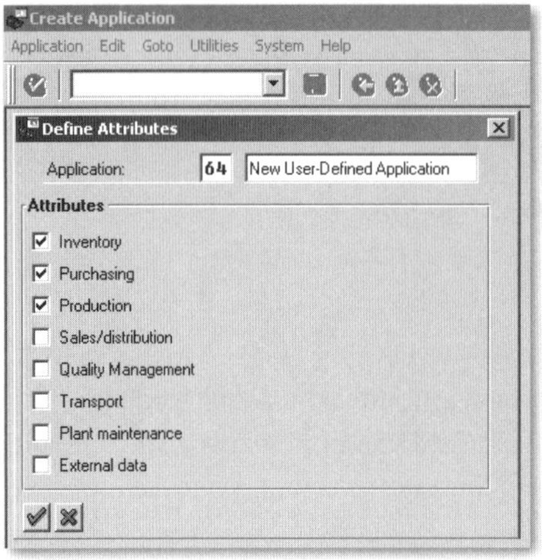

Figure 2.8 Addition of New User-Defined Application, Transaction OMOA

2.2.2 Types of Information Structures

The type of information structure is an important attribute; because once it is defined it cannot be changed. So it is vital that the person designing the information structure understand the difference between the various types, which are described next:

- **Standard Type**
  This type is used for the standard information structures that are predefined in SAP, i.e., the Purchasing Group information structure (S011). The standard type of information structure has the normal period structures—daily, weekly, monthly, and yearly. The standard type is identified with a blank in the type field.
- **Without Period Type**
  This type is used to ensure that the most current data is used. Without any period, current data is all that is available. The letter **C** identifies this type.
- **Without Update Type**
  This type is used for historical data stored in an information structure. If the structure has no update, then the data is never overwritten and acts like an archive table. This is useful when historical data needs to be referenced. The letter **D** identifies this type.
- **Standard with Stock Values Type**
  This type is similar to a standard type, but allows the periodic update of stock values, for example, at the end of a fiscal period. The letter **E** identifies this type.

- **Transfer to BW Type**
  This type is used solely to move information to the SAP Business Information Warehouse (SAP BW) system. These information structures cannot be used for analysis. More information on these particular information structures and SAP BW can be found in later chapters. The letter **T** identifies this type.

Planning Possible Indicator

The planning possible indicator (**Plng. possible** checkbox), seen in Figure 2.9, should be used if the information structure is used in flexible planning. This indicator cannot be changed after the information structure has been created; therefore, the designer of the structure should consider the requirement of the data in flexible planning during the initial design of the structure.

Once the initial naming and descriptions are entered for the new information structure, the next step is to add the characteristics and the key fields. Figure 2.9 shows the basic header information for the user-defined information structure entered previously and the two areas that need to be created next, namely, the characteristics and the key fields.

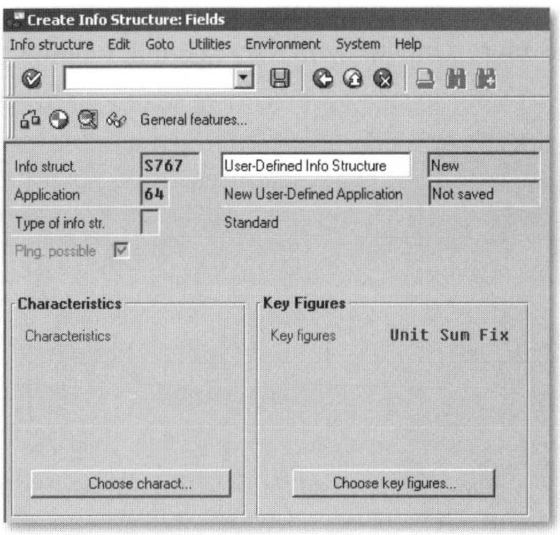

Figure 2.9 Header Data Entered for User-Defined Information Structure

To choose the characteristics associated with this information structure, you should click on the **Choose characteristics** button. This will display a selection of field catalogs and a list of available characteristics. This is shown in

Figure 2.10 where the chosen field catalog **Material (Purchasing)** has five **Field catalog fields** available (characteristics) from which to choose.

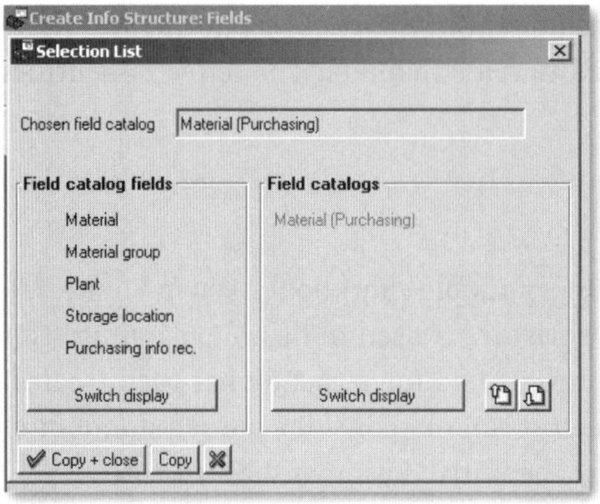

Figure 2.10 Field Catalogs and Characteristics Selected for Information Structure

After selecting a characteristic from this catalog, you can select another catalog and copy additional characteristics into the information structure.

The **Switch display** button at the bottom of the **Field catalogs** and **Field catalog fields** areas allows you to convert the display into the technical names that some consultants may be more familiar with. An example of this is shown in Figure 2.11.

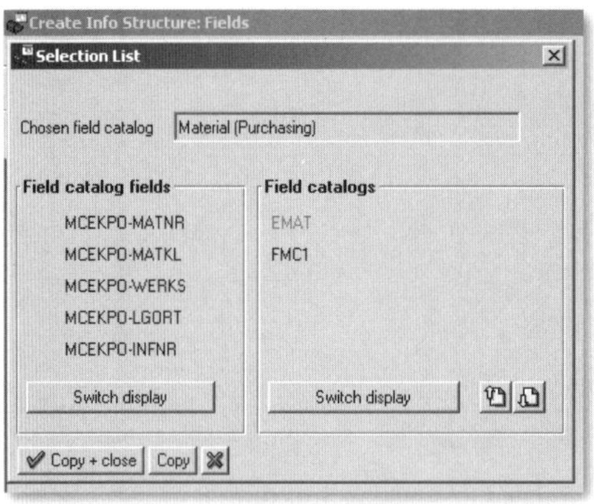

Figure 2.11 Switched Display That Allows Display of Technical Names for Catalogs and Catalog Fields

Once the characteristics for the user-defined information structure have been identified, the key figures for the information structure should be defined as well. Select the key figures in the same way as you did the characteristics. The fields that are selected from the available field catalogs and copied into the information structure are displayed in Figure 2.12.

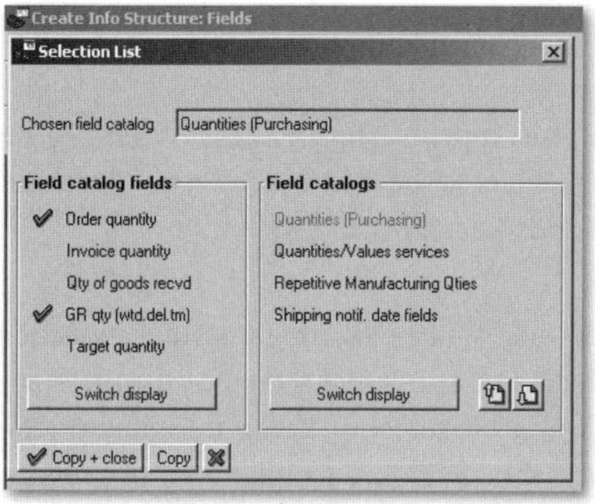

Figure 2.12 Selection of Key Figures for User-Defined Information Structure

Once the characteristics and the key figures are defined for the new information structure, the summary screen will be displayed, as shown in Figure 2.13. There are three fields to note next to the key figure selected for the structure. Let's take a closer look at these fields.

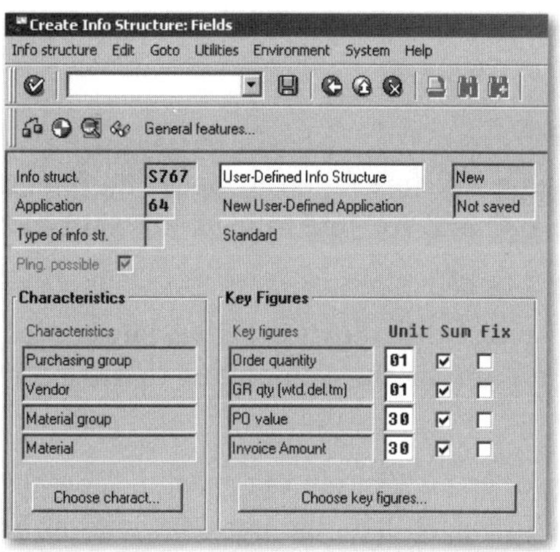

Figure 2.13 Selected Characteristics and Key Figures for User-Defined Information Structure

- **Unit Field**
  The **Unit** field shows what unit the key field will be updated in. For example in Figure 2.13, the key figure **Order quantity** will be updated in Unit

01, which is the base unit of measure. It could have been updated in a different unit of measure if required. The **PO value** field is updated in Unit 30, which is the local currency, but a different currency selection could have been made, such as the Purchase Order currency or the statistical currency.

- **Sum Indicator**
  The **Sum** indicator can be set if it is appropriate for the key field to be accumulated. Most fields will be able to be combined, e.g., Purchase Order Value, Invoice Amount, Goods Receipt Quantity, etc.
- **Fix Indicator for Planning**
  The **Fix** indicator can be selected only if the Planning Possible indicator (i.e., **Plng. possible**) has been selected on the initial screen of the information structure. This indicator should be set only if the designer of the structure wants to fix the values of the key figure for planning purposes.

After the appropriate indicators have been set for the key fields, the information structure should be checked to identify any inconsistencies that would prevent the information structure from being generated.

2.2.3 Generating a User-Defined Information Structure

Once the basic information has been entered into the user-defined information structure, the next task is to generate the structure so it can be used.

Checking the Information Structure

To check the user-defined information structure for errors, select the option from the main menu: **Info structure • Check.** You could also use the **Shift + F7** key, as shown in Figure 2.14.

If any inconsistencies or errors are found with the user-defined information structure, the system will return an error log that you can use to make corrections (see Figure 2.15).

The errors can be simple warnings or errors that must be fixed to allow the information structure to generate. In Figure 2.15, the warnings inform the user that there may be a potential problem if data with different units of measure are loaded into the structure. To prevent this problem from occurring, you can add another characteristic or key figure to ensure that there are no inconsistencies with the data.

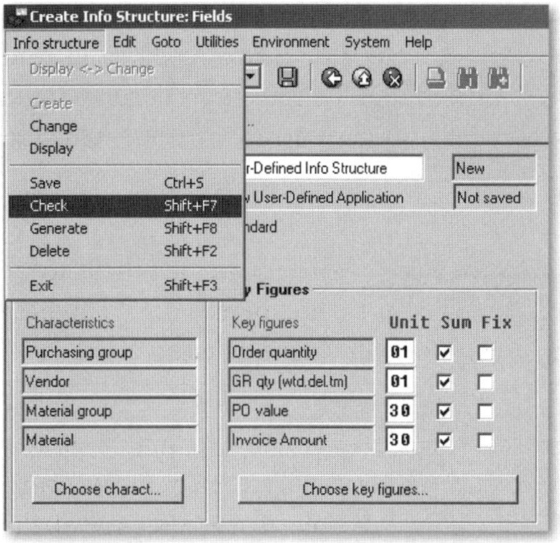

Figure 2.14 Checking Information Structure for Inconsistencies

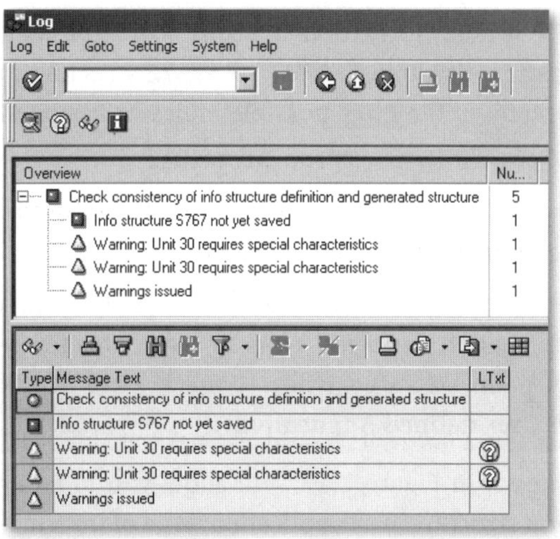

Figure 2.15 Using Error Log to Make Corrections

Generating the Information Structure

After the errors and warnings have been analyzed, you can generate the information structure. You can do this by using the selection from the header menu **Info structure • Generate,** or by using the **Shift+F8** key. After the information structure has been generated, the system produces a log of the generation, as shown in Figure 2.16.

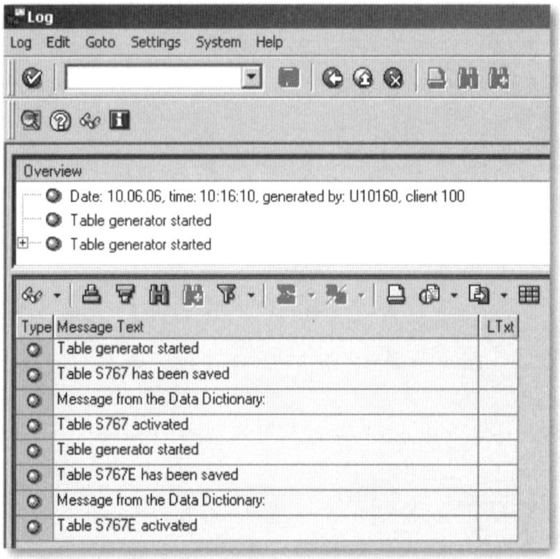

Figure 2.16 Log for Generated User-Defined Information Structure

In Figure 2.16, the log shows that the information structure **S767** has been generated as well as an information structure **S767E**. The **S767E** structure is generated for the planning hierarchy if the **Plng. possible** indicator has been set.

2.2.4 Changing a User-Defined Information Structure

If the information structure needs to be amended, you should use the Transaction MC22 to change the information structure. You can access this transaction by using the navigation path: **IMG • Logistics—General • LIS • Data Basis • Applications • Maintain User-defined Applications.**

The initial change screen, as shown in Figure 2.17, will allow you to enter only the name of the information structure. The application, type of information structure, and planning possible indicator cannot be changed.

The detailed information of the information structure is displayed, as shown in Figure 2.18. The user can change the key fields or the characteristics of the information structure, but can only do so using the fields available via the application, which cannot be changed.

Figure 2.18 also shows the options to review information, such as the technical field information, field documentation, and general features of the information structure.

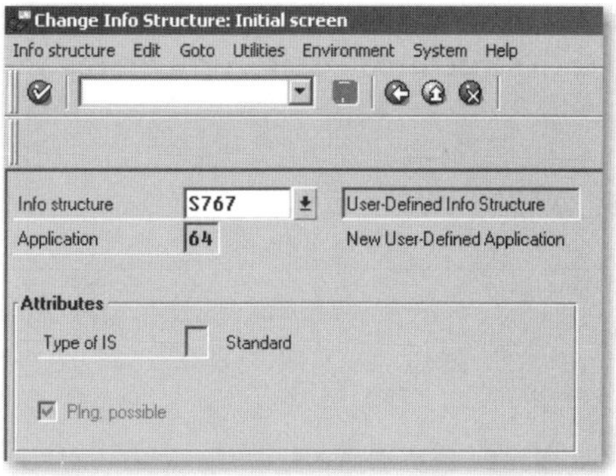

Figure 2.17 Initial Screen for Changing Information Structure, Transaction MC22

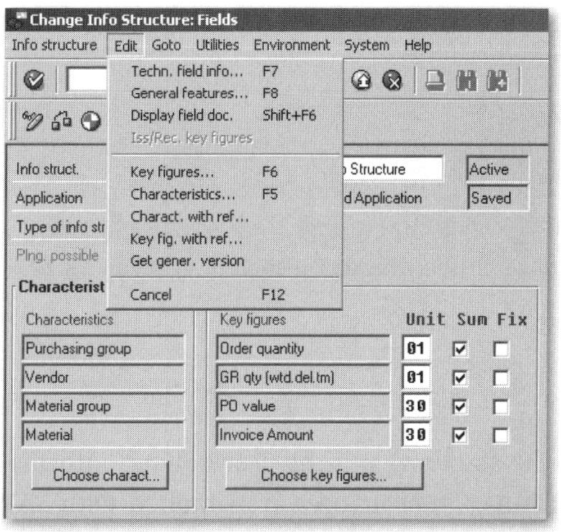

Figure 2.18 Detailed Information of User-Defined Information Structure

2.2.5 Display a User-Defined Information Structure

To display the user-defined information structure, you should use Transaction MC23. You can access this transaction in the IMG by using the navigation path: **IMG • Logistics—General • LIS • Data Basis • Information Structures • Maintain User-Defined Information Structures.**

2.2.6 Delete a User-Defined Information Structure

To delete an information structure, the user must perform this task using the change function, that is, Transaction MC22. This can be accessed in the IMG by using the navigation path: **IMG • Logistics—General • LIS • Data Basis • Information Structures • Maintain User-defined Information Structures**.

Figure 2.19 shows how to delete the information structure by choosing the delete option from the header menu **Info structure • Delete**, or by using the **Shift + F2** key.

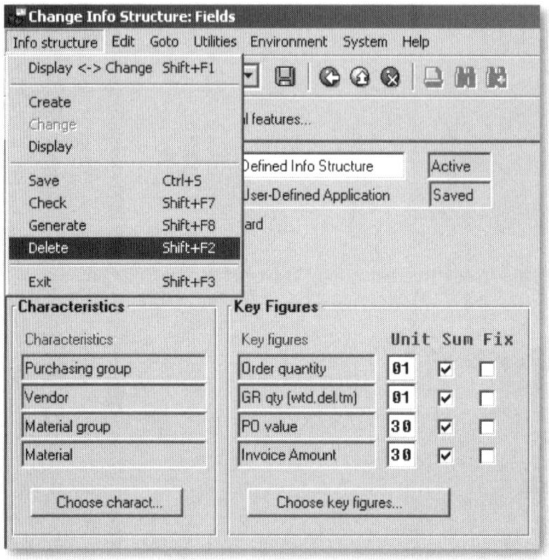

Figure 2.19 Deleting an Information Structure Using Change Function, Transaction MC22

2.3 Summary

In this chapter, I discussed both the standard and the user-defined information structures. The standard information structures are supplied with SAP and can be used with analyses to report on and monitor a wide range of logistics functions. Companies are becoming increasingly more complex in viewing their supply chain, and consequently, may use multiple indicators that require more than standard information structures. To use the flexibility of the LIS, user-defined information structures are created to produce the complex supply chain analyses that companies require. In Chapter 3, the standard analyses, sometimes called basic analyses, will be described in detail.

The Standard Analysis, sometimes called the Basic Analysis, is supplied with SAP to derive a standard analysis from the delivered information structure. The basic analysis lets the user view the data from the information structure using the selection criteria defined in the analysis.

3 Standard Analyses

In Chapter 2, I discussed the standard information structures that are available for the different SAP areas. The basic method to retrieve data from the SAP-defined information structures is via the standard analyses. There are a number of tools that can be used with the standard analysis, such as versions, drilldown, ABC analysis, and classification, that will be explained later on in this chapter and in subsequent chapters.

3.1 Basic Analyses

The SAP system is delivered with standard information structures and basic analyses for these structures. The analyses are predefined and allow any user to quickly run an analysis on a structure with minimum effort. For example, in the Purchasing Information System, there are a number of analyses for the Purchasing information structure (S012) that allow for various reviews of the information of that structure.

For the information structure S012, an analysis of the data can be made by Material, Material Group, or Vendor. For example, in Figure 3.1, the basic analysis is of purchasing values for vendors. The selection criteria are predefined, and any user who enters values for the purchasing organization, vendor, and period to review will instantly receive the analysis of the data, as shown in Figure 3.2. The transaction can be run by using transaction code MCE3, or by using the navigation path: **SAP Menu • Logistics • Logistics Controlling • Logistics Information System • Standard Analyses • Purchasing • Vendor.**

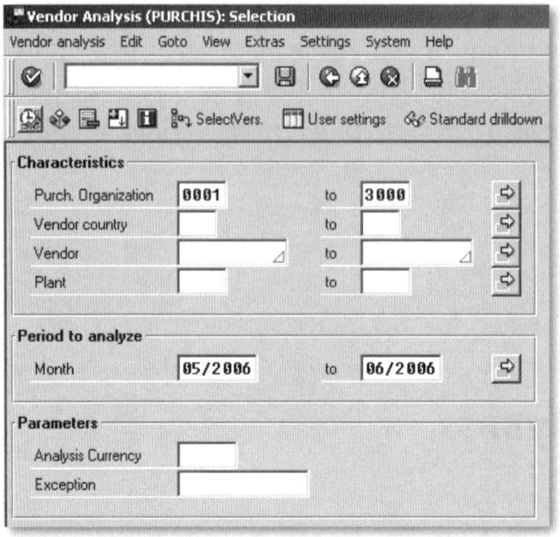

Figure 3.1 Basic Analysis Selection Criteria for Transaction MCE3 (Vendor Analysis of Purchasing Information Structure)

The information in Figure 3.2 is directly derived from the information structure. It shows that for the selected Purchase Organizations during period 05/2006 to 06/2006 there were four vendors with a total purchase order value of $ 5,044.00.

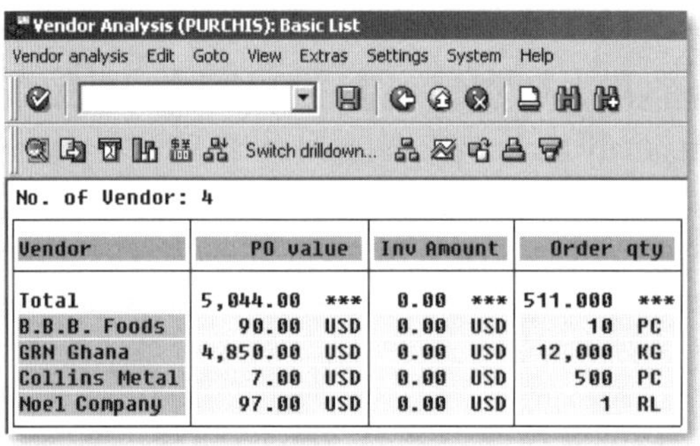

Figure 3.2 Basic Analysis of Data in Information Structure Defined by Selection Criteria Entered, Transaction MCE3

If a user performs the same analysis many times, the analysis selection criteria can be saved so the analysis can be run without the user having to enter the selection data again. This is known as a *selection version*. The analysis can be saved as a selection version after the results of the analysis are returned as shown in Figure 3.3.

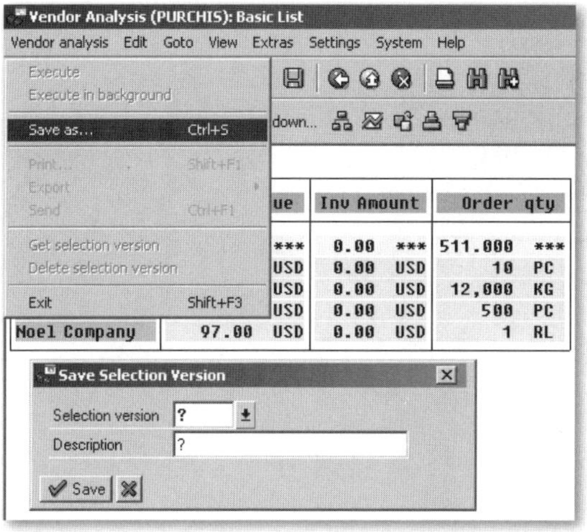

Figure 3.3 Menu Selection to Save Standard Analysis as a Selection Version for Easy User Retrieval

The selection can be saved by selecting the **Ctrl + S** key or by going to the header menu and selecting **Vendor analysis • Save as.** Once the dialog box opens, the selection version can be saved with a six-character version name and a 40-character version description. For a more detailed review of the selection versions, see Chapter 4.

3.2 Standard Analyses for Purchasing

There are a number of standard analyses used in Purchasing that provide analysis of the data in the information structures related to Purchasing: S011, S012, S013, and S015.

3.2.1 Purchasing Group

The standard analysis for purchasing groups derives its data from the information structure, S011. With this standard analysis, the Purchasing Organization, Purchasing Group, and Vendor are the characteristics that can be selected using the period that the user wants to define.

The selection criteria for this analysis are displayed in Figure 3.4. This transaction can be accessed using the transaction code MCE1, or using the navigation path: **SAP Menu • Logistics • Logistics Controlling • Logistics Information System • Standard Analyses • Purchasing • Purchasing Group.**

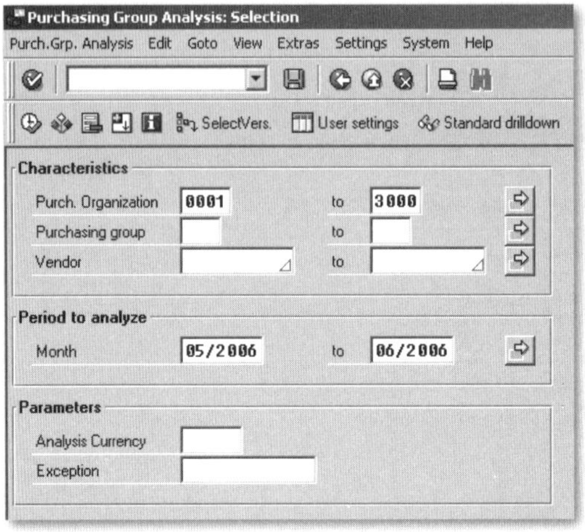

Figure 3.4 Selection Screen for Purchasing Group Standard Analysis, Transaction MCE1

Figure 3.5 shows the number of purchase orders and the purchase order value for the purchasing groups entered, during the period selected, in the selection criteria in Transaction MCE1.

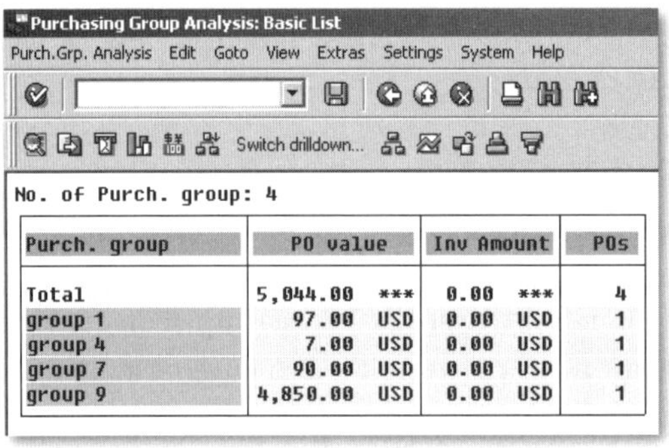

Figure 3.5 Results of Purchasing Group Standard Analysis, Transaction MCE1

3.2.2 Vendor

The standard analysis for vendors derives its data from the information structure S012. With the vendor standard analysis, the information retrieved from the information structure lets users analyze how much business vendors have done with certain purchase organizations, based on the period defined for the analysis.

The selection criteria for this analysis are displayed in Figure 3.6. This transaction can be accessed using transaction code MCE3, or by using the navigation path: **SAP Menu • Logistics • Logistics Controlling • Logistics Information System • Standard Analyses • Purchasing • Vendor.**

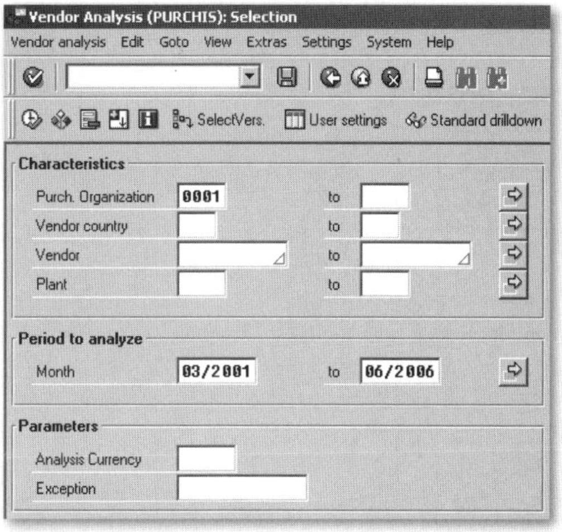

Figure 3.6 Selection Screen for Vendor Standard Analysis, Transaction MCE3

Figure 3.7 shows the one vendor associated with the selected purchasing organization during the period defined in the selection criteria. The results show the purchase order value and quantity of material ordered.

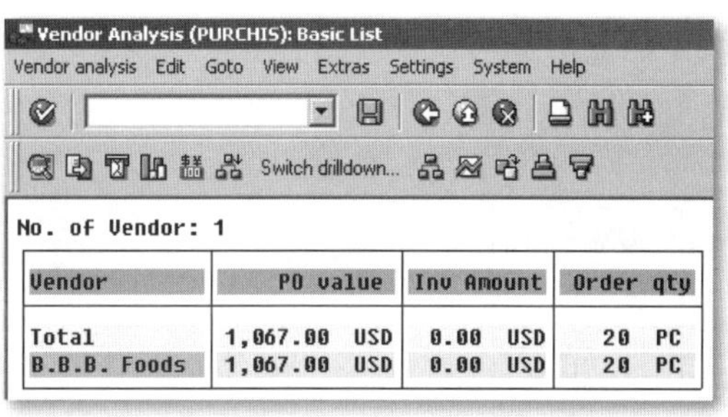

Figure 3.7 Results of Vendor Standard Analysis, Transaction MCE3

3.2.3 Material Group

The standard analysis for material groups also derives its data from the information structure S012. The standard analysis for material groups will report on the purchase order value and quantity of the company's material groups. Selecting a range of purchasing organizations, materials or plants can reduce the data retrieved from the information structure. The results will be based on the period defined for the analysis.

The selection criteria for this analysis can be seen in Figure 3.8. This transaction can be accessed using transaction code MCE5, or using the navigation path: **SAP Menu • Logistics • Logistics Controlling • Logistics Information System • Standard Analyses • Purchasing • Material Group.**

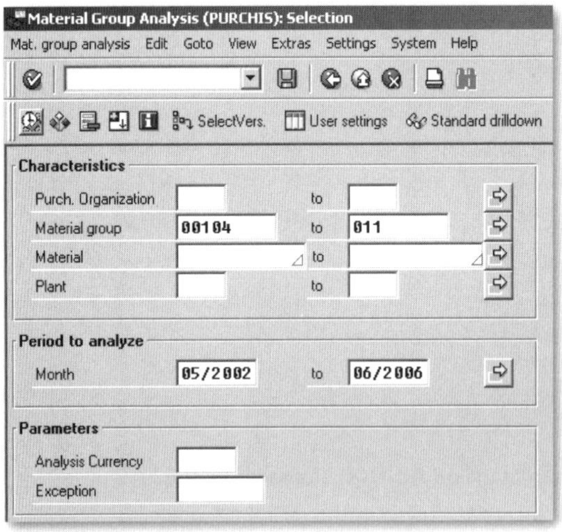

Figure 3.8 Selection Screen and Criteria for Material Group Standard Analysis, Transaction MCE5

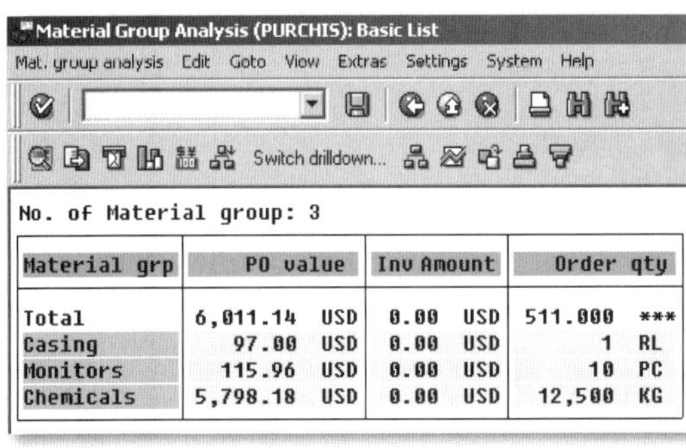

Figure 3.9 Results of Material Group Standard Analysis, Transaction MCE5

The data shown in Figure 3.9 shows the material groups from the selection criteria with the relevant purchase order values and order quantity.

3.2.4 Material

The standard analysis for materials also derives its data from the information structure S012. The standard analysis for materials will report on the purchase order value, good receipt totals, and order quantity of all materials or those from the selection criteria entered. The results will be based on the period defined for the analysis.

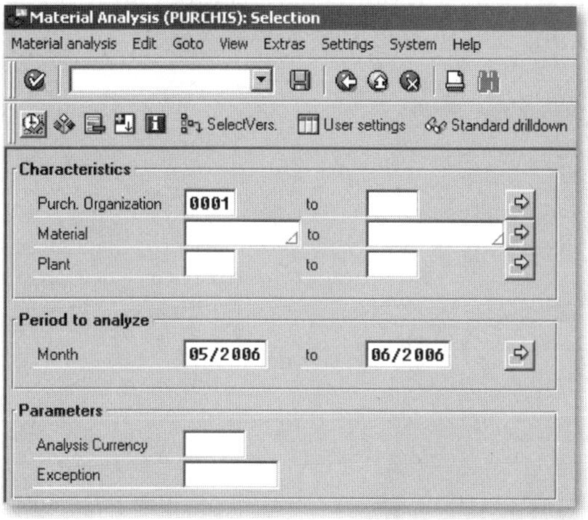

Figure 3.10 Selection Screen for Standard Analysis for Materials Based on Purchasing Information Structure, Transaction MCE7

The selection criteria for this analysis can be seen in Figure 3.10. This transaction can be accessed using Transaction MCE7, or using the navigation path: **SAP Menu • Logistics • Logistics Controlling • Logistics Information System • Standard Analyses • Purchasing • Material.**

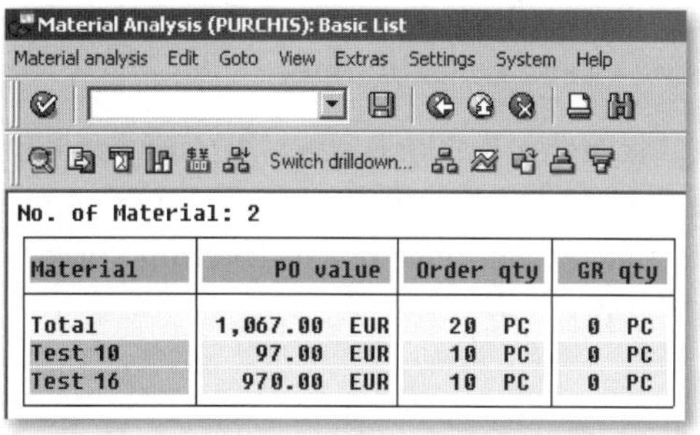

Material	PO value	Order qty	GR qty
Total	1,067.00 EUR	20 PC	0 PC
Test 10	97.00 EUR	10 PC	0 PC
Test 16	970.00 EUR	10 PC	0 PC

Figure 3.11 Results of Material Standard Analysis, Transaction MCE7

The results of the material standard analysis are shown in Figure 3.11. The results show two materials with the relevant purchase order value (**PO value**), order quantity (**Order qty**), and goods receipt quantity (**GR qty**).

3.2.5 Vendor Evaluation

If the client uses the vendor evaluation functionality, then this particular standard analysis can aid in creating data for subjective scoring in the configured vendor evaluation calculations. The standard analysis for vendor evaluation derives its data from the information structure S013.

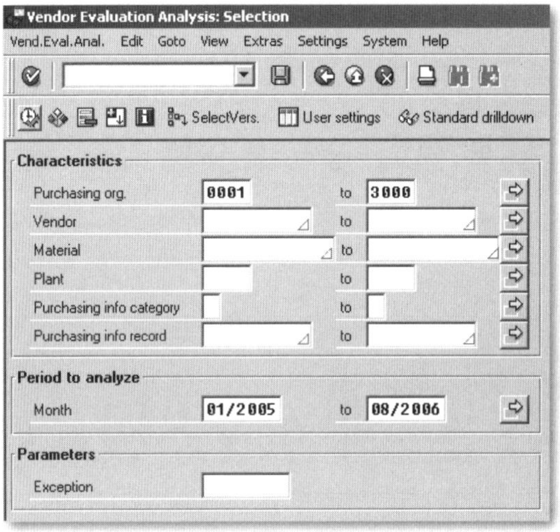

Figure 3.12 Selection Screen for Vendor Evaluation Standard Analysis Transaction ME6H

The selection criteria for this analysis can be seen in Figure 3.12. This transaction can be accessed using Transaction ME6H, or by using the navigation path: **SAP Menu • Logistics • Logistics Controlling • Logistics Information System • Standard Analyses • Purchasing • Vendor Evaluation.**

The results of the vendor evaluation standard analysis show certain percentage results. The results contain the two figures for quality reliability, two figures for on-time delivery, and two figures for shipping instruction correctness. These figures can be seen in Figure 3.13.

3.2.6 Subsequent Settlement

Subsequent settlement is the SAP functionality that allows rebate arrangements with vendors that are paid or settled at arranged dates, for instance, end of a quarter or one per year. The rebates will be based on some business volume, value, quantity, or a point structure. To verify the vendor's calculations, you can use the standard analysis with the S015 information structure.

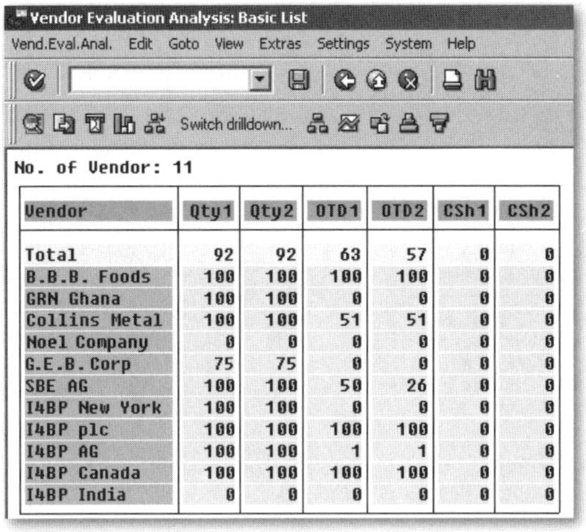

Figure 3.13 Results of Vendor Evaluation Standard Analysis, Transaction ME6H

The selection criteria for the subsequent settlement analysis can be seen in Figure 3.14. This transaction can be accessed using Transaction MCE+, or by using the navigation path: **SAP Menu • Logistics • Logistics Controlling • Logistics Information System • Standard Analyses • Purchasing • Subsequent Settlement.**

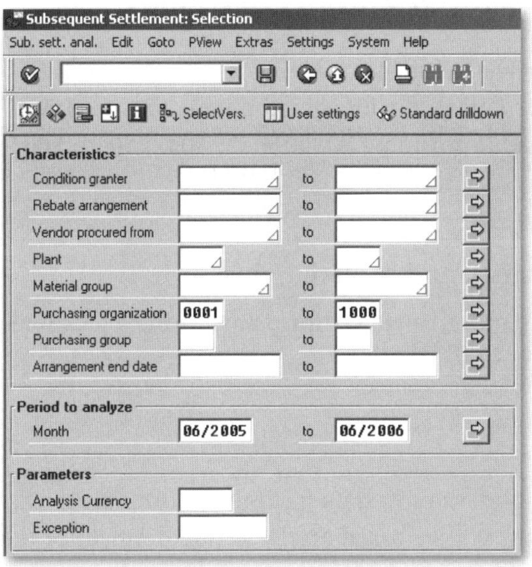

Figure 3.14 Selection Screen for Subsequent Settlement Standard Analysis, Transaction MCE+

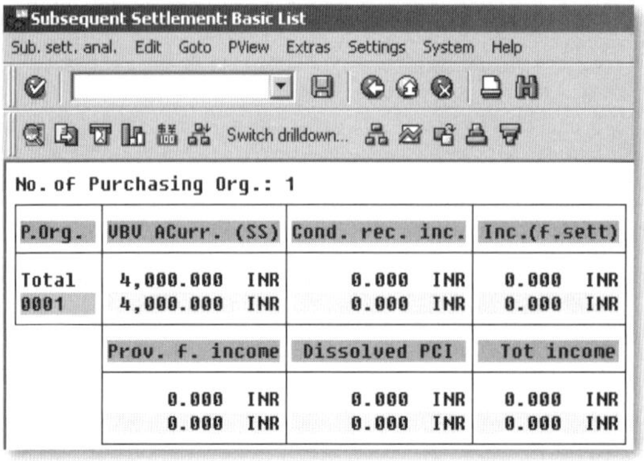

Figure 3.15 Results for Subsequent Settlement Standard Analysis, Transaction MCE+

The results of the subsequent settlement standard analysis show the values from the information structure, as shown in Figure 3.15. The fields shown are the Vendor Business Volume Value for the Condition Record, Income from Condition Record, Income Resulting from Final Settlement, Provision for Anticipated Income, Dissolved Provisions for Income, and Total Income. Now let's proceed to understanding standard analyses for inventory controlling.

3.3 Standard Analyses for Inventory Controlling

There are a number of standard analyses that are used in Inventory Controlling that provide analysis of the data in the information structures for Inventory and Warehouse Management including S031, S032, S033, S034, S035, S039, S090, S091, and S094.

3.3.1 Plant, Storage Location, and Material

This section will examine the standard analyses for plants, storage locations, and materials.

Plant

The standard analysis for a plant derives its data from the information structures S031 and S032. The results will be based on the period defined for the analysis.

The selection criteria for the plant analysis can be seen in Figure 3.16. This transaction can be accessed using transaction code MCBA, or using the navigation path: **SAP Menu • Logistics • Logistics Controlling • Logistics Information System • Standard Analyses • Stocks • Plant.**

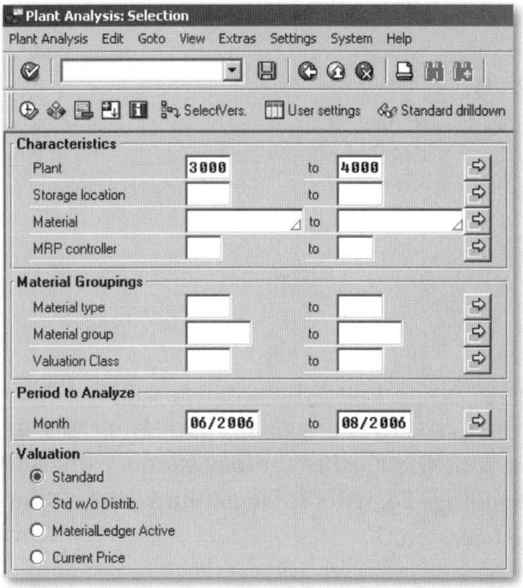

Figure 3.16 Selection Criteria for Standard Analysis for Plant Stock, Transaction MCBA

The results of the plant standard analysis show the values from the information structure, as shown in Figure 3.17.

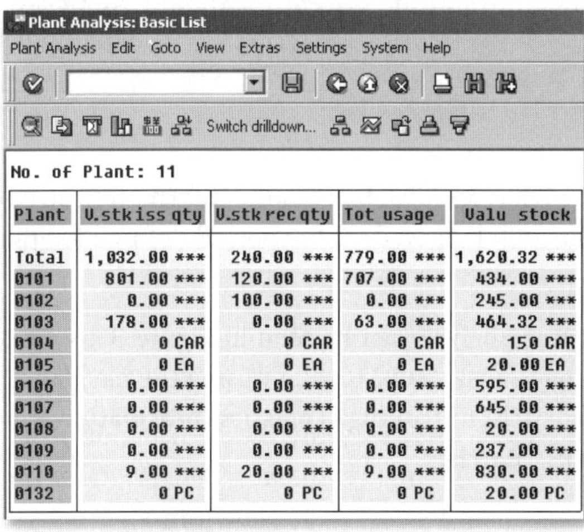

Plant	V.stkiss qty	V.stkrecqty	Tot usage	Valu stock
Total	1,032.00 ***	240.00 ***	779.00 ***	1,620.32 ***
0101	801.00 ***	120.00 ***	707.00 ***	434.00 ***
0102	0.00 ***	100.00 ***	0.00 ***	245.00 ***
0103	178.00 ***	0.00 ***	63.00 ***	464.32 ***
0104	0 CAR	0 CAR	0 CAR	150 CAR
0105	0 EA	0 EA	0 EA	20.00 EA
0106	0.00 ***	0.00 ***	0.00 ***	595.00 ***
0107	0.00 ***	0.00 ***	0.00 ***	645.00 ***
0108	0.00 ***	0.00 ***	0.00 ***	20.00 ***
0109	0.00 ***	0.00 ***	0.00 ***	237.00 ***
0110	9.00 ***	20.00 ***	9.00 ***	830.00 ***
0132	0 PC	0 PC	0 PC	20.00 PC

Figure 3.17 Results of Plant Standard Analysis, Transaction MCBA

The fields shown in Figure 3.17 are:

- **V.stk iss qty**
  Valuated stock issued quantity
- **V.stk rec qty**
  Valuated stock received quantity
- **Tot usage**
  Total usage quantity
- **Valu stock**
  Quantity of the valuated stock

Storage Location

The standard analysis for a storage location uses the same selection criteria described in the plant standard analysis. The storage location standard analysis is found using Transaction MCBC, or using the navigation path: **SAP Menu • Logistics • Logistics Controlling • Logistics Information System • Standard Analyses • Stocks • Storage Location**.

Material

The standard analysis for a material uses the same selection criteria described in the plant standard analysis. The material standard analysis is found using Transaction MCBE, or by using the navigation path: **SAP Menu • Logistics • Logistics Controlling • Logistics Information System • Standard Analyses • Stocks • Material**.

3.3.2 Batches

The standard analysis for batches derives its data from the information structures S034 and S035. The results will be based on the period defined for the analysis.

The selection criteria for the batch analysis can be seen in Figure 3.18. This transaction can be accessed using Transaction MCBR, or using the navigation path: **SAP Menu • Logistics • Logistics Controlling • Logistics Information System • Standard Analyses • Stocks • Batches**.

The results screen for the batch standard analysis, as shown in Figure 3.19, shows the results fields for batches in the plant: Valuated Stock Issued Quantity, Valuated Stock Quantity in the Plant, and Valuated Stock Received Quantity.

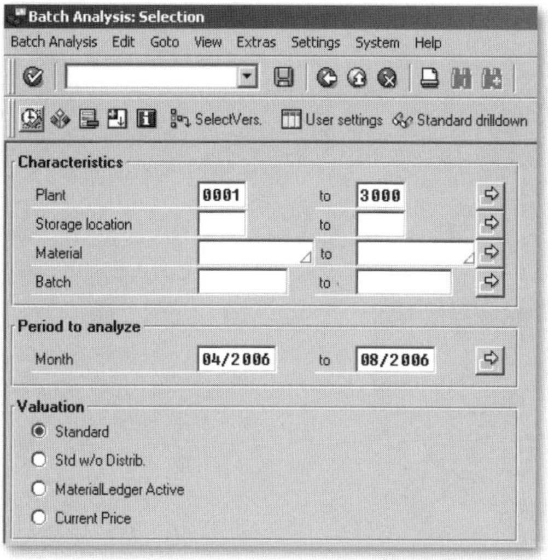

Figure 3.18 Selection Criteria for Batch Standard Analysis, Transaction MCBR

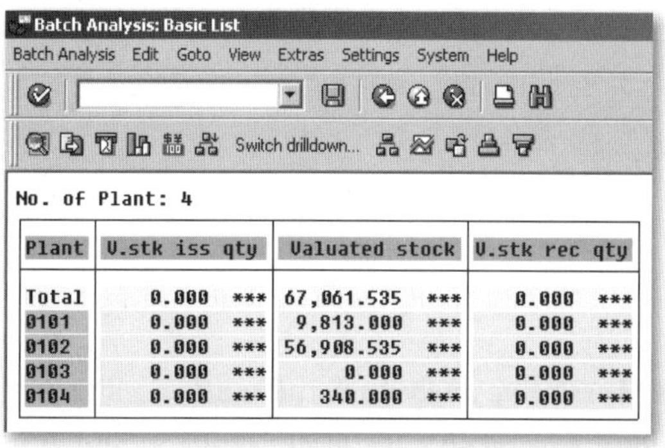

Figure 3.19 Resulting Fields for Batch Standard Analysis, Transaction MCBR

3.3.3 Material Groupings

There are five standard analyses that fall under the material groupings heading (in some older versions of SAP, this is called Material Pricing Groups). The standard analysis for these material group analyses derives its data from the information structures S031 and S032. The five material group analyses are as follows:

- **Materials Resource Planning (MRP) Controller**
  Transaction MCBG
- **Business Area**
  Transaction MCBI

- **Material Group**
  Transaction MCBK
- **Division**
  Transaction MCBM
- **Material Type**
  Transaction MCBO

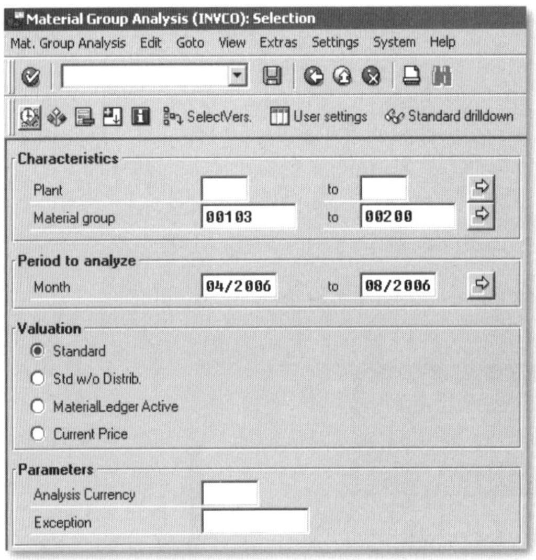

Figure 3.20 Selection Criteria Used for All Material Pricing Group Standard Analyses

The selection criteria screen for these five analyses is the same. To illustrate the selection criteria, the standard analysis for material groups is shown in Figure 3.20. You can also access the Transaction MCBK by using the navigation path: **SAP Menu • Logistics • Logistics Controlling • Logistics Information System • Standard Analyses • Material Groupings • Material Group**.

The results screen for the material group standard analysis, as shown in Figure 3.21, shows the results fields for the material group over the specified period. These are:

- **V.stk rec qty**
  Valuated stock received quantity
- **V.stk iss qty**
  Valuated stock issued quantity
- **Total usage**
  Total usage quantity

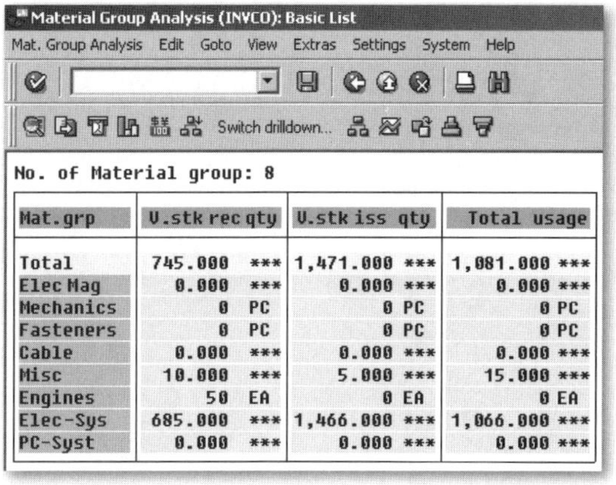

Mat.grp	V.stk rec qty	V.stk iss qty	Total usage
Total	745.000 ***	1,471.000 ***	1,081.000 ***
Elec Mag	0.000 ***	0.000 ***	0.000 ***
Mechanics	0 PC	0 PC	0 PC
Fasteners	0 PC	0 PC	0 PC
Cable	0.000 ***	0.000 ***	0.000 ***
Misc	10.000 ***	5.000 ***	15.000 ***
Engines	50 EA	0 EA	0 EA
Elec-Sys	685.000 ***	1,466.000 ***	1,066.000 ***
PC-Syst	0.000 ***	0.000 ***	0.000 ***

Figure 3.21 Results of Material Group Standard Analysis

3.3.4 Stock/Requirement Situation

There are two standard analyses that the user can execute for the stock/requirements situation: Current Situation, Transaction MCBZ; and Long-term Planning, Transaction MCB.

Current Situation

This standard analysis is used to review the current stock and requirements data from the MRP data. This standard analysis lets the user choose where the information for the analysis is derived from. In Figure 3.22, the selection criterion for the Transaction MCBZ is shown. The transaction has the option to allow data on an ad-hoc basis, which means directly for the current MRP run or from the information structure S094. In Figure 3.22, the **Ad-hoc evaluation** indicator must be set for the data to be taken from the current MRP data. If the indicator is not set, then the information structure is used.

However, to update the information structure S094 with the correct data, a program must first be executed. This program is called RMCBDISP, which can be executed via Transaction SE38.

The Transaction MCBZ can be reached by using the navigation path: **SAP Menu • Logistics • Logistics Controlling • Logistics Information System • Standard Analyses • Stocks • Current Requirement/Stock**.

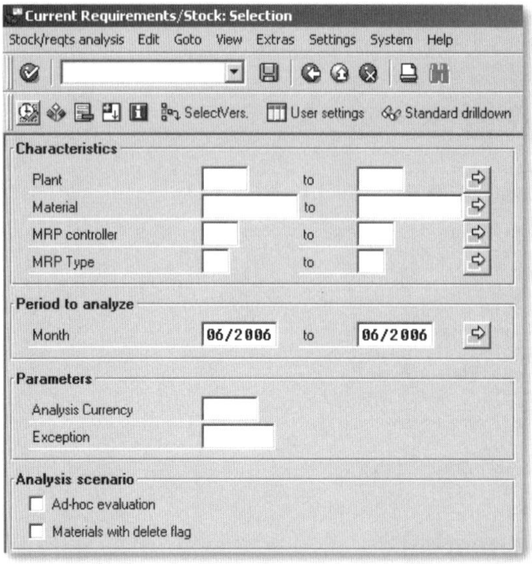

Figure 3.22 Selection Criteria for Current Requirements Standard Analysis, Transaction MCBZ

Long-term Planning

The long-term planning standard analysis is based either on the data from the latest MRP run or the information structure S094. This transaction uses the **Ad-hoc evaluation** indicator in the same manner as thc Current Requirements standard analysis.

The long-term planning standard analysis also uses a planning scenario, as shown in Figure 3.23. The planning scenario is used to determine the control parameters for long-term planning. These parameters include the plant used in long-term planning, the planning period, and the requirements versions to be planned.

The Transaction MCB can be reached by using the navigation path: **SAP Menu • Logistics • Logistics Controlling • Inventory Controlling • Standard Analyses • Stock/Requirement • Long-term Planning**.

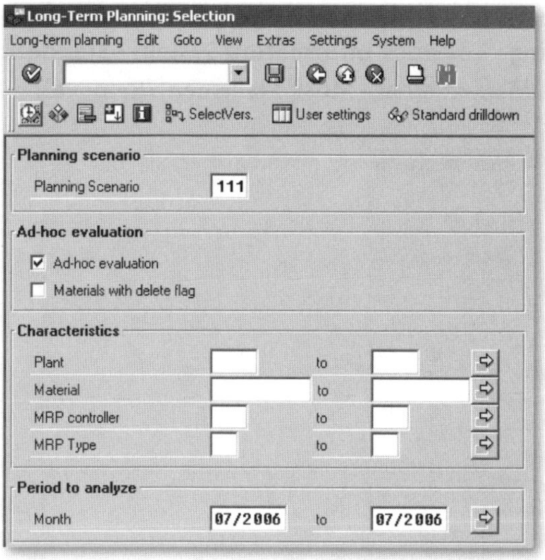

Figure 3.23 Selection Criteria for Long-Term Planning Standard Analysis, Transaction MCB

3.3.5 Warehouse Management

The standard analyses for Warehouse Management allow for a view of stock placement and removal and also for material placement and removal. There are five standard analyses for Warehouse Management and all of them use the information structure S091:

- **Stock Placements and Removals**
  Transaction MCL1
- **Quantities Flows**
  Transaction MCL5
- **Material Placements and Removals**
  Transaction MCL9
- **Material Flows**
  Transaction MCLD
- **Movement Types**
  Transaction MCLH

The standard analyses use the same selection criteria for querying the information structure S091. Figure 3.24 shows the selection criteria for Transaction MCL1, Stock Placements and Removals. This analysis allows the review of stock placements and removals for a warehouse, a material, or a movement type, etc.

The Transaction MCL1 can be reached by using the navigation path: **SAP Menu • Logistics • Logistics Controlling • Logistics Information System • Standard Analyses • Stocks • Warehouse Management • Stock Placement/Removal**.

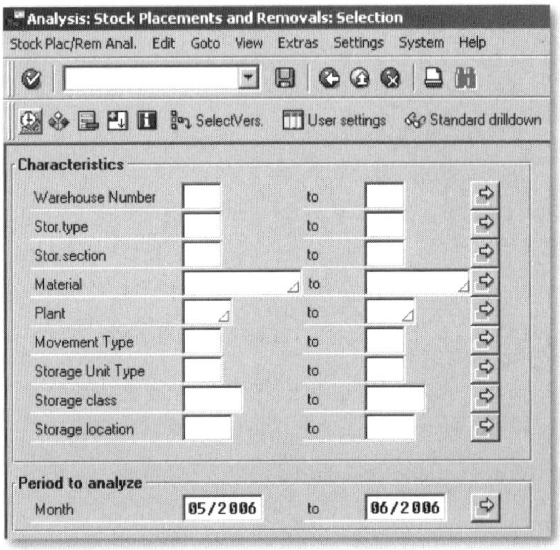

Figure 3.24 Selection Criteria for WM Standard Analysis, Stock Placements and Removals, Transaction MCL1

The results of the analysis, in Figure 3.25, show the amount of material that has been removed, placed in the warehouse, any return quantity and the number of placements and removals. The information structure can also produce analysis on the weight of the material placed and removed if the client needs it.

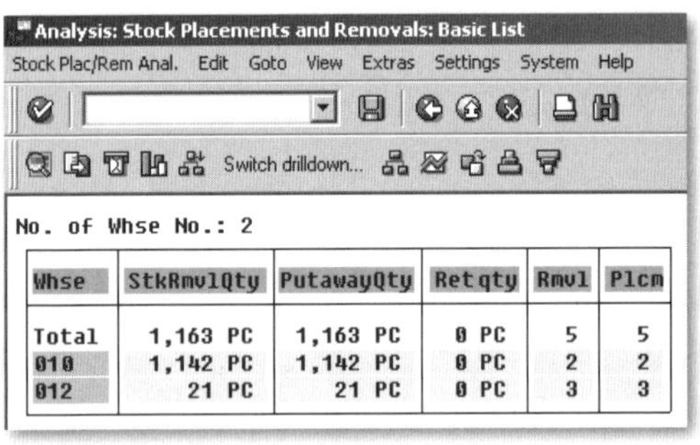

Figure 3.25 Resulting Analysis for WM Standard Analysis, Stock Placements and Removals, Transaction MCL1

3.4 Standard Analyses for Production

There are a number of standard analyses that are used for reviewing data in Production. These standard analyses review the data in the information structures related to Work Centers, Operations, Production Orders, etc. The relevant information structures are S021 through S029.

3.4.1 Work Center

The standard analysis for the work center is useful when the objective of production is to reduce the lead time for each work center. In the supply chain, any reduction in the time-to-customer is a benefit. This particular analysis shows the target and actual lead times for work centers at plants.

Figure 3.26 shows the selection criteria for the work center standard analysis, Transaction MCP7. This analysis of information structure S024 allows the selection of plant, planner group, and work center.

The Transaction MCP7 can be reached by using the navigation path: **SAP Menu • Logistics • Logistics Controlling • Logistics Information System • Standard Analyses • Production • Work Center**.

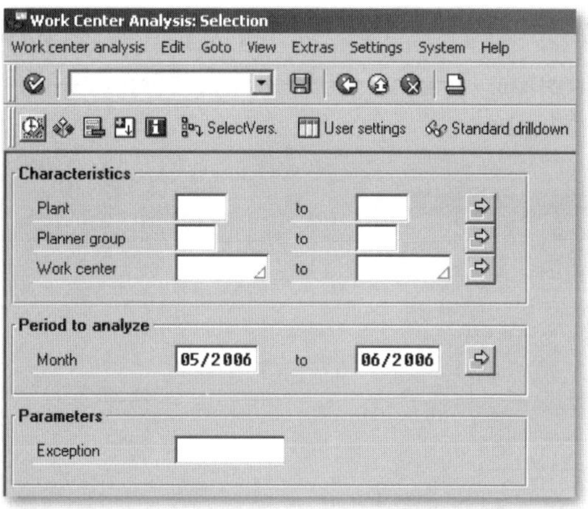

Figure 3.26 Selection Criteria for Work Center Standard Analysis, Transaction MCP7

The results of the standard analysis, as shown in Figure 3.27, allow the production staff to focus on situations where lead times need to be reduced to improve the lead time of the material to the customer.

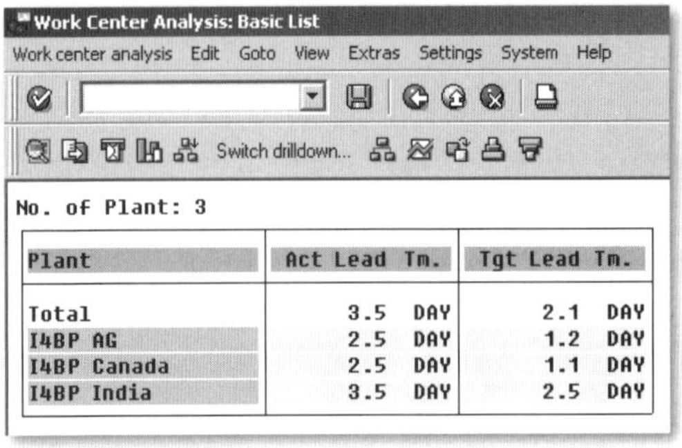

Figure 3.27 Actual and Target Lead Times of Work Centers by Plant from Transaction MCP7

3.4.2 Operation

The operations performed on a production order add up to make the lead time for the material to be completed. This standard analysis allows the production staff to review the target and actual lead time for operations at a given plant, work center, order, or for a selected material.

Figure 3.28 shows the selection criteria for the operation standard analysis, Transaction MCP1. This analysis of information structure S022 allows the selection of plant, work center, material, and production order.

The Transaction MCP1 can be reached by using the navigation path: **SAP Menu • Logistics • Logistics Controlling • Logistics Information System • Standard Analyses • Production • Operation.**

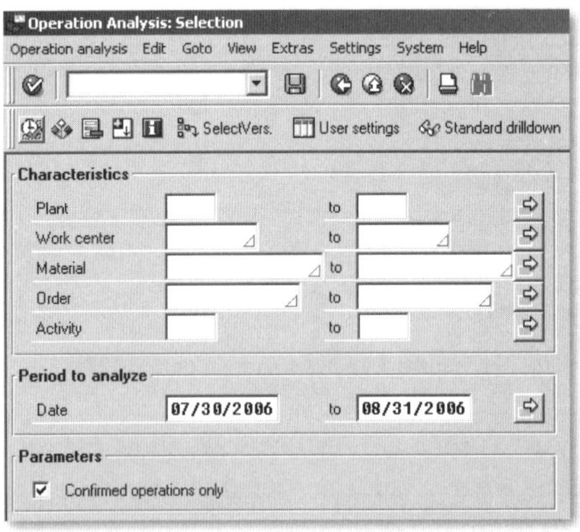

Figure 3.28 Selection Criteria for Operation Standard Analysis, Transaction MCP1

The resulting standard analysis for operations is similar to that in Figure 3.27 for work centers, in that it shows target and actual lead time for operations per plant.

3.4.3 Material

The material standard analysis queries the data in the information structure S023. The data can be selected at the plant, material, or MRP controller. Figure 3.29 shows the selection criteria for the operation standard analysis, Transaction MCP5, and can be reached by using the navigation path: **SAP Menu • Logistics • Logistics Controlling • Logistics Information System • Standard Analyses • Production • Material.**

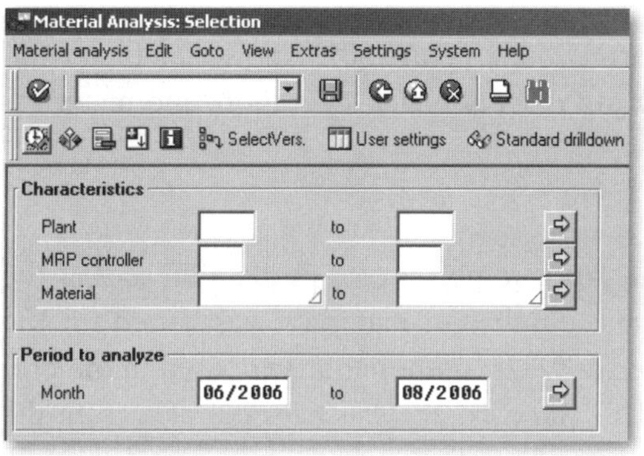

Figure 3.29 Selection Criteria for Material Standard Analysis, Transaction MCP5

The resulting data specifies the target lead time and the actual lead time for the material, similar to the results for work center and operation.

3.4.4 Production Order

The production order standard analysis allows the production staff to review the target against actual lead time. The more time the production order takes to complete over the target time, the less effective the company is at getting product to the customer.

Figure 3.30 shows the selection criteria for the standard analysis, Transaction MCP3, and can be reached by using the navigation path: **SAP Menu • Logistics • Logistics Controlling • Logistics Information System • Standard Analyses • Production • Production Order.**

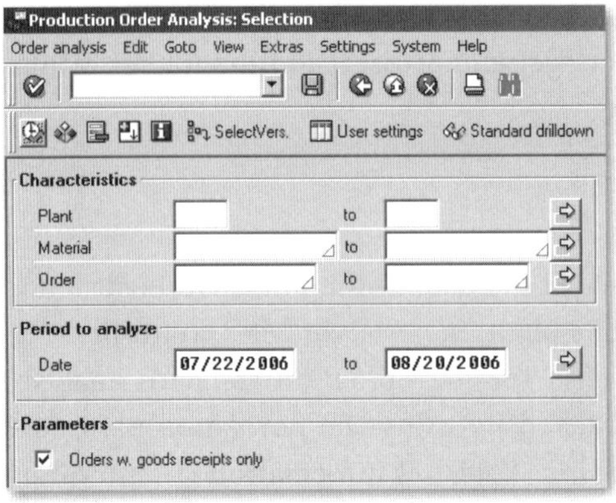

Figure 3.30 Selection Criteria for Production Order Standard Analysis, Transaction MCP3

The resulting data from the information structure S021 shows the target and actual lead time in days, similar to the work order, operation, and material.

3.4.5 Material Usage

The material usage standard analysis is important for production staff as the results of this show if the correct number of materials was issued for the requirements. It is also useful to see what components were used in the production of a certain material. This standard analysis uses the data from the information structure S026.

Figure 3.31 shows the selection criteria for the standard analysis, Transaction MCRE, and can be reached by using the navigation path: **SAP Menu • Logistics • Logistics Controlling • Logistics Information System • Standard Analyses • Production • Material Usage**.

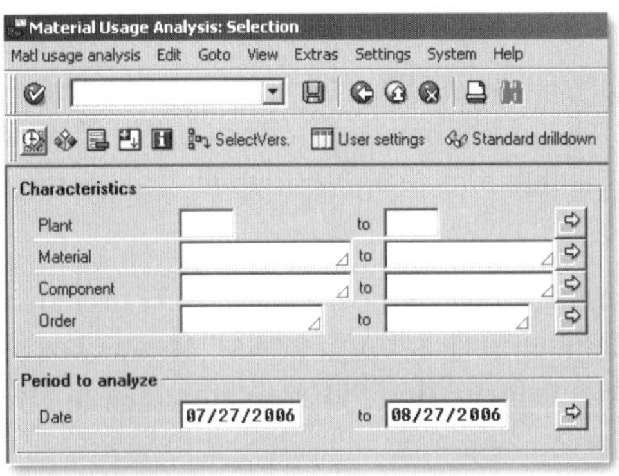

Figure 3.31 Selection Criteria for Material Usage Standard Analysis, Transaction MCRE

The results of the material usage standard analysis, as shown in Figure 3.32, allow the production staff to review the requirements and the withdrawal of materials to monitor production validity.

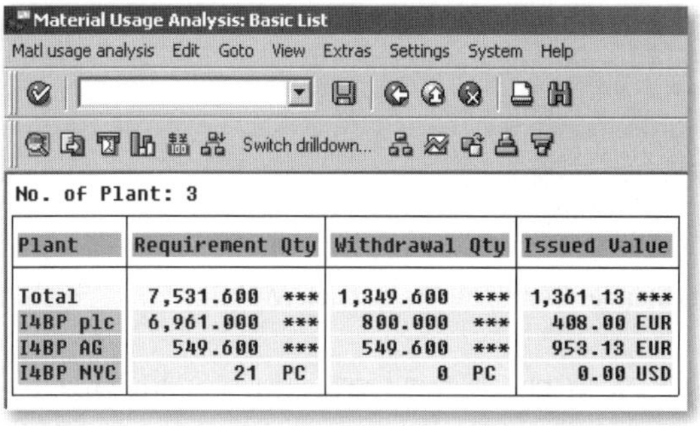

Figure 3.32 Results for Material Usage Standard Analysis, Transaction MCRE

3.4.6 Product Costs

The product costs standard analysis reviews the data in the information structure, S027. The analysis allows the costing department to review the material costs using the selection criteria of plant, material, or production order.

Figure 3.33 shows the selection criteria for the product costs standard analysis, Transaction MCRI, and can be reached by using the navigation path: **SAP Menu • Logistics • Logistics Controlling • Logistics Information System • Standard Analyses • Production • Product Costs.**

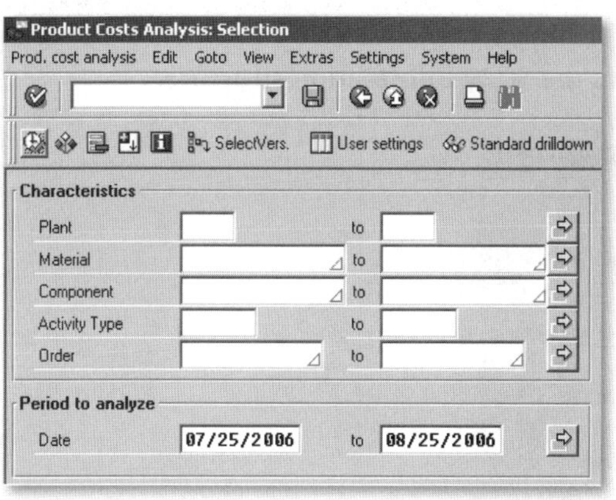

Figure 3.33 Selection Criteria for Product Costs Standard Analysis, Transaction MCRI

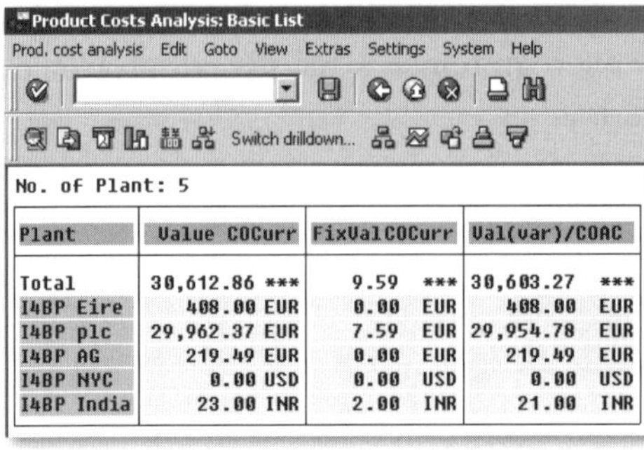

Figure 3.34 Results of Product Costs Standard Analysis, Transaction MCRI

The result of the analysis is shown in Figure 3.34. The three fields that are displayed in Figure 3.34 are:

- **Value COCurr**
  Total fixed and variable values for material components or activities in controlling area currency
- **FixVal COCurr**
  Value of the components or activity quantity that is valuated with the fixed price in controlling area currency
- **Val(var)/COAC**
  Value of the components or activity quantity in controlling area currency

3.4.7 Kanban

If your company uses Kanban, the Kanban standard analysis may help production staff to monitor the wait times in the Kanban process. The Kanban standard analysis uses data from the S029 information structure.

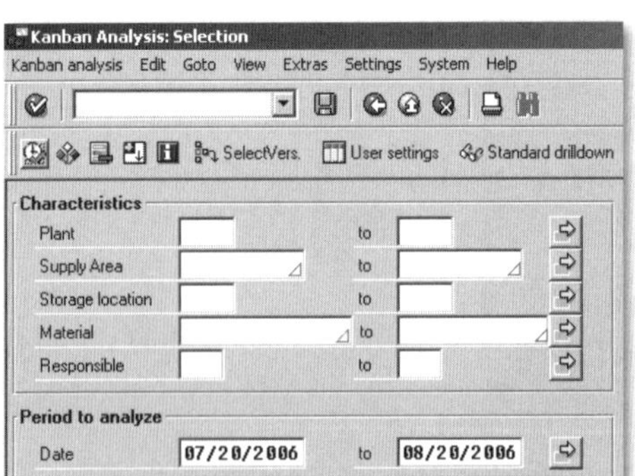

Figure 3.35 Selection Criteria for Kanban Standard Analysis

Figure 3.35 shows the selection criteria for the product costs standard analysis and can be reached by using the navigation path: **SAP Menu • Logistics • Logistics Controlling • Logistics Information System • Standard Analyses • Production • Kanban.**

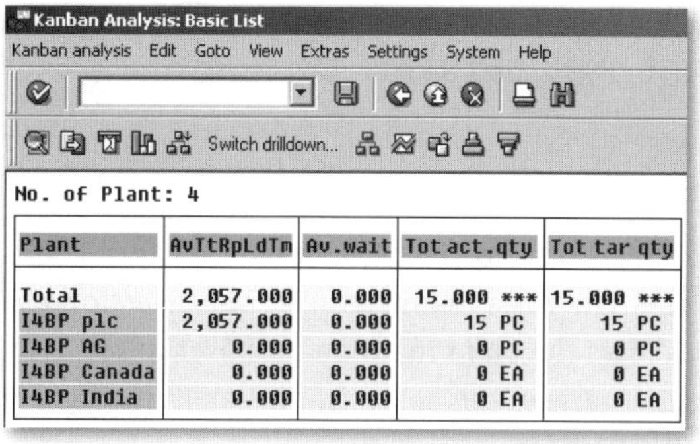

Figure 3.36 Results for Kanban Standard Analysis

The results fields for the Kanban standard analysis are shown in Figure 3.36. Definitions for the result fields are shown below:

- **Average Total Replenishment Lead Time**
  The total replenishment lead time is the sum of the times passed between the replenishment signal and the refilling of a Kanban. Using the sum of the replenishment lead-time and the number of completed replenishment operations, the average replenishment lead-time for a Kanban is calculated.
- **Average Wait Time**
  The total wait time is the sum of the times that all Kanban bins spend with the full status. This time plus the total time that all Kanban spent with this status is used to calculate the average wait time that a Kanban spends with the full status.
- **Total Actual Quantity**
  This is the sum of the material quantities that have actually been replenished using Kanban to which a goods receipt has been posted.
- **Total Target Quantity**
  This is the sum of the material quantities that would be replenished using Kanban, if a target quantity had been defined in the control cycle for each goods receipt for a container.

3.5 Standard Analyses for Plant Maintenance

There are a number of standard analyses that are defined for reviewing data in Plant Maintenance (PM). These standard analyses review the data in the information structures related to manufacturers, locations, damage analysis, breakdowns, etc. The relevant information structures in Plant Maintenance are S061, S062, S063, S065, S070, S115, and S116.

3.5.1 Manufacturer

The standard analysis for a manufacturer allows the plant maintenance teams to perform a total analysis on the data for a manufacturer. The selection criteria, as shown in Figure 3.37, allows the plant maintenance user to select by manufacturer, material, or year to narrow the analysis. This analysis queries data from the S062 information structure.

The standard analysis on manufacturers can be run by executing Transaction MCI2 and can be reached by using the navigation path: **SAP Menu • Logistics • Logistics Controlling • Logistics Information System • Standard Analyses • Plant Maintenance • Manufacturer**.

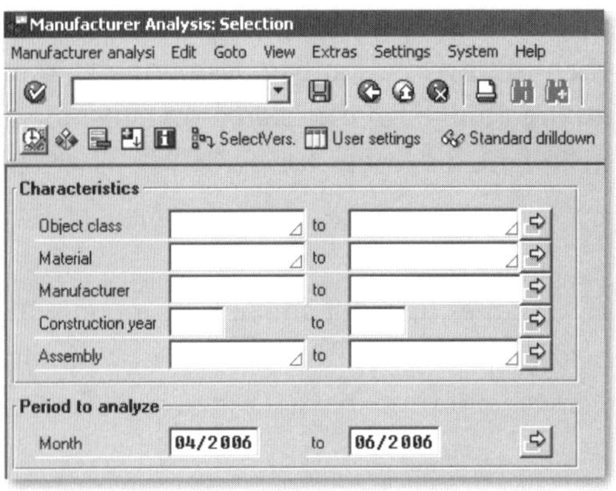

Figure 3.37 Selection Criteria for Manufacturer Standard Analysis, Transaction MCI2

The result of this analysis produces a large amount of data for review. The result fields include:

- Number of Notifications to the Manufacturer
- Number of Recorded Breakdowns that occur for objects supplied by the relevant manufacturer
- Number of Recorded Maintenance Orders

- Sum of the Planned Costs for Maintenance Orders
- Total Actual Costs of Maintenance Services
- Total Plant Maintenance Costs for Internal Personnel
- Total Plant Maintenance Costs for External Contractors
- Total Plant Maintenance Costs for Internal Materials
- Total Plant Maintenance Costs for External Materials
- Sum of Plant Maintenance Costs that result from Services
- Total of Miscellaneous Plant Maintenance Costs
- Sum of the Actual Revenues for Plant Maintenance Services

3.5.2 Location

The standard analysis for a plant maintenance location allows the maintenance staff to review and monitor the costs and notifications that arise from specific or various locations.

The selection criteria, as shown in Figure 3.38, allows the maintenance user to select by plant, plant section, location, functional location, or specific equipment to narrow down the analysis further. This analysis queries data from the S061 information structure.

The standard analysis on PM locations can be run by executing Transaction MCI3 and can be reached by using the navigation path: **SAP Menu • Logistics • Logistics Controlling • Logistics Information System • Standard Analyses • Plant Maintenance • Location.**

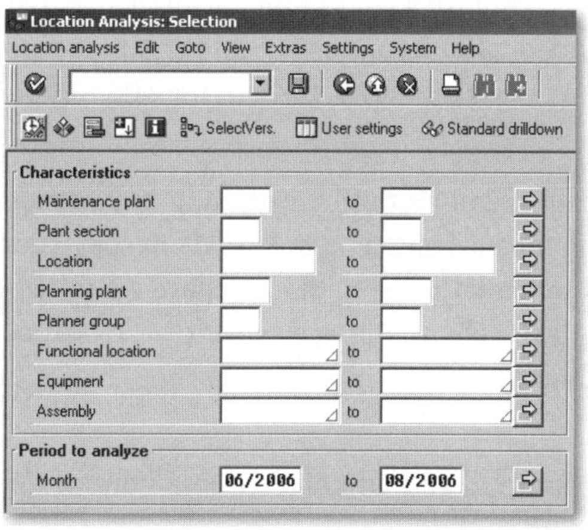

Figure 3.38 Selection Criteria for PM Location Standard Analysis, Transaction MCI3

The resulting analysis produces a significant quantity of data to review. The result fields are the same as those found for the standard analysis for a manufacturer, described in Section 3.5.1.

3.5.3 Damage Analysis

The damage analysis standard analysis allows the maintenance staff to review the data for specific notification types, functional locations, or actual equipment. This is useful to determine whether or not there is recurring damage with particular equipment or in a certain functional location.

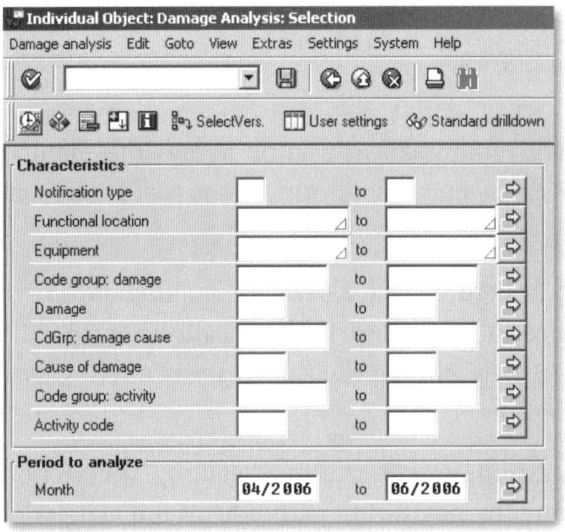

Figure 3.39 Selection Criteria for Damage Analysis Standard Analysis, Transaction MCI5

The selection criteria, as shown in Figure 3.39, allows the maintenance user to select by notification type, functional location, or specific equipment to restrict the analysis further. This analysis queries data from the S063 information structure.

The damage analysis standard analysis can be run by executing Transaction MCI5, and can be reached by using the navigation path: **SAP Menu • Logistics • Logistics Controlling • Logistics Information System • Standard Analyses • Plant Maintenance • Damage Analysis**. The resulting fields for MCI5 can be seen in Figure 3.40. The data includes:

- **Damage**
  The number of times damage occurred and was entered in a notification for describing the recorded damage

- **Causes of Damage**
  The number of cause of damage codes recorded for a technical object to explain the recorded cause of damage in the notification
- **Activities**
  The number of activity codes recorded to describe the executed activities in the notification

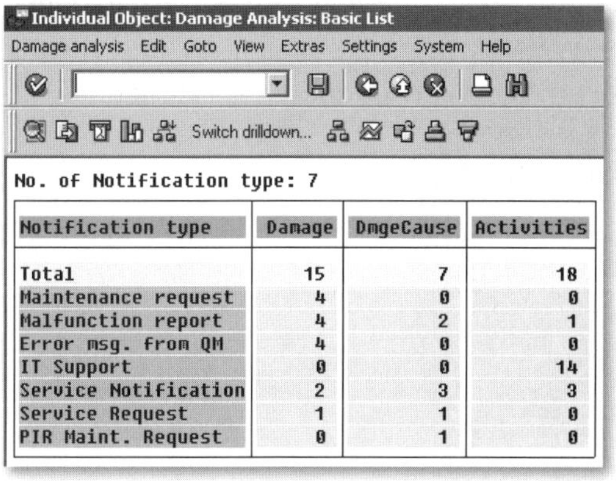

No. of Notification type: 7

Notification type	Damage	DmgeCause	Activities
Total	15	7	18
Maintenance request	4	0	0
Malfunction report	4	2	1
Error msg. from QM	4	0	0
IT Support	0	0	14
Service Notification	2	3	3
Service Request	1	1	0
PIR Maint. Request	0	1	0

Figure 3.40 Resulting Fields for Damage Analysis, Standard Analysis, Transaction MCI5

3.5.4 Breakdown Analysis

The breakdown standard analysis is similar to the damage analysis, but this analysis refers specifically to the breakdown of equipment and the costs involved in maintenance. This analysis is useful for maintenance staff working on equipment warranty and replacement.

The selection criteria, as shown in Figure 3.41, allows the maintenance user to select by functional location or specific equipment to narrow down the analysis further. This analysis queries data from the S070 information structure.

The breakdown standard analysis can be run by executing Transaction MCI7 and can be reached by using the navigation path: **SAP Menu • Logistics • Logistics Controlling • Logistics Information System • Standard Analyses • Plant Maintenance • Breakdown Analysis**. The resulting data for the breakdown analysis is shown in Figure 3.42. Detailed descriptions of the fields are given below:

- **Actual Breakdowns**
  The number of breakdowns that actually occurred with a technical object.

- **Mean Time to Repair**
  The mean of the sum of the actual periods of time for correcting a technical object malfunction, or the actual times it took to repair the object.
- **Mean Time Between Repairs**
  The mean of the sum of the times between the termination of a machine breakdown and the commencement of the next one.

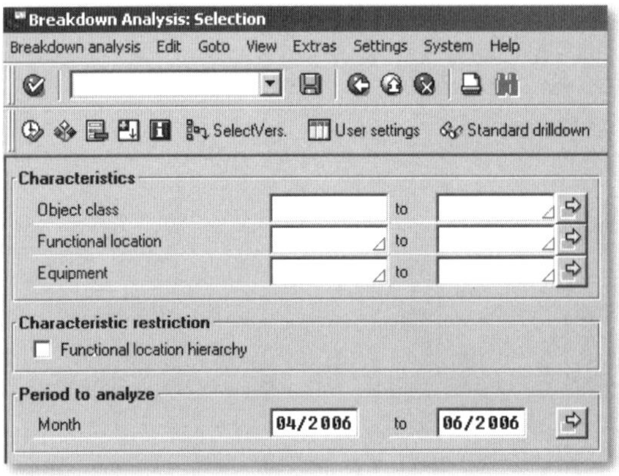

Figure 3.41 Selection Criteria for Breakdown Standard Analysis, Transaction MCI7

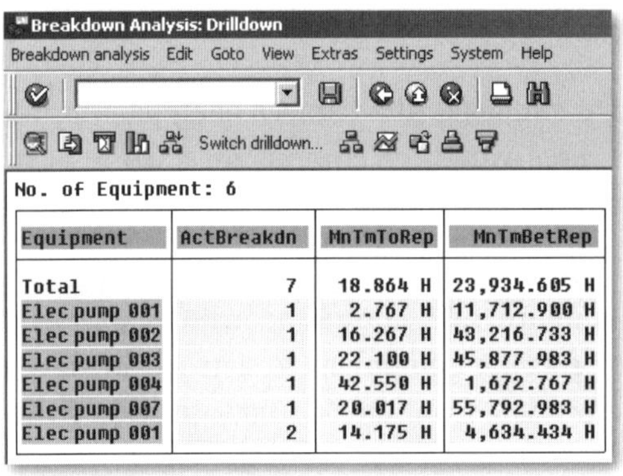

Figure 3.42 Resulting Data for Breakdown Standard Analysis, Transaction MCI7

3.6 Standard Analyses for Quality Management

A number of standard analyses are used for reviewing data in Quality Management. These standard analyses review the data in the information structures related to Lots, Error Analysis, etc. The relevant information structures in Quality Management are S068, S069, and S097 through S104.

3.6.1 Lots

There are three standard analyses for Lots, which are:

- **Material**
  Transaction MCV3, information structure S069
- **Vendor**
  Transaction MCV1, information structure S068
- **Customer**
  Transaction MCOO, information structure S104

Figure 3.43 shows the selection criteria for Transaction MCV1, which is the review of lots for vendors. This can be found using the navigation path: **SAP Menu • Logistics • Logistics Controlling • Logistics Information System • Standard Analyses • Quality Management • Vendor • Lots**.

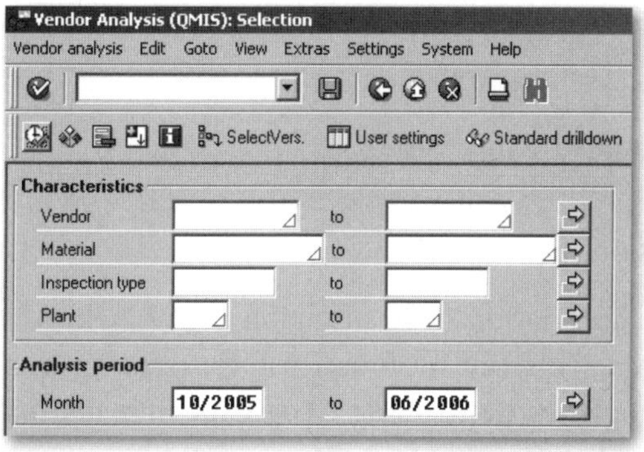

Figure 3.43 Selection Criteria for Lot Standard Analysis for Vendors, Transaction MCV1

The results that are returned by the analysis shown in Figure 3.43 are listed below:

- **Mean Value Quality Score**
  The mean of the number of inspection lots whose quality scores lie within the class range.
- **Rejection Rate**
  The total number of rejected inspection lots (usage decision is not okay).
- **Rejected Quantity Rate**
  The total lot quantities of all rejected inspection lots (usage decision is not okay).
- **Skipped Lots Rate**
  The total number of skipped inspection lots.

- **Skipped Quantity Rate**
  The total lot quantities of all skipped inspection lots.
- **Sample Quantity Rate**
  This indicates the cumulative, inspected amount.
- **Defective Quantity Rate**
  This is the sum of the defective quantity for all inspection lots.
- **Mean Lead Time**
  The mean of the total lead times of all of the inspection lots that have not been canceled.

3.6.2 Error Analysis

There are three standard analyses for error analysis, which are:

- **Material**
  Transaction MCXX, information structure S100
- **Vendor**
  Transaction MCVX, information structure S102
- **Customer**
  Transaction MCOX, information structure S103

Figure 3.44 shows the selection criteria for the Transaction MCVX, which is the review of errors for vendors. This can be found using the navigation path: **SAP Menu • Logistics • Logistics Controlling • Logistics Information System • Standard Analyses • Quality Management • Vendor • Error**.

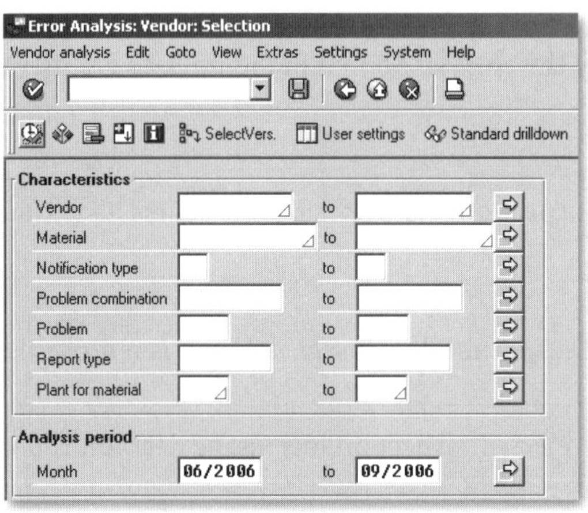

Figure 3.44 Selection Criteria for Error Standard Analysis for Vendors, Transaction MCVX

The results that are returned by the error standard analysis shown in Figure 3.45 are listed below:

- **Problem Frequency**
  Frequency with which a code is used in the defect items
- **Mean Defect Value**
  Mean value of the total defect valuations
- **Total Defect Value**
  Total of the defect valuations for all defect positions
- **Problem Items**
  Number of defect items that contain defect codes

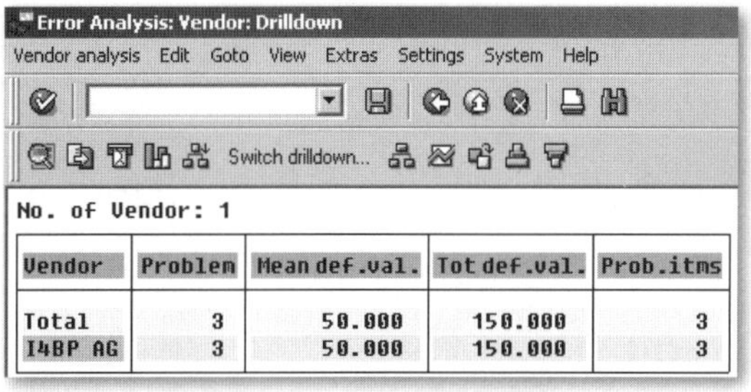

Figure 3.45 Results of the Errors Standard Analysis for a Vendor, Transaction MCVX

3.7 Summary

In this chapter, I tried to show you that the predefined standard analyses combined with the predefined information structures offer a vast range of analytical data that can be used by personnel from all user groups to aid them in their daily positions. The logistics reports in SAP are integral to the supply chain and are available to the logistics department without requiring additional configuration or ABAP programming. In Chapter 4, the functionality of selection versions will be discussed as will their usefulness for the everyday user.

A selection version allows users to either save the data from a standard analysis that they have executed or to predefine the selection fields of the analysis. By predefining the key figures, users can create many selection versions for the same standard analysis.

4 Selection Versions

When discussing standard analyses in Chapter 3, I described an analysis that could be saved as a selection version on the results screen. In this chapter, I will elaborate on the method by which a user can create, change, and use selection versions.

4.1 Create a Selection Version

In Chapter 3, the method of creating a selection version was to save the standard analysis in the results screen. In this section, I'll describe another method of creating a selection version.

A selection version can be created directly from the LIS menu in SAP, as shown in Figure 4.1. The transaction to perform this action is MCMO, and it can be found using the navigation path: **SAP Menu • Logistics • Logistics Controlling • Logistics Information System • Standard Analyses • Selection Version • Create.**

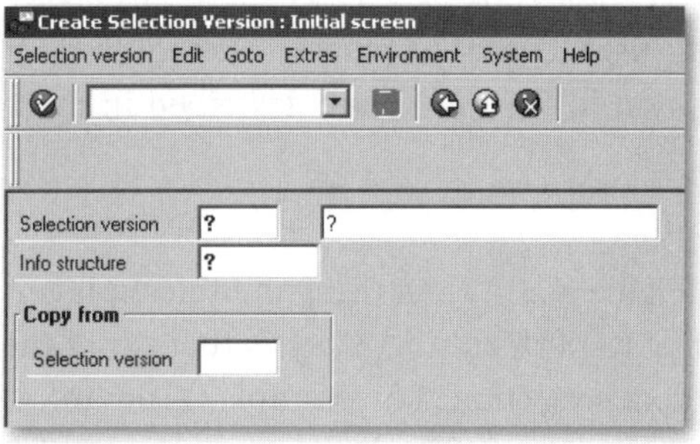

Figure 4.1 Initial Screen to Create Selection Version, Transaction MCMO

When creating a selection version using the LIS menu, three entries are required:

- **Selection Version Name**
  A five-character alpha-numeric field
- **Selection Version Description**
  A 40-character description
- **Information Structure**
  The number of the information structure for which the selection version is to be valid

When using this method of creating a selection version, knowledge of the information structures, as well as the key figures and characteristics, is required. For this example, the information structure to be referenced is the S012 Purchasing information structure, as shown in Figure 4.2.

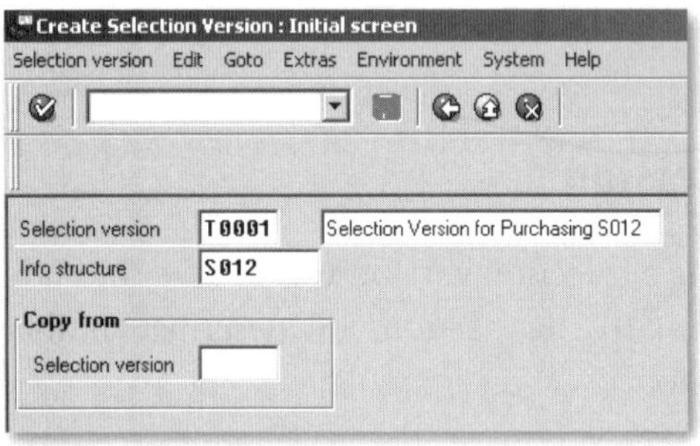

Figure 4.2 Information Added into Initial Screen for Transaction MCMO

4.1.1 Definition

After the user has entered the initial information into the transaction, the **Definition** screen for the selection version is displayed, as shown in Figure 4.3. The **Definition** screen allows the user to add the parameters required for his selection version. The fields shown in Figure 4.3 are described in more detail below.

- **Analysis Currency**
  This is seen as **Analysis Curr.** in Figure 4.3. When using the selection version, the user can enter a currency to perform the analysis that is not the currency originally used in the data collection. For example, if the information structure is updated in US Dollars (USD), but there is a need for the analysis to be performed in Canadian Dollars, the user can enter the analysis currency CDN in this field.

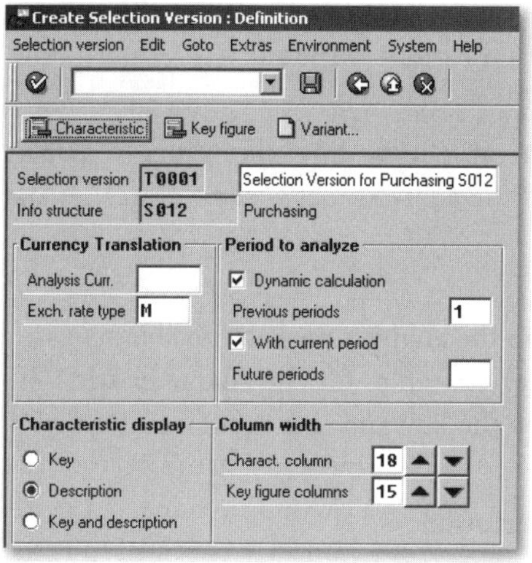

Figure 4.3 Definition Screen for Transaction MCMO

- **Exchange Rate Type**
  This is seen as **Exch. rate type.** If the user enters an analysis currency into the selection version, she will need to enter an exchange rate type as well. The default for this field is **M**, which is the average rate, or mean between the bank buying rate and the bank-selling rate.

  The exchange rate type can be configured by using Transaction OB07, and can be found using the SAP menu navigation path: **IMG • Controlling • Cost center Accounting • Planning • Basic Settings for Planning • Define Exchange Rate Types.**

- **Dynamic Calculation of Time of Analysis**
  Dynamic calculation was also seen in Figure 4.3. If the user creating the selection version sets this indicator, then the system will dynamically determine the period to be analyzed from the current date. For instance, if this version should always analyze the last six months from the date the analysis is carried out, this indicator should be set.

- **Previous Periods for Selection Version**
  The field, **Previous periods** allows the number of periods to be entered that the analysis will retrieve data.

- **With Current Period**
  The **With current period indicator** set, the current period will be included in the selection time period for analysis.

- **Future Periods for Selection Version**
  In the **Future periods** field, the number of future periods to be analyzed

can be entered. For example, if the next fiscal year was to be analyzed and the period is a month, then 12 would be entered in the field.

- **Characteristic Display**
  In **Characteristic display**, the user can choose how she wants to display the characteristics in the output of the analysis. Let's take a closer look at these options below:
  - **Characteristic Display as a Key**
    If this option is selected, then, in the analysis results, the characteristic will be displayed as the key. For example, for the characteristic Vendor, the vendor number may be the key and this is what is displayed, e.g., 109903.
  - **Characteristic Display as a Description**
    If this option is selected, then, in the analysis results, the characteristic will be displayed as the description. For example, for the characteristic Vendor, the vendor number may be the key, but it is the vendor description that is displayed, e.g., Hastie & Son LLC.
  - **Characteristic Display as a Key and Description**
    If this option is selected, then, in the analysis results, the characteristic will be displayed with the key and description, e.g., 109903, Hastie & Son LLC.
- **Column Width**
  Two column widths can be determined, which are:
  - Width of the column for the characteristics
  - Width of the column for the key figures

4.1.2 Characteristics

Once the definitions for the selection version are complete, the characteristics and the key figures can be selected. The user can access the characteristics by selecting the following from the header menu, **Edit • Choose Characteristics**. A dialog box opens, displaying the characteristics to be selected, as shown in Figure 4.4.

From the **Choose Characteristics** screen, a number of the available characteristics can be selected. The characteristics in the right column in Figure 4.4 can be selected and moved individually, or as a group to the selection criteria column on the left. Once the user has decided on the characteristics, she should select the appropriate checkbox to continue.

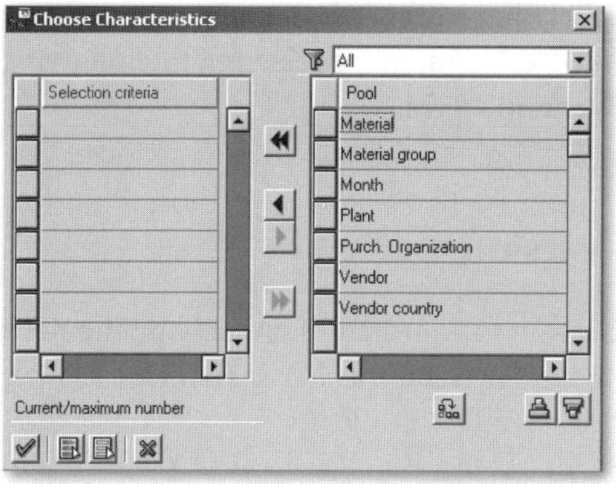

Figure 4.4 Choose Characteristics Screen for User-Defined Selection Version

4.1.3 Key Figures

The key figures can be accessed by selecting the following from the header menu: **Edit • Choose Key Figures.** A dialog box will be displayed on the selection screen, from which the key figures can be selected, as shown in Figure 4.5.

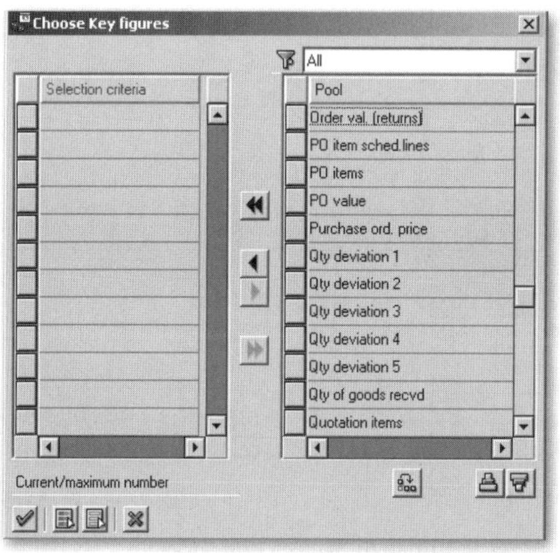

Figure 4.5 Choose Key Figures Screen for User-Defined Selection Version

From the **Choose Key Figures** screen, a number of the available key figures can be selected. The key figures in the right column in Figure 4.5 can be selected and moved individually, or as a group to the selection criteria column on the left. Once the user has determined the key figures, she should select the appropriate checkbox to continue.

After the characteristics and key figures have been selected, the user can save the selection version by using the **Ctrl + S** keys, or by selecting the following from the header menu: **Selection Version • Save**.

4.2 Change a Selection Version

After a selection version has been created and tested, there may be the need to amend some part of it, that is, to add or change a characteristic or key figure.

To change the selection version, the user can use the Transaction MCMP, which can be found using the navigation path: **SAP Menu • Logistics • Logistics Controlling • Logistics Information System • Standard Analyses • Selection Version • Change**.

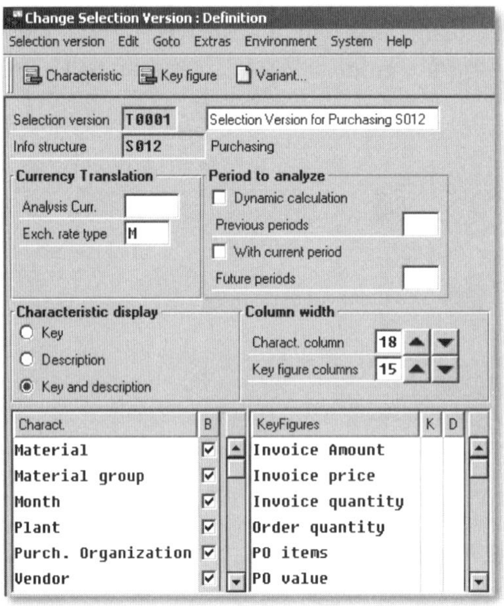

Figure 4.6 Definition Screen for Selection Version Change, Transaction MCMP

4.2.1 Delete Characteristic or Key Figure

In Figure 4.6, the characteristics and key figures are displayed. The user can delete the characteristics or key figures by using the icons or by using the header menu: **Edit • Delete Characteristic** or **Edit • Delete Key Figure**.

4.2.2 Create Variant for Selection Version

As part of the change functionality, the user can create a variant for the selection version. A variant allows values to be entered into the selection version and saved in the variant. The variant is created by using the **F7** function key or by accessing the header menu: **Edit • Variant • Create.**

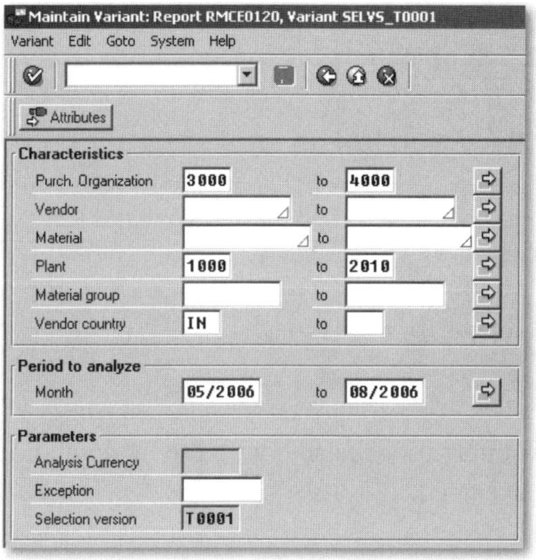

Figure 4.7 Variant Creation Screen for Selection Version, Transaction MCMP

The variant creation for the selection version, as shown in Figure 4.7, allows the specific selection criteria to be entered. For instance, in Figure 4.7, the variant entered is a range of Purchase Organizations, 3000 to 4000, and a range of plants from 1000 to 2010. The next part of the variant is to select which attributes are to be used for each field. To access the attributes screen, select the **Attributes** button or use the header menu: **Edit • Attributes.**

In Figure 4.8, the attributes for each field can be selected. Ranges of attributes can be used, as listed below:

- **Protect**
  If this indicator is set, then the field in the variant is protected from being changed when the variant is being executed. This means that a user cannot change the variant value in the selection version.
- **Hide**
  If this indicator is set then the field will not be visible when the selection version variant is executed and therefore cannot be changed by the user.

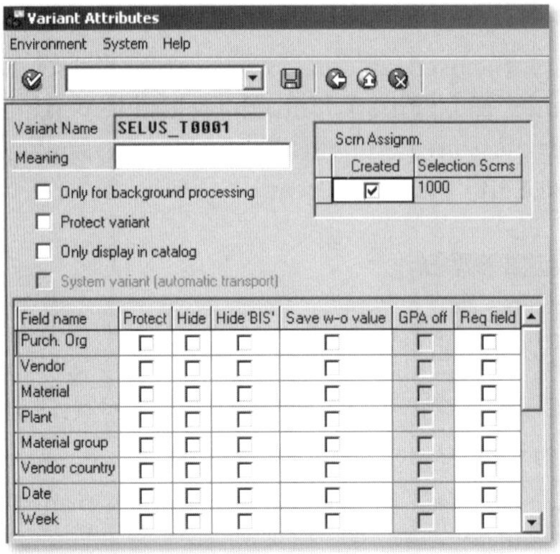

Figure 4.8 Attributes That Can Be Selected for Each Field of Variant

- **Hide BIS**
  If this indicator is set, then the intervals associated with the field will not be shown when the variant is executed.
- **Save Without Values**
  When this indicator is set, this field will not overwrite any content of the field in the existing selection version. For example, if the Purchasing Group field has a value 007 in it prior to the variant being imported, then this value will not be overwritten with the Purchasing Group value in the variant.
- **GPA Off**
  If this indicator is set, the user parameter (GPA) is not required to be imported into the field.
- **Required Field**
  If this indicator is set, then the field in the variant will require a value to be entered for it. After the indicators have been set, the variant can be saved by using the **Save** icon or the **Ctrl + S** keys.

4.3 General Overview of Selection Versions

The general overview transaction for selection versions gives a total view of all applications with the LIS. The user can review all versions within an application and execute from the screen.

The general overview Transaction MCKO can be found using the navigation path: **SAP Menu • Logistics • Logistics Controlling • Logistics Information System • Standard Analyses • Selection Version • General Overview.**

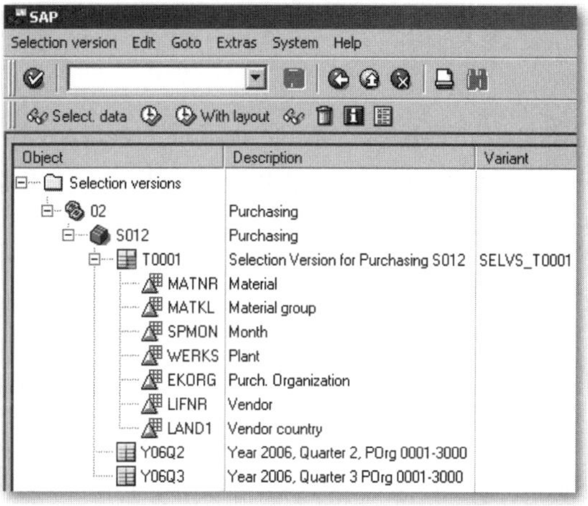

Figure 4.9 General Overview for Selection Versions, Transaction MCKO

The general overview, as shown in Figure 4.9, shows all the available selection versions for the applications. In this figure, Application 02 is shown, which is Purchasing, followed by the information structure S012. For Information Structure S012, three selection versions are available. Using the legend, shown in Figure 4.10, the user can see that the selection version T0001 is without data, while Y06Q2 and Y06Q3 are selection versions with data.

Beneath the selection version T0001 are a number of characteristics without data, as per the legend in Figure 4.10. In addition to the characteristics, it is noted that there is a variant for selection version T0001, which was created in the previous section.

Figure 4.10 Legend for General Overview of Selection Versions, Transaction MCKO

Selection versions can be executed through the general overview by selecting from the header menu: **Selection version • Execute** or **Selection version • Execute** with variant.

4.4 Summary

This chapter shows you that a selection version can be used to create a version of a standard analysis that contains field information relevant for a department or user group, which can be used over and over again. Using the general overview transaction is important in providing visibility of the selection versions currently created for a particular area. This allows personnel to review selection versions in order to assess their usefulness before they establish the need to create further versions and therefore requiring additional work.

In Chapter 5, the focus will be on the drilldown functionality within the standard analyses.

Once the data has been retrieved for a certain analysis in the LIS, the data can be reviewed at certain levels; this is obtained by drilldown functionality. There are two types of drilldown, one using characteristics, the other using a specified hierarchy.

5 Drilldown

Data that is retrieved using a standard analysis can be reviewed at the top level, but then it can be further reviewed at lower levels via the drilldown functionality. Drilldown allows the reviewer to see the data at a more specific criteria level based on either characteristic drilldown or hierarchy drilldown or a combination of both.

5.1 Characteristic Drilldown

The *characteristic drilldown* allows the reviewer of the data to analyze the data at lower levels by certain characteristics. These characteristics can be items such as Material, Vendor, Equipment, Work Center, etc.

For example, if a standard analysis is performed for a Vendor analysis in the Purchasing Information System, Transaction MCE3, the drilldown can be by the characteristic **Vendor**. This is the top level of the drilldown. The next level of the drilldown can be another characteristic, **Material**. This shows the data at *this* characteristic level.

5.1.1 Standard Drilldown

For standard analyses, there are standard drilldowns that can be used by the data reviewer that are predefined for them to use. In Figure 5.1, the selection criteria for Transaction MCE3 is shown. There is a button identified, **Standard drilldown.** If this is executed, a dialog box will appear with the information on the standard drilldown, as shown in Figure 5.1.

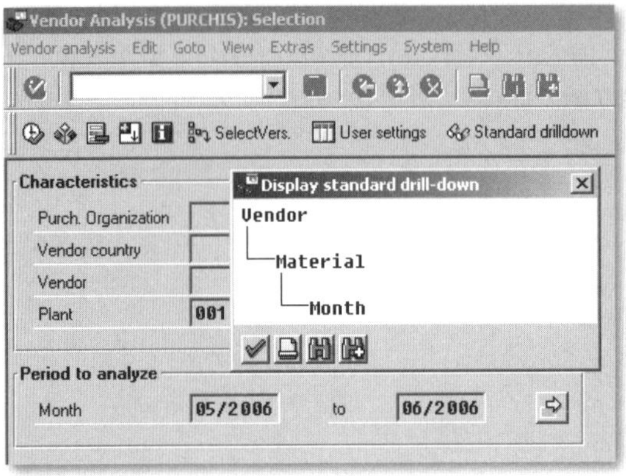

Figure 5.1 Standard Drilldown for Vendor Analysis, Transaction MCE3

The standard drilldown shows that there are three characteristics that will be used to display the data: **Vendor**, **Material**, and **Month**.

Therefore, once the information for the **Vendor** characteristic level is displayed in Transaction MCE3, as shown in Figure 5.2, the next drilldown can be obtained by selecting one of the vendors from the resulting data and from the header menu: **View • Standard Drilldown.**

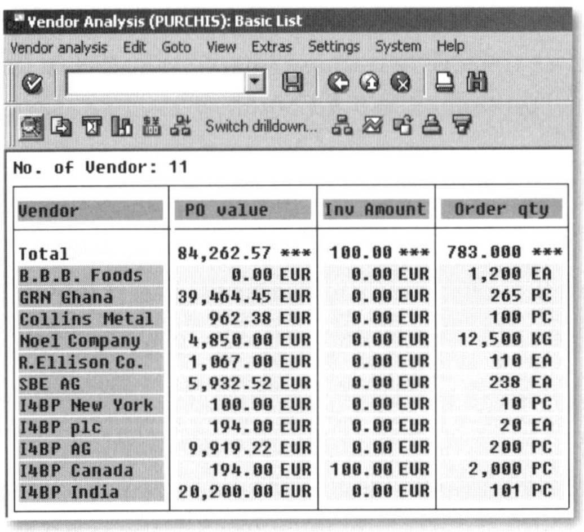

Figure 5.2 Vendor Analysis Data Retrieved, Transaction MCE3

The next characteristic level to be displayed according to the drilldown shown in Figure 5.1 is for **Material**. The material data will be shown for the vendor **GRN Ghana**, which is selected as shown in Figure 5.2.

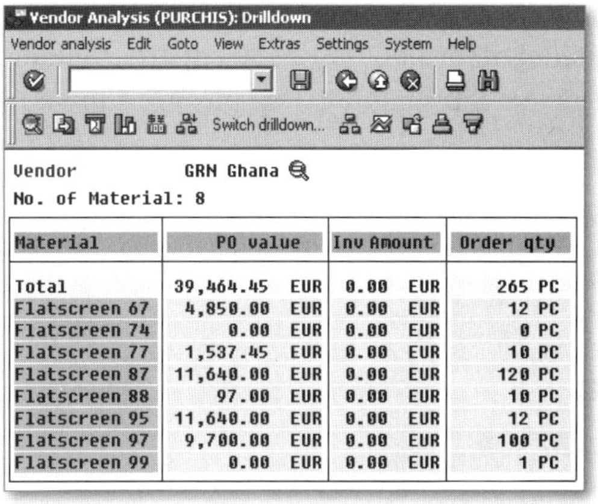

Material	PO value	Inv Amount	Order qty
Total	39,464.45 EUR	0.00 EUR	265 PC
Flatscreen 67	4,850.00 EUR	0.00 EUR	12 PC
Flatscreen 74	0.00 EUR	0.00 EUR	0 PC
Flatscreen 77	1,537.45 EUR	0.00 EUR	10 PC
Flatscreen 87	11,640.00 EUR	0.00 EUR	120 PC
Flatscreen 88	97.00 EUR	0.00 EUR	10 PC
Flatscreen 95	11,640.00 EUR	0.00 EUR	12 PC
Flatscreen 97	9,700.00 EUR	0.00 EUR	100 PC
Flatscreen 99	0.00 EUR	0.00 EUR	1 PC

Figure 5.3 Standard Drilldown Screen, Transaction MCE3

The materials shown in Figure 5.3 have been supplied by that particular vendor. According to the standard drilldown, there is one more level that can be reviewed, the period level. Again, by selecting a material from the data and then choosing **View • Standard Drilldown** from the header menu, the period data for that material is shown (see Figure 5.4).

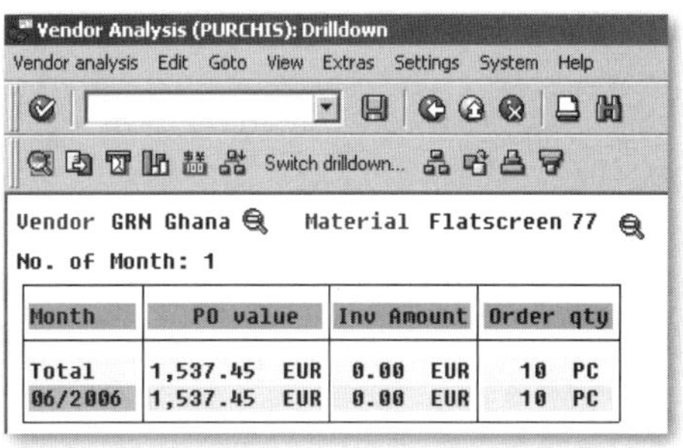

Month	PO value	Inv Amount	Order qty
Total	1,537.45 EUR	0.00 EUR	10 PC
06/2006	1,537.45 EUR	0.00 EUR	10 PC

Figure 5.4 Standard Drilldown to Period Date for Material for Vendor Analysis, Transaction MCE3

5.1.2 Change Drilldown

Once a characteristic drilldown has been executed as was shown in Figure 5.2, the data is displayed for the top level of the drilldown. You can change the drilldown so that the SAP standard drilldown is not used.

Using the same transaction for vendor analysis, MCE3, and the same initial selection criteria, the resulting analysis is shown in Figure 5.2. At this interval, the analyst can change the drilldown by selecting the following from the header menu: **View • Change** drilldown.

A dialog box will appear and show the reviewer the characteristics, which can be chosen instead of the standard drilldown characteristic, **Vendor**, which is grayed out. The header menu choice and dialog box are shown in Figure 5.5.

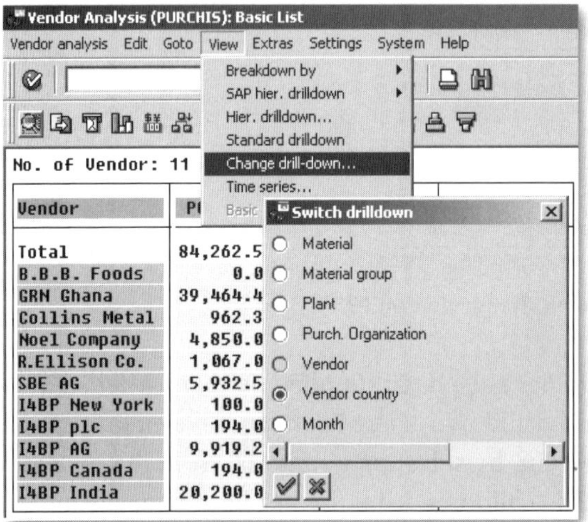

Figure 5.5 Dialog Box to Allow a Change of Characteristic for the Drilldown of the Vendor Analysis, Transaction MCE3

From the dialog box shown in Figure 5.5, the reviewer can change the drilldown from vendor to one of the six other characteristics listed. For this example, the reviewer has chosen a **Vendor country**, and a new analysis results screen is displayed showing the four countries of the relevant vendors. Figure 5.6 shows the values for the four countries: **Germany**, Great Britain (**GB**), **India**, and the **US**.

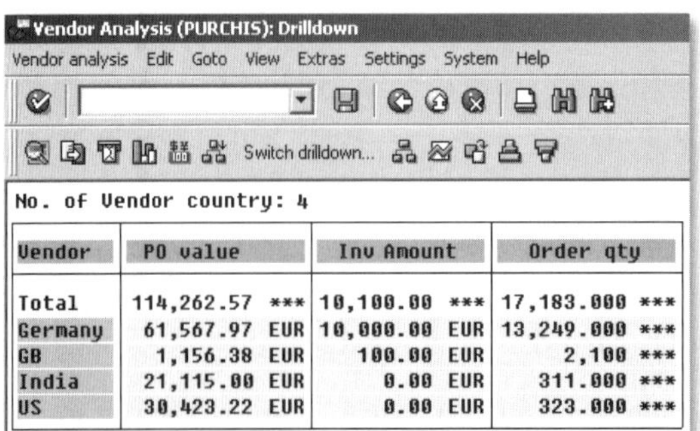

Figure 5.6 Vendor Country Drilldown of the Data After the Drilldown Was Changed from Vendor, Transaction MCE3

Please note that once the drilldown has been changed from the initial characteristic, the reviewer cannot continue a standard drilldown from that analysis.

5.2 Hierarchy Drilldown

The *hierarchy drilldown* allows the reviewer of the data to analyze the data at lower levels by a structured hierarchy. These hierarchies include Material Class, Product Group, Functional Location Hierarchy, Vendor Class, etc.

SAP has supplied a number of predefined hierarchies that can be used with various information structures, which are listed below:

5.2.1 SAP Defined Hierarchy Drilldowns

Let's take a look at these drilldowns:

- **Purchasing Information System**
  Vendor Class, Material Class, Product Group, and Product Hierarchy
- **Inventory Controlling**
  Product Group, Material Class, and Product Hierarchy
- **Shop Floor Information System**
  Work Center Hierarchy, Material Class, Product group, and Product Hierarchy
- **Quality Management Information System**
  Vendor Class, Material Class, Customer Class, Customer Hierarchy, and Product Hierarchy
- **Plant Maintenance Information System**
  Functional Location Hierarchy, Classification of Functional Locations, Classification of Equipment, and Product Hierarchy
- **Sales Information System**
  Product Group, Customer Class, Material Class, Customer Hierarchy, and Product Hierarchy

5.2.2 Executing a Hierarchy Drilldown

To run an SAP-defined hierarchy, a standard analysis should be run from the LIS menu. In this example, the Material Group analysis, Transaction MCE5, has been chosen. This can be found using the navigation path: **SAP Menu •**

Logistics • Logistics Controlling • Logistics Information System • Standard Analyses • Purchasing • Material Group.

After entering the relevant selection criteria in the initial screen, the analysis is executed and the results data is displayed. To run the SAP hierarchy, the selection is made from the header menu: **View • SAP Hierarchy Drilldown** and then the hierarchy options are shown. In this case, as shown in Figure 5.7, the predefined hierarchy selections are **Vendor Class**, **Material Class**, and **Product Group**.

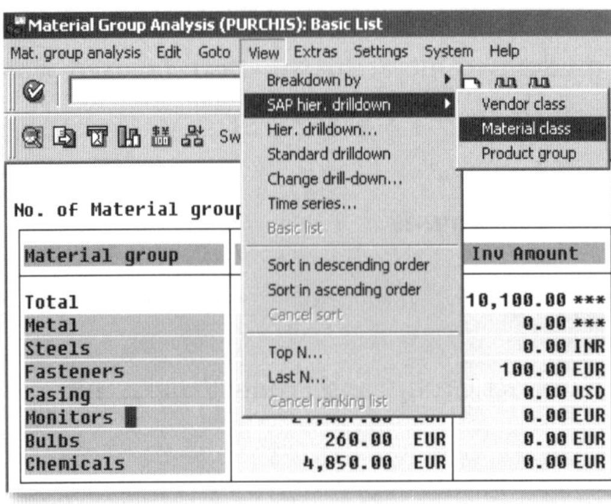

Figure 5.7 SAP-Defined Hierarchy Drilldowns Available, Transaction MCE5

The hierarchy drilldown allows the data reviewer to choose a line item from the results shown in Figure 5.7 and drill down using the hierarchy. In this case, the line item, **Monitors**, is highlighted by placing the cursor on that line. The **Material class** hierarchy has been selected as the basis for the drill-down.

The resulting hierarchy analysis, as shown in Figure 5.8, displays the results of the top level of the Material Class hierarchy drilldown for the **Material Group**, **Monitors**.

The data reviewer can display the hierarchy that she is drilling down into by selecting **Extras • Display Hierarchy** from the header menu. This shows all the levels of the hierarchy down to the object level (see Figure 5.9). The hierarchy drilldown will allow the user to review data at all of these levels of the hierarchy down to the **Material** level, as shown in Figure 5.9.

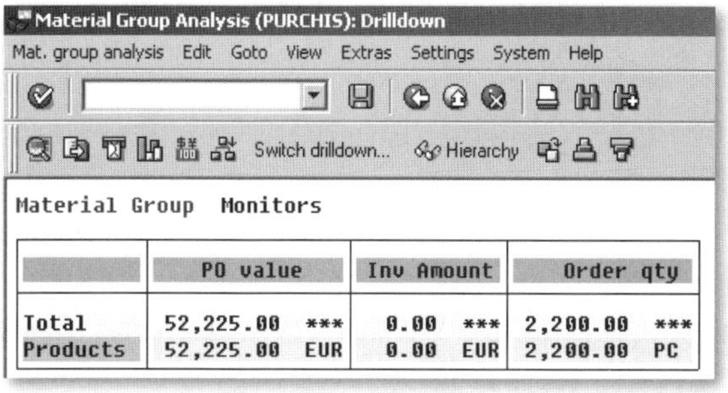

Figure 5.8 Top Level of Material Class Hierarchy for Material Group Standard Analysis, Transaction MCE5

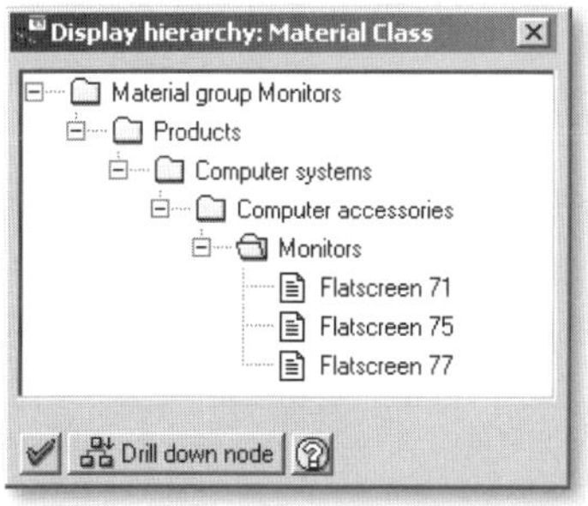

Figure 5.9 Material Class Hierarchy for Material Group, Monitors

5.3 Switching Information Structures

Within the drilldown, the analyst can move from one information structure to another, based on the information being analyzed. In the example of MCE5 and the **Material Group Monitors**, as was shown in Figure 5.8 and Figure 5.9, you can use information from another information structure to further analyze the information on the material group.

To switch to another information structure, use the menu path from the header menu: **Goto • Other info structure** as shown in Figure 5.10. A dialog box opens, from which the data reviewer can choose another information structure.

The display of available information structures, as shown in Figure 5.11, allows the data analyst to choose a structure that will provide more data on the materials from the hierarchical analysis.

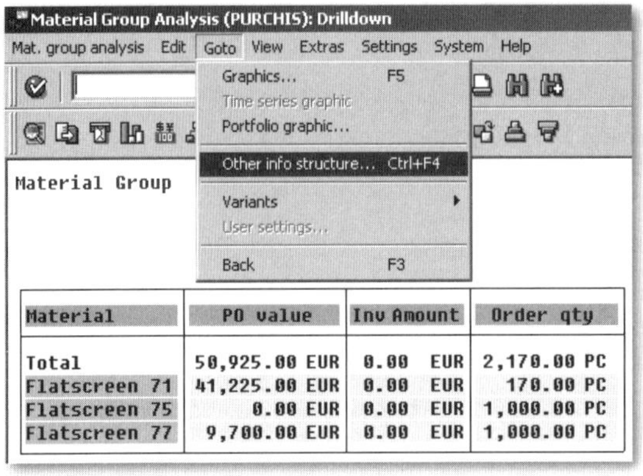

Figure 5.10 Path to Switch to Another Information Structure to Perform Further Data Analysis

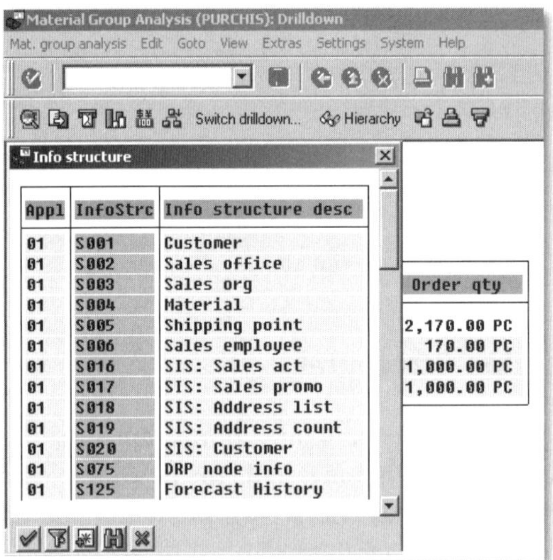

Figure 5.11 Available Information Structures to Choose to Switch to Material Group Analysis

After selecting an information structure to switch to, the transaction will access the new information structure and provide further information on the objects from the previous hierarchy drilldown. In this example, the data analyst has chosen the **Material** information structure (**S004**).

The data, shown in Figure 5.12, from the new information structure (S004) is shown for the materials derived by the Material Group analysis and the information structure S012.

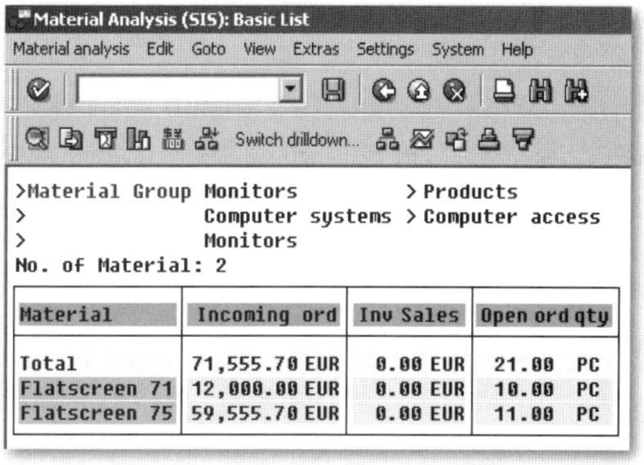

Figure 5.12 Data from Information Structure (S004)

5.4 Selection Log

When executing a drilldown, you can review the selections that have been made and you can also view statistics regarding the analysis by accessing the Selection log. You can also select the Selection log by using the menu path: **Extras • Selection Log**.

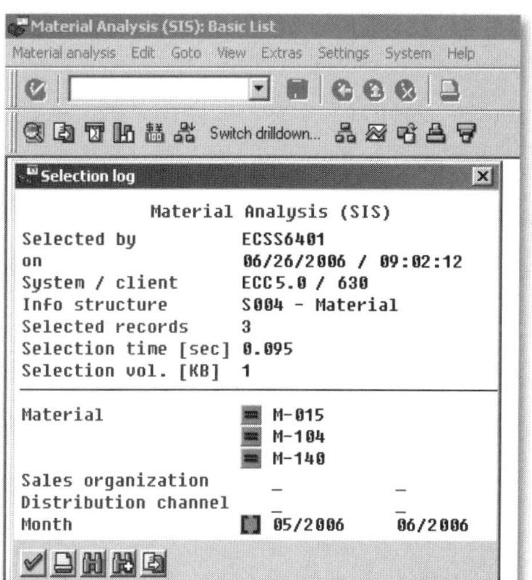

Figure 5.13 Selection Log for the Material Group Selection Analysis

The information displayed in the **Selection log**, shown in Figure 5.13, allows the analyst to review what information structure is being used, what selection has been made, and what selection criteria was used.

5.5 Summary

In this chapter, I have discussed two types of drilldown within a standard analysis. A drilldown can allow an analyst to review data at the top level and then review the lower levels via the drilldown functionality. Drilldown allows the analyst to see the data at a more specific criteria level based on either characteristic drilldown or hierarchy drilldown.

In Chapter 6, the focus will be on the use of ABC analysis to rank the results of a standard analysis.

The ABC analysis is performed on the basic list of a standard analysis where the results are to be ranked. The ABC analysis classifies the characteristic values in the order of importance based on the relevant key figures.

6 ABC Analysis

Once the result, or basic list, of a standard analysis is displayed, the data analyst can review the data, which may include exporting the data to an external system, or performing more analysis in SAP. One example of further analysis in SAP is the use of ABC analysis. This functionality can be accessed from the basic list of a standard analysis and allows the characteristic data to be ranked in order of importance based on the key figures.

Many companies use ABC analysis to rank objects, for instance, materials for cycle counting, etc. Companies can rank their objects by using the ABC analysis of the data from the standard analyses.

6.1 Create an ABC Analysis

The ABC analysis can be accessed from the basic list of a standard analysis. This means that the data analyst entered some values into the selection criteria of a standard analysis and the results are displayed in the basic list.

For this example, the standard analysis for Material, Transaction MCE7, is used. This can be found using the navigation path: **SAP Menu • Logistics • Logistics Controlling • Logistics Information System • Standard Analyses • Purchasing • Material**.

Once the selection criterion has been entered and the transaction executed, the basic list will display the relevant data. To execute the ABC analysis, select a column of data to be analyzed and then access ABC analysis from the header menu: **Edit • ABC analysis** (see Figure 6.1).

Once the ABC analysis has been selected, a dialog box opens, displaying a list of strategies, one of which can be chosen as the strategy for the ABC analysis.

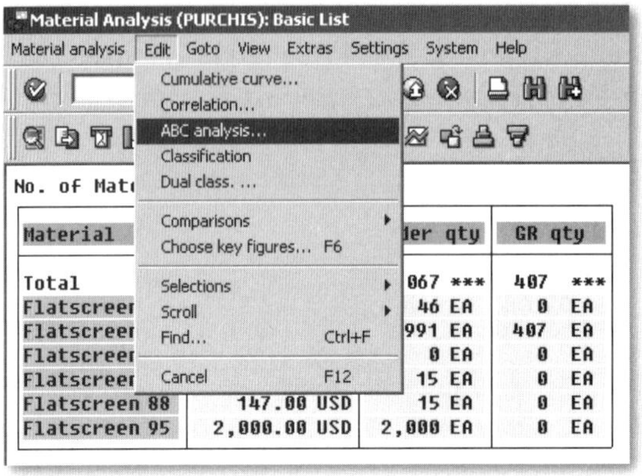

Figure 6.1 ABC Analysis Option from Header Menu of Material Standard Analysis, Transaction MCE7

6.1.1 Strategies for an ABC Analysis

Figure 6.2 shows you the four strategies available to the data analyst that can be used to perform the ABC analysis. These are examined below.

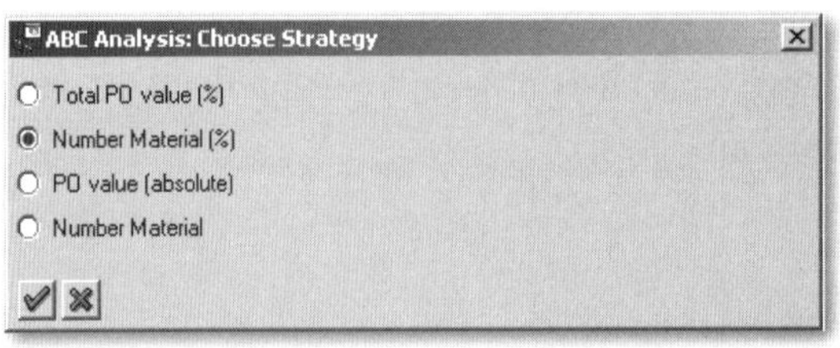

Figure 6.2 ABC Analysis Strategies on Material Standard Analysis, Transaction MCE7

- **Total of the Key Figure as a Percentage**
  This strategy **Total PO Value (%)**, will display the assigned A, B, or C segments as a percentage of the total value of that key figure. The strategy sorts the values and then the characteristic values, which make up the first defined percentage of the total key figure value, are assigned to the A segment. The next defined percentage is assigned to the B segment. The characteristic values that make up the final assigned percentage are assigned to the C segment.
- **Number of Characteristic Values as a Percentage**
  This strategy **Number Material (%)**, calculates the number of characteristic values assigned to the A, B, and C segments, and these values are given as a percent of the total number. This is the strategy that is chosen in Figure 6.2.

- **Absolute Key Figure**
  With this strategy **PO value (absolute)**, the analyst can define the boundaries between the A, B, and C segments. For example, the analyst can define that all characteristic values with a key figure value of more than 100 are assigned to the A segment, all characteristic values with a key figure value of less than 100 but more than 30 are assigned to the B segment, and all characteristic values with a key figure value of less than 30 are assigned to the C segment.
- **Number of Characteristic Values**
  This strategy **Number Material**, allows the user to define the number of characteristic values for the A and B segments. This strategy assumes that all remaining characteristic values are assigned to the C segment.

6.1.2 Strategy Parameters

Subsequent to the selection of the ABC analysis strategy, a dialog box will be displayed allowing analysts to keep the default parameters or to define their own.

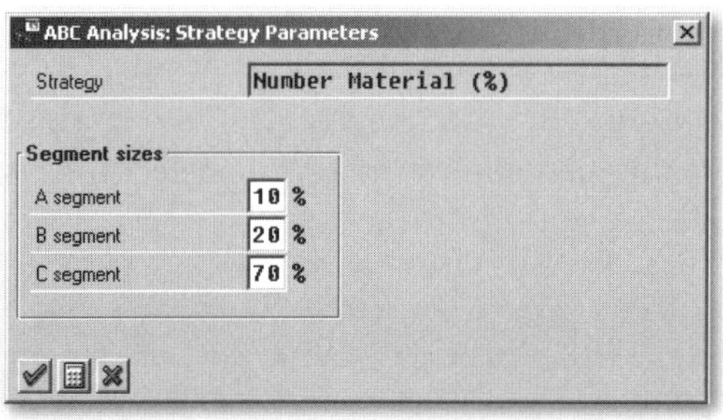

Figure 6.3 Strategy Parameters for ABC Analysis on Material Standard Analysis, Transaction MCE7

In Figure 6.3, the parameters for the ABC analysis can be entered. The default parameters for the particular strategy are displayed: 10 % for A, 20 % for B, and 70 % for C. If the analyst requires the percentages to be different for the analysis, he can change the percentage split on this screen.

6.1.3 Graphic Display of ABC Analysis

After reviewing the strategy parameters, the ABC analysis is executed. A graphical display of the results is returned, as shown in Figure 6.4.

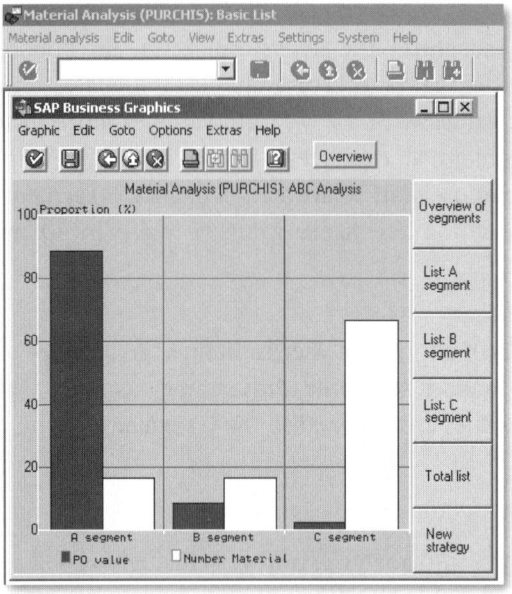

Figure 6.4 Graphical Display Showing ABC Analysis for Material Standard Analysis, Transaction MCE7

The ABC analysis graphic display, Figure 6.4, shows the Purchase Order Value and Number of Materials split into the three segments. There is also a set of icons to the right of the graphic that allows the user to select further analysis from the following options:

- Overview of segments
- List: A segment
- List: B segment
- List: C segment
- Total list
- New strategy

Now, let's examine these in more detail.

Overview of Segments

The overview of the segments shows the analyst the complete picture of the ABC analysis. The overview, shown in Figure 6.5, displays the number of materials per segment, the purchase order value per segment, and the respective percentages.

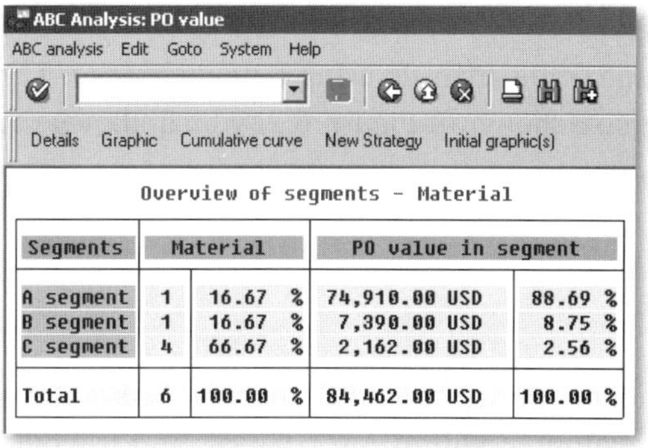

Figure 6.5 Overview of A, B, and C Segment Data for Material Standard Analysis

List of Segments

There are three options for the analyst to choose from; the list of objects is displayed for each of these segments. Figure 6.6 shows the three segment lists, **A**, **B**, and **C**.

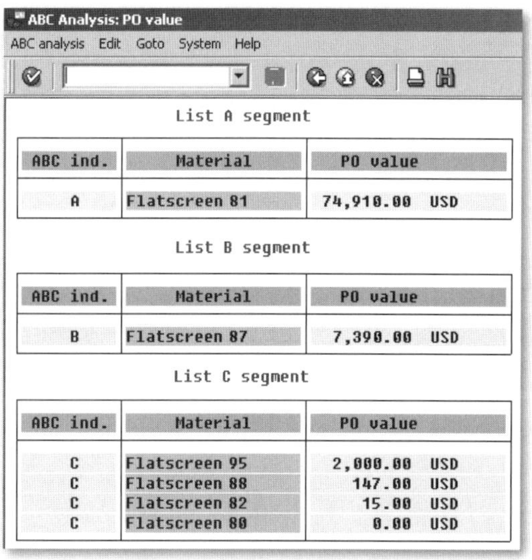

Figure 6.6 Three Segment Lists for the Material Standard Analysis

Total list

The total list will display all the objects that are in the A, B or C segments.

New strategy

The analyst has the choice to repeat the analysis using a new strategy. The program will display the dialog box shown in Figure 6.2, which allows the analyst to choose a new strategy.

6.2 Summary

This chapter addressed the functionality of the ABC analysis. There are a number of strategies that can be adopted within ABC analysis and it would greatly benefit the data analyst to understand the results that these different strategies can provide. The graphical displays are also useful when they provide good clear results, and manipulating the ABC analysis to do this can provide the kind of visual results that management often demands. In Chapter 7, I'll discuss the classification of standard analyses and how this functionality can show trends in the reported data.

Classification of the standard analysis allows the data analyst to review the results and to identify trends or visible relationships within the returned data. This classification functionality creates classes of values with reference to one key figure.

7 Classification Functionality

The classification functionality is useful for reviewing data and quickly sorting information into classes where the values are similar. For example, in production data where the scrap totals per order vary by small amounts, classification makes identifying the worst and best performing orders very clear-cut, especially with large data volumes. The system defines six classes for the initial review, but the analyst can define as few as three. The system also initially defines the class boundaries for the six classes; however, the analyst can change this, as they review the raw data. The analyst can change the number of classes depending on the analysis they are trying to perform for a particular investigation. Some instances would require few classes, others may require more.

The classification functionality can be executed from the basic list resulting from a standard analysis. For this example, the standard analysis for Vendor Analysis, Transaction MCE3, has been used.

From the basic list, as shown in Figure 7.1, a key figure column, for example, Purchase Order value (**PO value**) or Order quantity (**Order qty**) should be selected. The classification function can be executed from the header menu on the basic list: **Edit • Classification**.

The classification function sorts the data into classes or groups that fall within the class boundaries. Initially, the classes are defined by the six-class system. The class limits are defined by the system based on the total data that it is sorting.

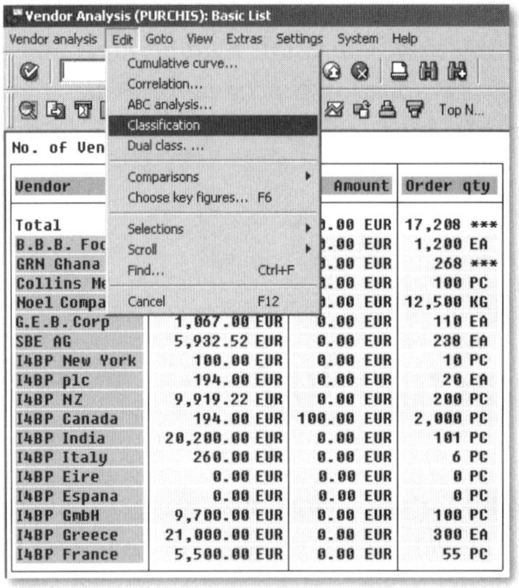

Figure 7.1 Classification Function Selected from Header Menu of Basic List for Vendor Analysis, Transaction MCE3

7.1 Graphical Display of Classification

The classification functionality initially returns a graphical display of the key figure column selected. Figure 7.2 shows the graphical display of the classification of the PO value key figure.

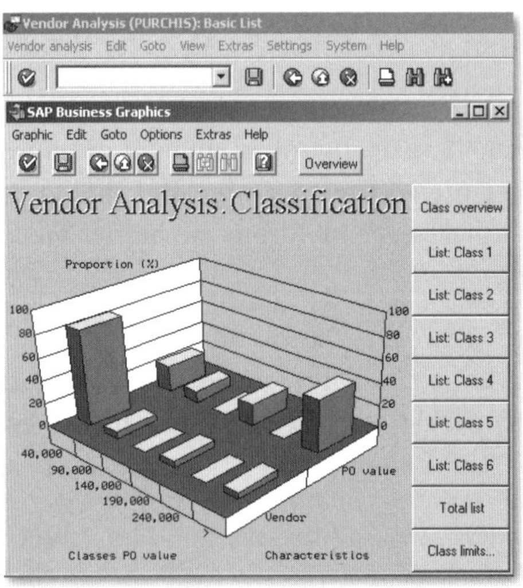

Figure 7.2 Graphical Display of Classification Functionality for Vendor Analysis, Transaction MCE3

The graphical display of the classification in Figure 7.2 shows the pictorial view of the classes. To the right of the graphic in this figure are nine options that the analyst can review. Let's take a look at these now.

7.1.1 Class Overview

The **Class overview** shows the analyst the six classes, as defined by the system, and what values have been selected for each of those classes. The system has created this overview for both the PO value and the vendors.

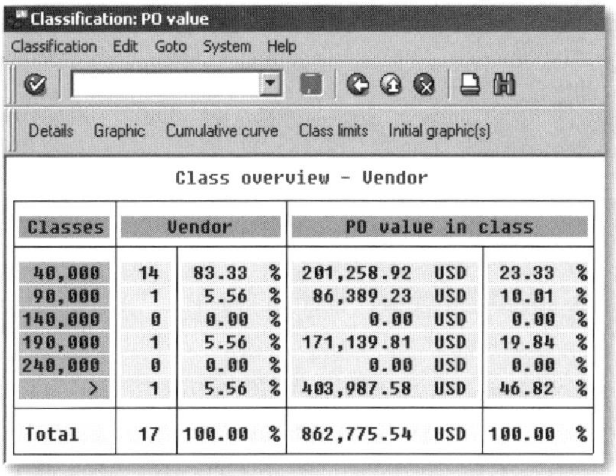

Classes	Vendor		PO value in class			
40,000	14	83.33 %	201,258.92	USD	23.33	%
90,000	1	5.56 %	86,389.23	USD	10.01	%
140,000	0	0.00 %	0.00	USD	0.00	%
190,000	1	5.56 %	171,139.81	USD	19.84	%
240,000	0	0.00 %	0.00	USD	0.00	%
>	1	5.56 %	403,987.58	USD	46.82	%
Total	17	100.00 %	862,775.54	USD	100.00	%

Figure 7.3 Overview for Classification of Vendor Analysis Standard Analysis

The overview, shown in Figure 7.3, gives the analyst a reference of the grouping of the data based on the SAP-defined classes and class boundaries. The analyst can review this and decide to move the boundaries or change the number of classes from the six defined in SAP.

To review the classes in greater detail, the analyst can return to the initial graphic. From this display, the analyst can review the information in each of the six classes.

7.1.2 Class List

The analyst can review the contents of each of the six classes using the icons to the right of the initial graphical display. In Figure 7.3, the overview of the classification shows that **Class 1** has a total of 14 vendors, which is 83.33 % of the total. The analyst can review this and determine that the class boundaries are not justified and that a review of the Class 1 vendors should be made.

Then, the analyst can select **Class 1** (located to the right of the graphical display in Figure 7.2) to view a list of the class contents.

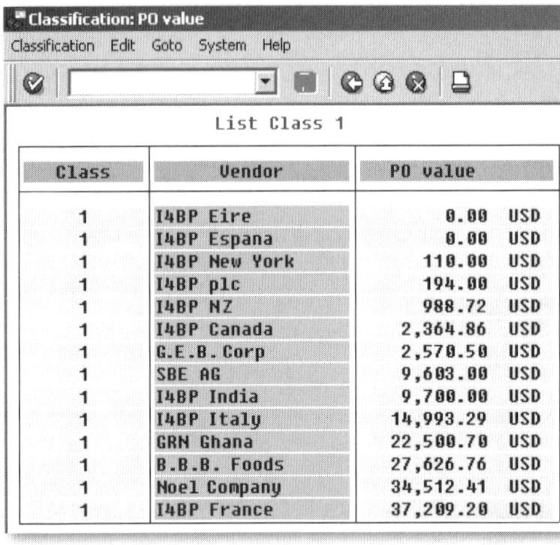

Class	Vendor	PO value
1	I4BP Eire	0.00 USD
1	I4BP Espana	0.00 USD
1	I4BP New York	110.00 USD
1	I4BP plc	194.00 USD
1	I4BP NZ	988.72 USD
1	I4BP Canada	2,364.86 USD
1	G.E.B. Corp	2,570.50 USD
1	SBE AG	9,603.00 USD
1	I4BP India	9,700.00 USD
1	I4BP Italy	14,993.29 USD
1	GRN Ghana	22,500.70 USD
1	B.B.B. Foods	27,626.76 USD
1	Noel Company	34,512.41 USD
1	I4BP France	37,209.20 USD

Figure 7.4 Contents of Class 1 as Defined by Classification Function in SAP

The **Class 1** display, as shown in Figure 7.4, identifies the vendors that have been allocated to Class 1 based on the class boundaries set by SAP. After reviewing the vendors in the class, the analyst can decide that the class boundaries should be changed, or the number of classes reduced to make the classification more realistic.

7.1.3 Class Limits

Initially in the classification functionality, the number of classes and the class limits are predefined by the system and sometimes the data is skewed towards one particular class or classes. To rectify this problem, the analyst can change one or both elements.

To review or change the number of classes or class limits, the analyst can select the Class Limits icon from the initial graphic, Figure 7.2. After the class limits have been selected, a dialog box opens, displaying the current number of classes used and offers the analyst the opportunity to change the number of classes to as few as three, as shown in Figure 7.5.

Subsequent to the number of classes being reviewed or changed, the class limits for the key value are displayed. The limits can be amended to reflect the data analyst's specific requirements, based on his analysis of the data.

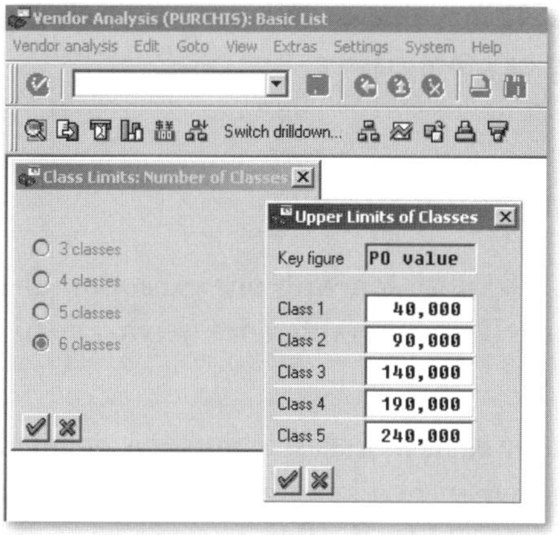

Figure 7.5 Changing Number of Classes and Class Limits to Meet Analyst's Requirements

When satisfied with the class limits, the analyst can execute this new version of class limits and a new graphical display of the vendor analysis is displayed, as shown in Figure 7.6. From there, the analyst can review the classification data and make further changes if necessary.

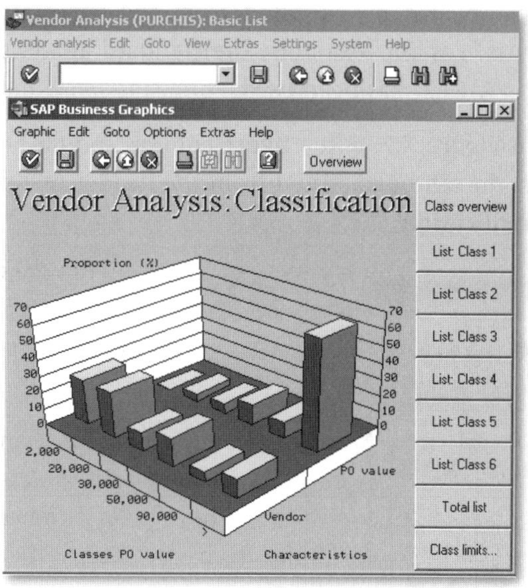

Figure 7.6 Graphical Display for Classification of Vendor Analysis Based on Amended Class Limits

The graphical display of the data in Figure 7.6 shows the six classes identified with the title, *Classes PO value*. This display shows that the data is more evenly distributed across the classes. This is due to the class limits being amended to avoid skewed data in one or more classes.

7.2 Dual Classification Functionality

Dual classification is similar to typical classification with one exception: the characteristic values are segmented into classes with reference to two key figures rather than one key figure.

Dual classification allows an analyst to review issues where the detailed examination of problems is simplified when two key figures are used. For example, in the SAP Plant Maintenance (SAP PM) module, analysis of equipment with the key figure of recorded notifications may be further assisted by using another key figure, such as completed notifications, to analyze equipment problems on a deeper level. The dual classification process produces a matrix based on the basic list results. The matrix shows the cross-reference between the two classifications and the analyst can see from the results where anomalies may exist.

The dual classification functionality can be executed from the basic list resulting from a standard analysis. For this example, the standard analysis for Material analysis, Transaction MCE7, has been used.

From the basic list, as shown in Figure 7.7, a key figure column should be selected. The classification function can be executed from the header menu on the basic list: **Edit • Dual Classification**.

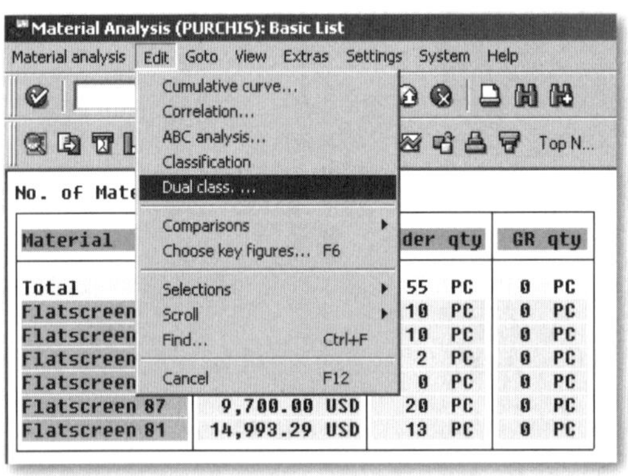

Figure 7.7 Classification Function Selected from Header Menu of Basic List for Material Analysis, Transaction MCE7

When the analyst selects dual classification, a dialog box opens, displaying a number of key figures that the analyst can choose two from (see Figure 7.8).

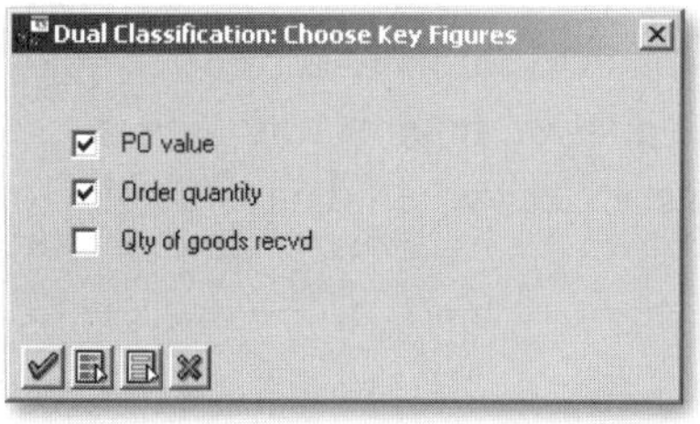

Figure 7.8 Key Figure Choice for Dual Classification of Material Analysis, Transaction MCE7

7.3 Graphical Display of Dual Classification

The result of the dual classification is a graphical display, as shown in Figure 7.9, similar to those found in single classification. The SAP system defaults to six classes and defines the class limits for the data.

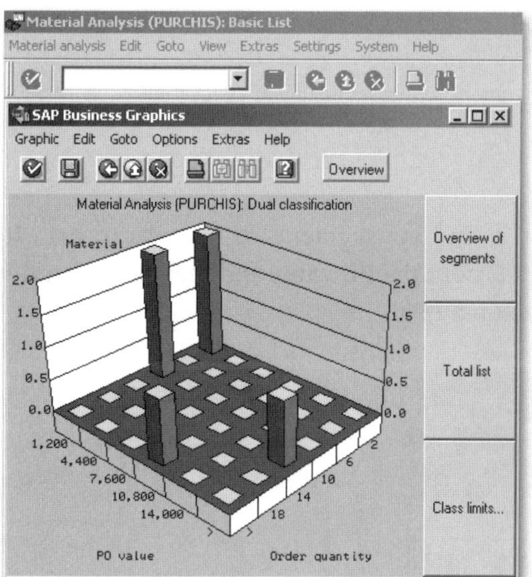

Figure 7.9 Dual Classification Graphical Display for Material Analysis

The three options available to the analyst are: to review the segment data, review the total list, and review the class limits. These options are discussed more fully in the next sections.

7.3.1 Overview of Segments

The segment data shows a matrix of material data with respect to the two sets of classification classes defined by the system. In Figure 7.10, the number of materials is shown for both classes for PO value and for Order quantity. The values in the matrix indicate to the analyst, in very simple terms, in what areas the data lies. In this way, it is very clear when data is outside of the norm and needs to be investigated.

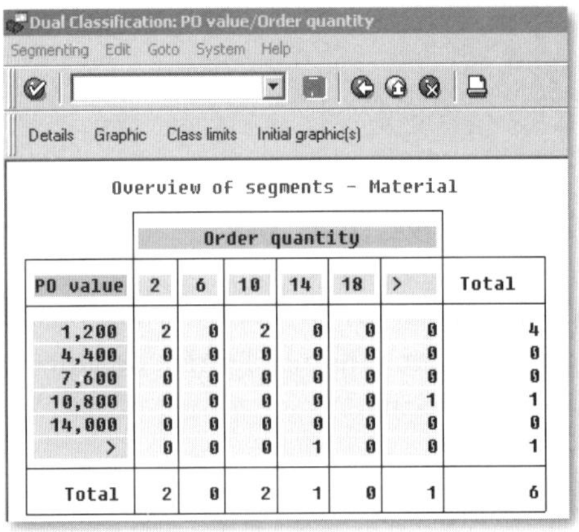

	Order quantity						
PO value	2	6	10	14	18	>	Total
1,200	2	0	2	0	0	0	4
4,400	0	0	0	0	0	0	0
7,600	0	0	0	0	0	0	0
10,800	0	0	0	0	0	1	1
14,000	0	0	0	0	0	0	0
>	0	0	0	1	0	0	1
Total	2	0	2	1	0	1	6

Figure 7.10 Material Data and its Assignment to Classes in Dual Classification

7.3.2 Total List

The total list shows information from both segments in a matrix format. In the example shown in Figure 7.11, both the **PO value** and the order quantity (**Order qty**) are displayed for each material.

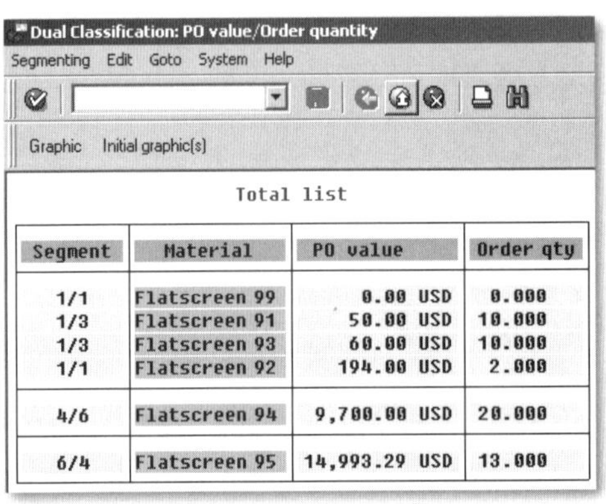

Segment	Material	PO value	Order qty
1/1	Flatscreen 99	0.00 USD	0.000
1/3	Flatscreen 91	50.00 USD	10.000
1/3	Flatscreen 93	60.00 USD	10.000
1/1	Flatscreen 92	194.00 USD	2.000
4/6	Flatscreen 94	9,700.00 USD	20.000
6/4	Flatscreen 95	14,993.29 USD	13.000

Figure 7.11 Segment List for Dual Classification of Material Analysis, Transaction MCE7

7.3.3 Class Limits

The class limits are the parameters of the class that has been created. For example, the class limits in Figure 7.9 show limits for the PO Value as 0 to 1200, 1201 to 4400, etc. The class limits can be changed for both sets of classes and can be accessed using the **Class limits...** button on the initial graphical display as seen in Figure 7.9.

As with the single classification method, the system defaults to six classes, but the analyst can reduce this default number to three. In addition, the analyst can change the class limits for either or both segments.

7.4 Summary

In this chapter, I discussed using single classification and dual classification to group together similar key figures. This classification tool is powerful for the analyst, because it can combine similar results, which may highlight issues that need to be further investigated, such as high purchase order quantities or high notifications in Plant Maintenance. Dual classification gives the analyst another level of analysis in which to highlight issues in the supply chain.

In Chapter 8, the focus changes from the standard analyses, which we have been discussing, to the flexible analyses, which afford analysts greater freedom to create and manipulate data.

Flexible analysis lets the data analyst create a more personalized data retrieval and review procedure using evaluations and evaluation structures. In addition, the functionality of the SAP Report Writer allows for the creation of customized reports.

8 Flexible Analysis

Rapidly changing business conditions found in industries such as financial companies and fast moving consumer products require rapid decision-making. Flexible analyses provide a solution for rapid decision-making and provide the tools necessary for a more personalized and complex review of data within SAP. The standard analysis and predefined information structures that are delivered with SAP enable the analyst to quickly retrieve information that may be relevant to the issues that arise in the supply chain.

Unfortunately, for some complex supply chain monitoring, the predefined information structures or the standard analyses are not suitable. The flexible analysis tools, however, do allow for a more customizable view of the data in the information systems and, with the SAP Report Writer, the ability to deliver personalized reporting becomes a reality.

8.1 Overview of Flexible Analysis

In a standard analysis, the data is defined in an information structure and retrieved by the standard analysis. In a flexible analysis, the data is defined in an evaluation structure and an evaluation is executed to retrieve the data from the structure.

In addition, each standard information structure has an evaluation structure that is named the same. Therefore, a standard information structure can be used in flexible analyses, if required.

The SAP Report Writer functionality used with flexible analysis is more commonly used for reporting in the SAP FI/CO module. The functionality available with flexible analysis is a subset of the functionality used in accounting. We'll address those limitations later on in this chapter.

The advantages of using flexible analysis are that the analyst can include data from sources that are not available in the standard information structures. This flexibility allows the analyst to create structures that extract data from part of the information structure and combine this data with the data from regular data dictionary tables not used in the LIS. The importance of this is that when the client asks for data reporting outside of the standard LIS, you can help meet the client's request by using flexible analysis.

8.2 Evaluation Structures

Much like an information structure is the data source of data for standard analyses, the evaluation structure is the data source for the flexible analysis evaluation. The evaluation structure can be defined from fields in one data dictionary table or can comprise fields from several tables. An evaluation structure consists of characteristics and key figures, and allows the analyst to use the functionality of the Report Writer.

An evaluation structure can be created using Transaction MC27 or located by using the navigation path: **SAP Menu • Logistics • Logistics Controlling • Logistics Information System • Flexible Analyses • Evaluation Structure • Create**.

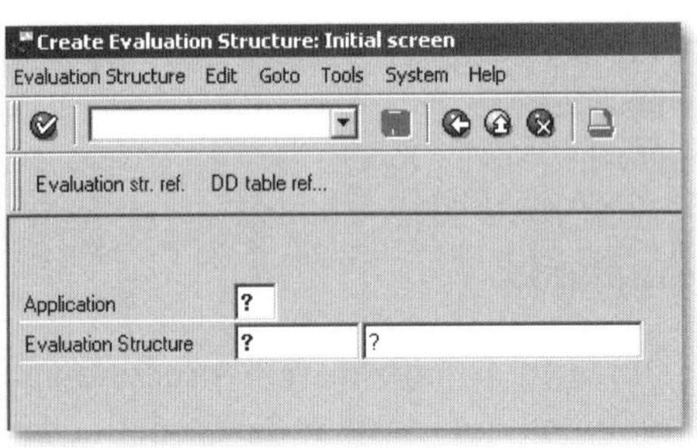

Figure 8.1 Initial Screen for Creation of an Evaluation Structure, Transaction MC27

The creation of an evaluation structure, as shown in Figure 8.1, requires entry of an application area, evaluation structure name, and structure description.

8.2.1 Application Area

The application area refers to a defined area of the LIS. For example, Purchasing is 02, Inventory Controlling is 03, Plant Maintenance is 07, etc.

8.2.2 Evaluation Structure Name

This eight-character alphanumeric field should be prefixed by the letters **ZF** to indicate that it is an evaluation structure, for example, ZF003PUR.

8.2.3 Evaluation Structure Description

The evaluation description is a 30-character alphanumeric field that describes the evaluation structure being created. More information on the evaluation structure and how it relates to the flexible analysis evaluation will be described in the following chapters.

8.3 Evaluations

An evaluation is similar to a standard analysis, but the evaluation refers to an evaluation structure, not to an information structure. The evaluation is created from characteristics and key figures, and derives the data from the evaluation structure. Evaluations can provide more flexibility for the analyst, because the use of formulas can be introduced to provide more specific analysis.

An evaluation can be created using Transaction code MC11, or found using the navigation path: **SAP Menu • Logistics • Logistics Controlling • Logistics Information System • Flexible Analyses • Evaluation • Create**.

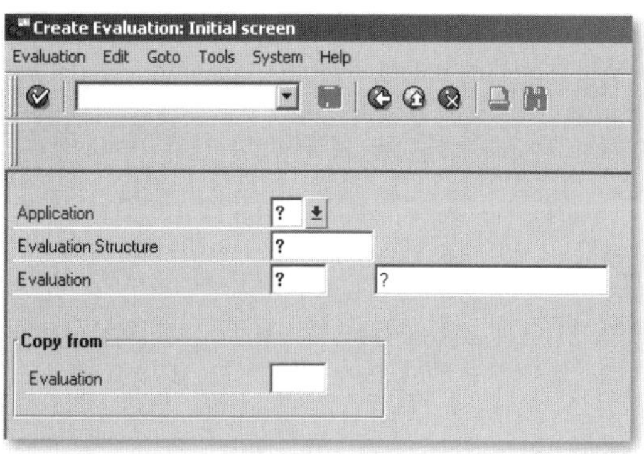

Figure 8.2 Initial Screen for Creation of an Evaluation, Transaction MC11

The creation of an evaluation, as shown in Figure 8.2, requires entry of an application area, an evaluation structure name, the name for the evaluation, and an evaluation description. For descriptions for the application area and the evaluation structure, see Section 8.2.

8.3.1 Evaluation Name

The evaluation name can be four alphanumeric characters. The protocol in many clients is that the evaluation begins with a **Z**. However, this may not be suitable for all clients.

8.3.2 Evaluation Description

The evaluation description must be added for each evaluation. This description can be up to 35 characters in length. More information on evaluations and how they function within flexible analysis will be described in the following chapters.

8.4 Summary

This chapter has briefly shown the key elements of the flexible analysis functionality. The evaluation structure and the evaluation are similar to the information structure and the standard analysis. However, the flexible analysis tool can provide more depth to data analysis by combining information from different tables and the use of formulas.

In Chapter 9, I'll discuss the purpose and function of the evaluation structure, and in the subsequent chapters, I'll explain more fully the role of the evaluation itself.

The evaluation structure defines what data is available to the evaluation for analysis. The structure can refer to a standard information structure, another evaluation structure, or a table in the data dictionary. The structure consists of characteristics and key figures.

9 Evaluation Structure

The evaluation structure is similar to the standard information structure in that it consists of characteristics and key figures. It is key to be able to help the client pinpoint specific data that may be available only in data dictionary tables and to use that data in the LIS. It is important to define the evaluation structure to include that data, as well as data from standard information structures.

9.1 Create an Evaluation Structure

In Chapter 8, the initial screen for creating an evaluation structure was introduced. In this section, we'll explore the details of creating an evaluation structure.

An evaluation structure can be created using Transaction MC27, or found using the navigation path: **SAP Menu • Logistics • Logistics Controlling • Logistics Information System • Flexible Analyses • Evaluation Structure • Create**.

For this example, the Purchasing application area is used, as shown in Figure 9.1. In addition, the evaluation structure name and description have been entered. Two options on this screen allow the analyst to create the evaluation structure:

- With reference to another Evaluation Structure (**F5** key)
- With reference to a Data Dictionary Table (**F6** key)

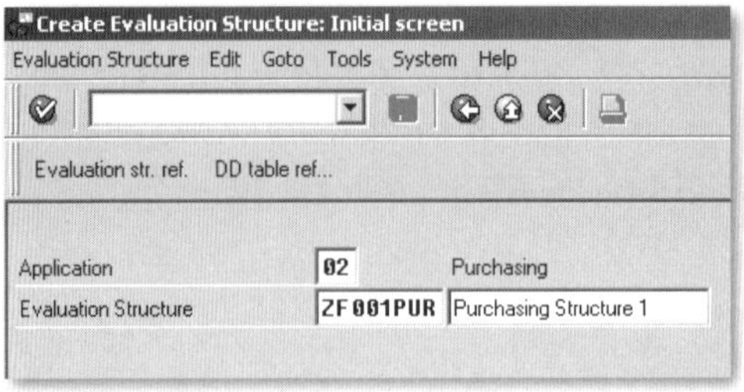

Figure 9.1 Initial Screen for Creation of an Evaluation Structure, Transaction MC27

The following sections will show you how the analyst can use each of these options to create an evaluation structure.

9.1.1 Create Evaluation Structure with Reference to an Evaluation Structure

After the initial information has been entered for the evaluation structure, the analyst can select the **F5** key and create an evaluation structure with reference to another evaluation structure.

The evaluation structures available to the analyst are those in the application area that were entered. In this example, it would be those evaluation structures displayed in the Purchasing area.

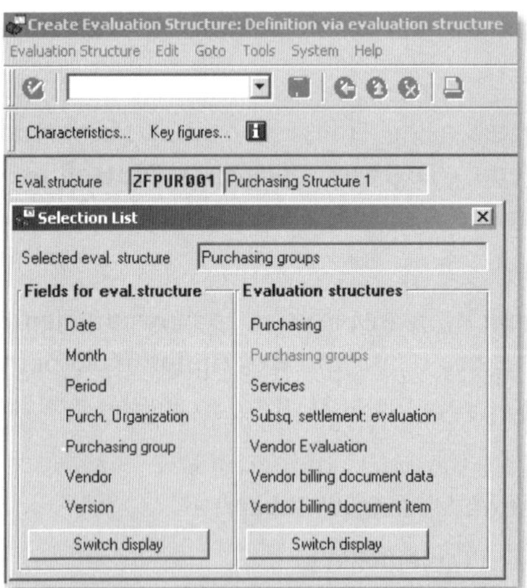

Figure 9.2 Evaluation Structures and Characteristics Available for the New Evaluation Structure

This screen allows the analyst to select information from other evaluation structures. In some cases, these evaluation structures are, in fact, the same as the standard information structures, since each information structure has a corresponding evaluation structure with the same information. In Figure 9.2, the analyst would have selected the **Characteristics** option on the screen or selected **Edit • Characteristics** from the header menu.

Each of the available evaluation structures is shown from the purchasing area. As each evaluation structure is selected, the corresponding characteristics are displayed in the left column.

Once the characteristics are selected, the key figures can be determined by using the **Key figures** option on the screen, or by selecting **Edit • Key Figures** from the header menu.

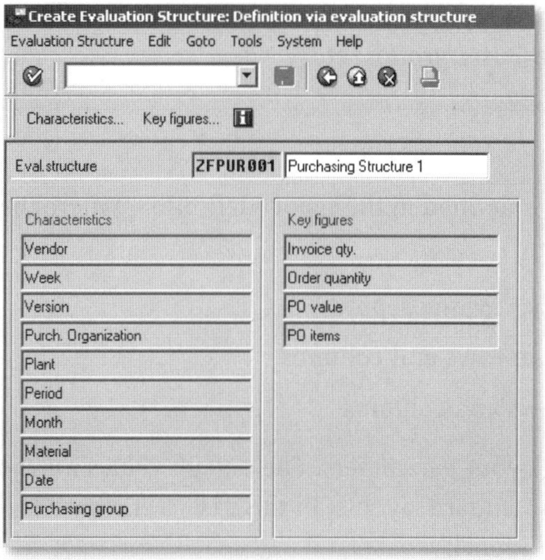

Figure 9.3 Characteristics and Key Figures Selected for New Evaluation Structure with Reference to Existing Structures

When the evaluation structures are shown, the key figures can be selected, and then they can be copied over to the new evaluation structure, as shown in Figure 9.3. The final option on the screen is the technical information option. This can also be selected by choosing **Edit • Technical Info** from the header menu. The technical information, shown in Figure 9.4, allows the analyst to view certain technical aspects of the evaluation structure.

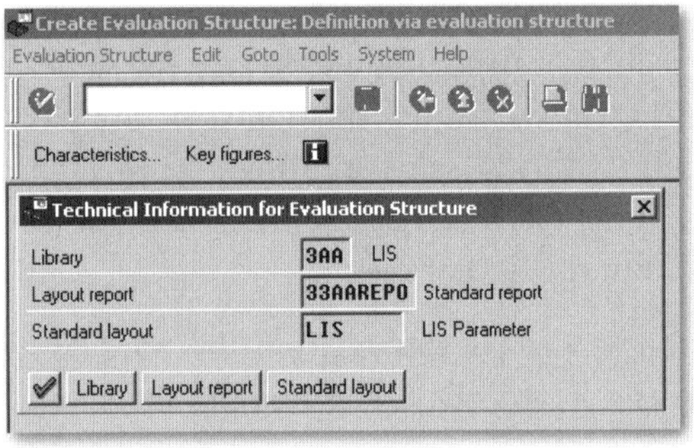

Figure 9.4 Technical Information of New Evaluation Structure, Transaction MC27

Library

The library defines which characteristics and key figures are to be used in a report. When a report is created, it must be assigned to a library. The library can hold reports for certain areas, user groups, etc.

Layout Report

The structure of a layout report is defined in the report definition, where the analyst can define the following:

- The limitation of characteristics for the report
- Which characteristics appear in rows and columns
- Which subtotals appear in rows and columns

The report layout is defined by layout parameters. The default values for the parameters can be derived from standard layouts. In this case, a standard layout is highlighted for the layout report.

Standard Layout

Generally a report has a significant number of layout parameters. These parameters are used to control the layout of the data in the report. Instead of entering these parameters each time a report is created, standard layouts are used and referenced. A standard layout provides default values for report layouts that can be customized.

9.1.2 Create Evaluation Structure with Reference to a Data Dictionary Table

In Transaction MC27, subsequent to the initial information being entered for the evaluation structure, the analyst can select the **F6** key or use the icon to create an evaluation structure with reference to a data dictionary table.

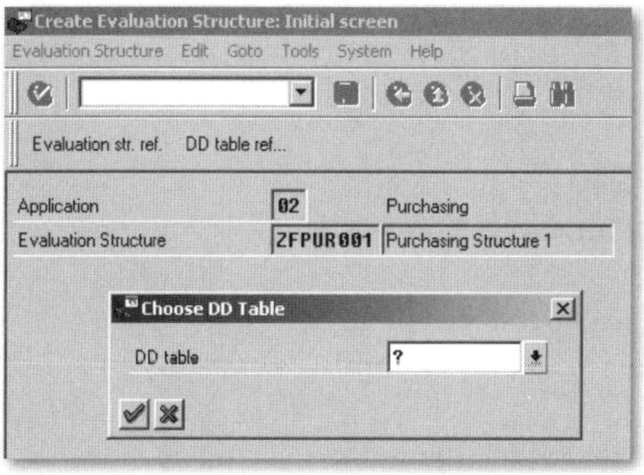

Figure 9.5 Table Selection Screen for Creating an Evaluation Structure Based on a Table

After selecting the option to base the evaluation structure on a table, a dialog box opens, prompting the analyst to enter the name of the table, as shown in Figure 9.5.

If the analyst wants to review the tables, he should select the **F4** key or the down arrow next to the field in order to display the search selection criteria, as shown in Figure 9.6.

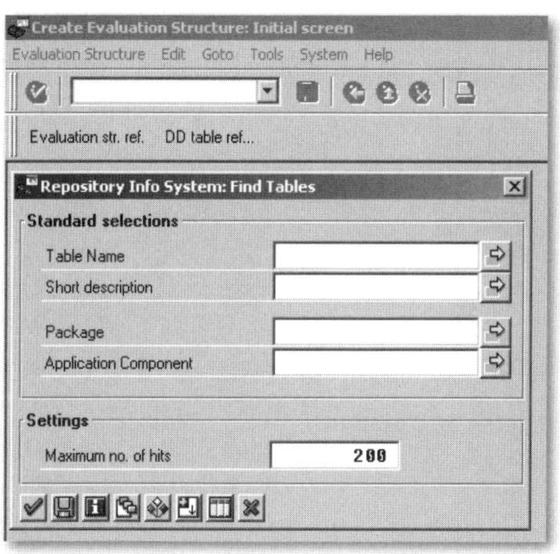

Figure 9.6 Search Selection Criteria for Data Dictionary Table to Use as Evaluation Structure Basis

The search can be accessed via table name, description, package, or application component.

Package

A *package* is a type of folder that contains ABAP Workbench Objects. When an object, such as a program or table, is created, it must be assigned to a package. The first character of a package determines what function a package has, as seen below:

- **A through S and U through X**
  Standard SAP packages and not available for new object
- **T**
  Private test packages
- **Y and Z**
  Available for new customer objects and available for transports
- **$**
  Local package and not available for transport

Examples of the packages are shown in Figure 9.7.

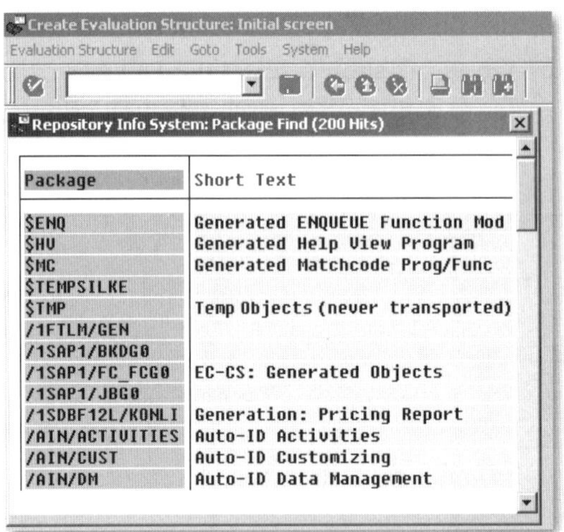

Figure 9.7 A Selection of Packages Available in the SAP System

Application Component

The application component refers to an element of the SAP system. For example, the SAP MM module consists of an application component that includes many subcomponents, as shown in Figure 9.8. The application components are structured in a hierarchy and there are many levels down to access specific functionality in the application component. For example, MM-PUR-REQ refers to Purchase Requisitions and PM-EQM-FL refers to Functional Locations in Plant Maintenance.

The application component is a useful tool in determining which table you may require for an evaluation structure, because it allows you to select a table at the right level, even if you don't know the name of that table.

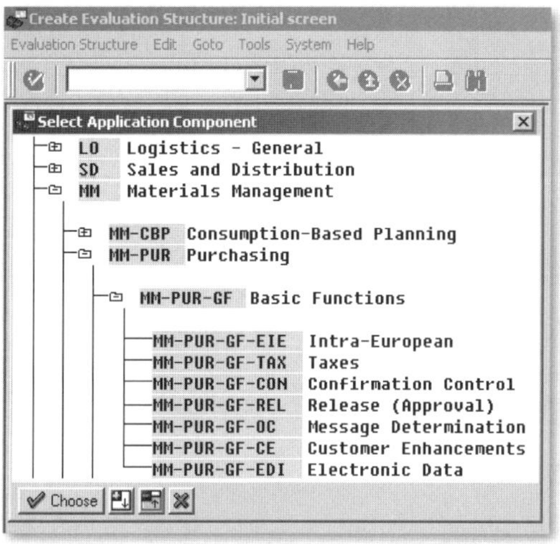

Figure 9.8 Application Components and Subcomponents, Transaction MC27

After the analyst has selected a table, he can continue to create the evaluation structure. The next phase in creating the evaluation structure is to select the characteristics and the key figures to complete the evaluation structure.

As the evaluation structure now references a data dictionary table, the characteristics now available will be from that table. In this example, the Purchase Order Header table, **EKKO**, has been selected as the reference data dictionary table, DD Table in Figure 9.9. When the Characteristics icon or the **F5** key has been selected, the available characteristics from the **EKKO** table will be displayed, as shown in Figure 9.9.

The analyst can select the key figures by clicking on the Key Figures icon or using the **F6** key. The key figures are then copied into the evaluation structure. Once the characteristics and the key figures are chosen, the evaluation structure can be generated, as shown in Figure 9.10, by using the menu path: **Evaluation Structure • Generate**.

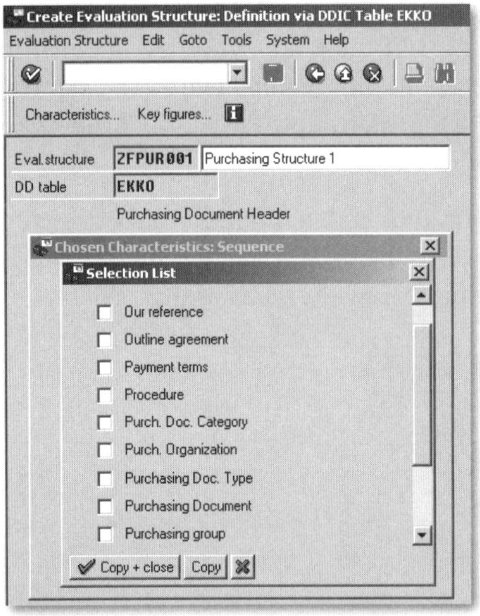

Figure 9.9 Characteristics Available, Referenced to EKKO Table, for Evaluation Structure

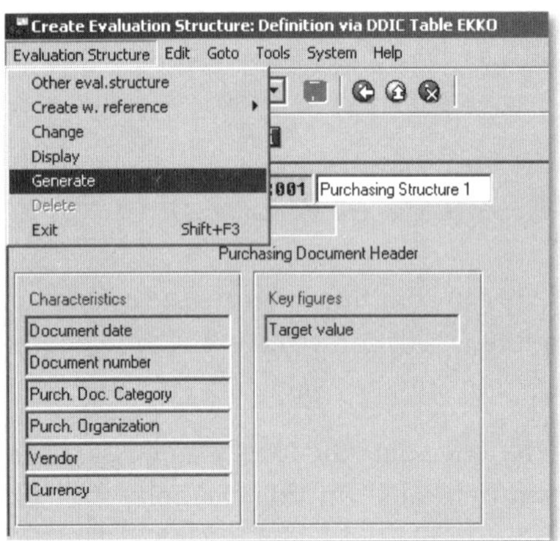

Figure 9.10 Menu Path to Generate Evaluation Structure for Use

After the evaluation structure is generated, the system will return the analyst to the initial screen and there will be a message on the screen to indicate that the evaluation structure was generated.

9.2 Change an Evaluation Structure

After an evaluation structure has been created and evaluated, there may be a need to change the evaluation structure. Perhaps, it needs more characteristics or different key figures to produce the desired results.

The transaction to change the evaluation structure is MC28, or it can be found using the navigation path: **SAP Menu • Logistics • Logistics Controlling • Logistics Information System • Flexible Analyses • Evaluation Structure • Change**. The characteristics and key figures can be moved or deleted, or new ones can be added.

9.2.1 Add a Characteristic

To add a characteristic to the evaluation structure, the Characteristics icon can be chosen or the **F5** key. The current list of characteristics is displayed and to add another characteristic click on the **Selection list** button. A list of available characteristics will be displayed, as shown in Figure 9.11. The characteristics already chosen will be check-marked. The analyst can select any of the other characteristics. In Figure 9.11, the **Purchasing group** characteristic has been selected for inclusion in the evaluation structure.

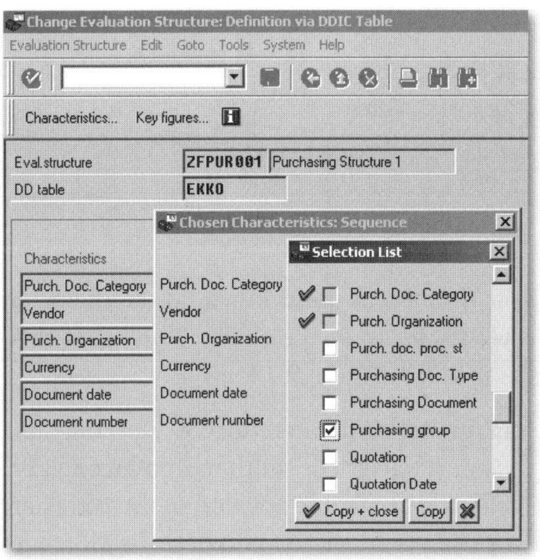

Figure 9.11 Characteristics Already Part of Evaluation Structure and Those Chosen to Be Added

Once all the new characteristics have been selected, click on the **Copy + close** button and the new characteristics will be displayed in the characteristics list.

9.2.2 Delete a Characteristic

To delete a characteristic from the evaluation structure, select the Characteristics icon or the **F5** key. The list of characteristics that are currently part of the evaluation structure is displayed. To delete a characteristic, select it and click on the Delete icon or the **Shift + F2** key (see Figure 9.12).

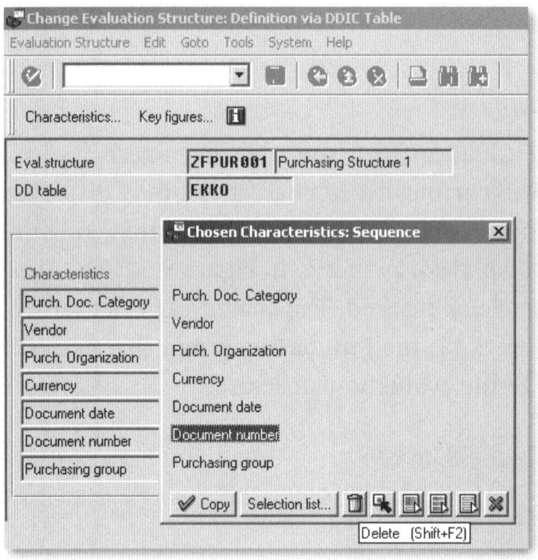

Figure 9.12 Deletion of a Characteristic from an Evaluation Structure

9.2.3 Move a Characteristic

You can move the characteristic to a different position within the characteristic list by selecting the **Characteristics** icon or the **F5** key. The list of characteristics is displayed in the dialog box in Figure 9.12.

Within the dialog box, you can move a characteristic by selecting that characteristic using the **F9** key. The characteristic will then be highlighted. Next, place your cursor on the characteristic in the position in the list where you want the highlighted characteristic to move to and select the **Shift + F4** key. The highlighted characteristic will be moved and the other characteristics will be moved sequentially.

9.2.4 Add a Key Figure

To add a key figure to the evaluation structure, **Key figures** can be selected or you can use the **F6** key. The list of key figures is displayed, and to add another key figure click on the **Selection list** button. A list of available key figures will be displayed, as shown in Figure 9.13. The key figures already chosen will be check-marked, which appears in green. The analyst can select any of the other key figures. In Figure 9.13, the **Exchange rate** key figure has been selected for inclusion in the evaluation structure.

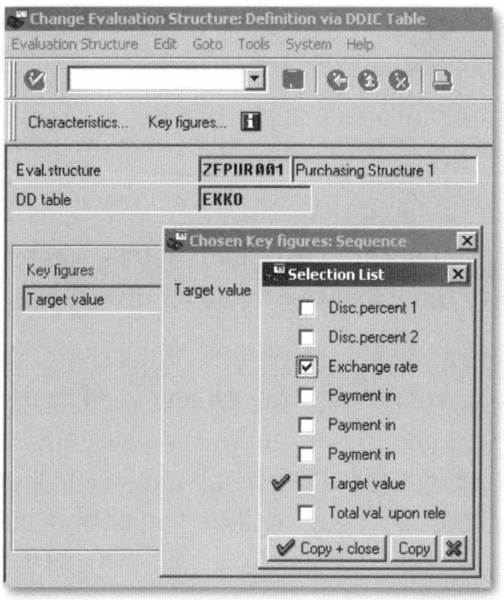

Figure 9.13 Key Figures Already Part of Evaluation Structure and Those Chosen to Be Added

When all the new key figures have been chosen, click on the **Copy + close** button and the new key figures will be displayed in the key figures list.

9.2.5 Delete a Key Figure

To delete a key figure from the evaluation structure, select **Key figures** or the **F6** key. The list of key figures already part of the evaluation structure is shown. To delete a key figure, select it and the Delete icon or the **Shift + F2** function keys (see Figure 9.14).

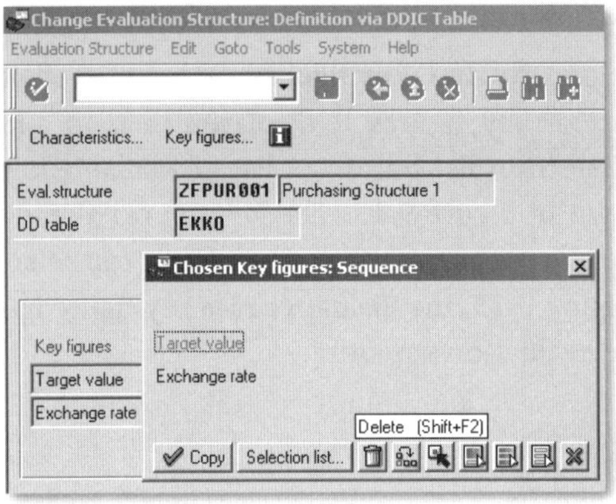

Figure 9.14 Deletion of a Key Figure from an Evaluation Structure

9.2.6 Move a Key Figure

You can move the key figure to a different position within the key figures list by selecting **Key figures** or the **F6** key. The list of key figures is displayed in the dialog box in Figure 9.14.

To move a key figure, select that key figure by using the **F9** key. The key figure will then be highlighted. Then place the cursor on the key figure in the position in the list where you want the highlighted key figure to move to and select the **Shift + F4** key. The highlighted key figure will be moved and the other key figures will be moved sequentially.

9.2.7 Generating and Transporting Evaluation Structures

Once all the changes have been made to an evaluation structure, the structure will need to be regenerated. Every time an evaluation structure is changed, it should be generated. Use the menu path: **Evaluation Structure • Generate**, as shown in Figure 9.10.

When the evaluation structure is generated, it can also be included in a transport. A system message appears: **Include the evaluation structure in a transport request?** (see Figure 9.15), which is displayed after the **Generate** menu option has been selected.

If an analyst requires that the evaluation structure be included in a transport request, the system will prompt her for a transport request number or for a new transport request to be created.

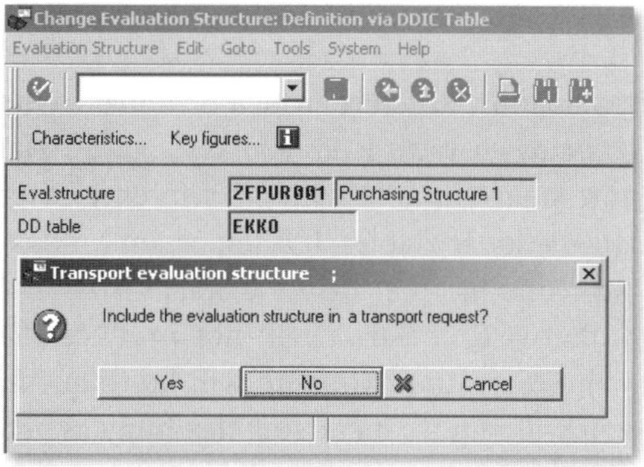

Figure 9.15 System Message Allowing Evaluation Structure to Be Included in a Transport Request

9.3 Combining Data

Note that there may be a situation where the data that the analyst requires is from two distinct data dictionary tables. Figure 9.2 shows that an evaluation structure can select characteristics from different evaluation structures; however, an evaluation structure can use only one data dictionary at a time. If an analyst has a complicated data retrieval requirement and needs data from two or more data dictionary tables, he can use a relatively straightforward means of combining the data. This scenario may occur when two areas of the supply chain have data required in the evaluation, such as Purchasing and Production.

If the analyst requires data from Table XX and Table YY to be combined for a single evaluation structure, the procedure is as follows:

1. Create an evaluation structure ZF001 referencing Table XX.
2. Create an evaluation structure ZF002 referencing Table YY.
3. Create an evaluation structure ZF003 referencing evaluation structures ZF001 and ZF002.
4. Create an evaluation for evaluation structure ZF003, which has data for Table XX and Table YY.

9.4 Summary

In this chapter, we discussed the evaluation structure, which is similar to the information structure in that it contains characteristics and key figures. The flexibility of the evaluation structure stems from its ability to reference other evaluation structures as well as data dictionary tables. It is important for flexible analysis that the evaluation structure has the correct characteristics and key figures for the evaluation; otherwise, the data will not produce the desired results. Modifications to the evaluation structure will be frequent, because in your role as analyst, you will require increasing flexibility as you become more experienced with the capabilities of the flexible analysis tool.

In Chapter 10, I will focus on the evaluation itself, which is used to extract the data from the evaluation structure.

An evaluation allows the analyst to retrieve the required data from the evaluation structure and to format that data in the preferred manner. This functionality also provides the flexibility necessary for the analyst to perform calculations within the evaluation to produce the desired results.

10 Evaluations

An *evaluation* is the tool that allows the user (in this case, the analyst) to retrieve and report on the data in a more flexible manner than the standard analysis functionality. Once an analyst has experience in creating evaluations and evaluation structures, the delivered reports are an excellent tool for management to monitor the supply chain. Different companies use different criteria for monitoring their unique supply chain characteristics. The purpose of the evaluation is to provide the data in the most accurate, timely and concise format possible. For example, a key supply chain report may be the level of sales in relation to the production equipment breakdowns, or the price of purchased materials in relation to the quality of purchased materials.

10.1 Create an Evaluation

The evaluation must refer to a specific evaluation structure. As explained in Chapter 9, an evaluation structure can refer to another evaluation structure or a data dictionary table. Therefore, the evaluation will have access to the data defined in the evaluation structure. It is best to check that the evaluation structure you are referencing contains the specific characteristics or key figures that are required for reporting.

The evaluation is created using Transaction MC11 and can be found using the navigation path: **SAP Menu • Logistics • Logistics Controlling • Logistics Information System • Flexible Analyses • Evaluation • Create.**

10.1.1 Create Evaluation—Initial Screen

The evaluation has to be defined in an application area and must refer to an evaluation structure. In addition, it will require a name and a description, as shown in Figure 10.1.

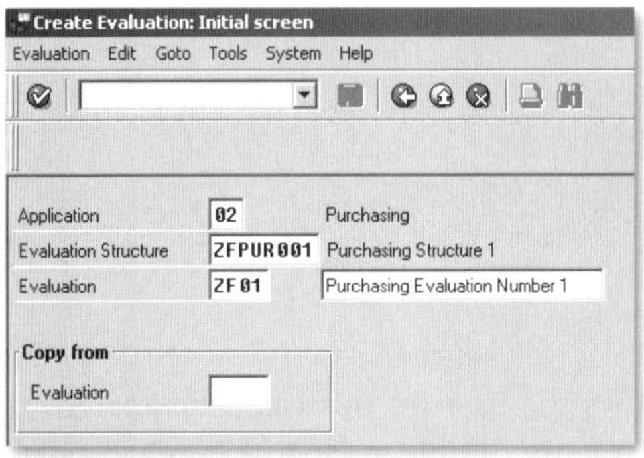

Figure 10.1 Initial Screen for Creating Evaluation, Transaction MC11

The application area has to be decided upon and, for this example, the Purchasing application area, **02**, has been selected.

Which evaluation structure you choose is important, because it contains the references to the characteristics and key figures that will be required for the evaluation. The key figures are also important, because they are the values that are being reported on, which is what the client will want to review.

The evaluation name can be defined as a four-character alphanumeric string. Some clients may require the evaluation to commence with a certain character, a Z, for example. Check with the client's data integrity or data standards team before you start creating evaluations. An example of an evaluation name may be Z45A.

The evaluation description can be defined with up to 35 alphanumeric characters. Again, check with the client's data integrity or data standards team for existing protocols.

10.1.2 Define Characteristics

After the analyst has entered the initial information regarding the evaluation, she can assign the characteristics from the evaluation structure. The characteristics for the defined evaluation structure can be displayed for selection by using the Characteristics icon, by using the **F5** function key, or from the header menu by choosing **Edit • Characteristics.**

Because there is only one evaluation structure assigned, the characteristics are displayed on the selection list. Only these characteristics can be used for selection. Figure 10.2 shows the **Selection List** of characteristics and the characteristics that have been selected (i.e., those characteristics with a checkmark).

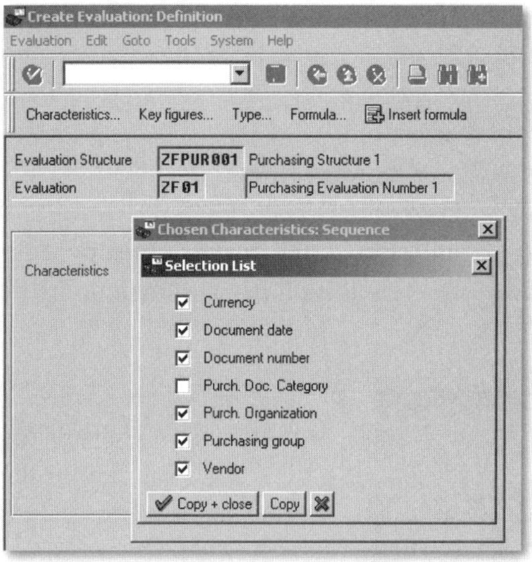

Figure 10.2 Selection List of Characteristics for Use in an Evaluation, Transaction MC11

Once the analyst has selected the correct characteristics, she can copy these characteristics to the evaluation and close the selection list.

10.1.3 Define Key Figures

The key figures can be selected from the evaluation structure using either **Key figures**, using the **F6** function key, or from the header menu by choosing **Edit • Key Figures**. The **Selection List** of available key figures, which are defined in the evaluation structure, is shown in Figure 10.3. As you can see, there are only two key figures to select from: **Exchange rate** and **Target value**. In other evaluation structures, there may be many more key figures to select from.

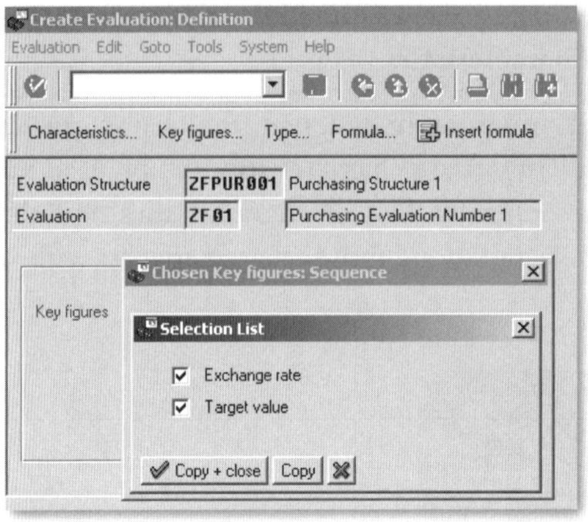

Figure 10.3 Key Figures Selected for Evaluation in Transaction MC11

Once the correct key figures have been selected, the analyst can copy these key figures to the evaluation and close the selection list as shown in Figure 10.4.

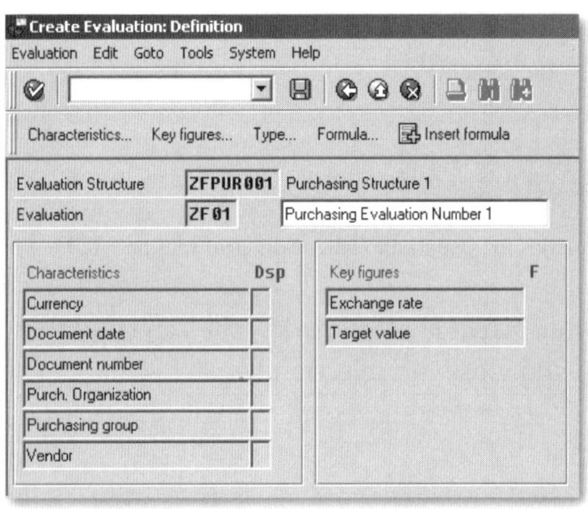

Figure 10.4 Characteristics and Key Figures Selected for Evaluation

10.1.4 Define a Characteristic Display Type

A characteristic in an evaluation can be assigned a display type, which can format the way in which the data is displayed on a report. There are a number of different display types that can be assigned to a characteristic. A display type formats the characteristic and defines the comparison that can be made between key figures.

To define a display type for a characteristic, the characteristic must be selected and the Display Type icon selected, or you can use the **F7** function key or select **Edit • Type** from the header menu.

A dialog box will appear with the available display types for the characteristic. The display types are referred to as **Type Selection for Purch. Organization** in Figure 10.5.

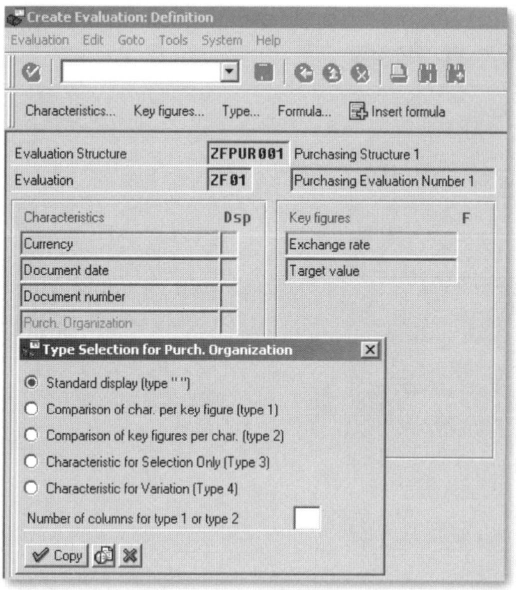

Figure 10.5 Display Types for the Selected Characteristic, Transaction MC11

Standard Display Type

The standard display type displays the characteristics in the order that they are defined in the characteristics selection within the evaluation. The standard list display is the default for the characteristic. This is primarily used when no comparisons are to be made between characteristics and if the client wants raw data.

Columnar Comparison of Characteristic per Key Figure (Type 1)

This display type allows the analyst to take a characteristic and compare the values of that characteristic against each other using the value of the key figures. For example, using the characteristics shown in Figure 10.4, the analyst could select the Purchasing Organization. The analyst could then decide how many purchasing organizations he wishes to compare. The purchasing organizations will appear alongside each key figure of the evaluation. The **Number of columns for type 1 or type 2** field in Figure 10.5 will contain the number of columns required. The default for this display type is **2**.

Once the evaluation is saved, it can be executed. The evaluation containing the columnar comparison would require the analyst to enter the purchase organizations (**Purch.Org.**) to be compared, as shown in Figure 10.6.

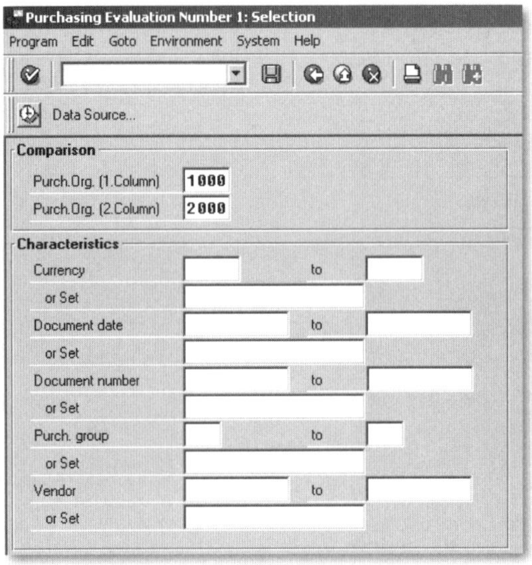

Figure 10.6 Initial Screen of Executing an Evaluation with a Columnar Comparison Display Type

In Figure 10.6, the comparison of the purchasing organization characteristic is for only two purchasing organizations: **Purch.Org (1.Column)** and **Purch.Org. (2.Column)**. The resulting data, as shown in Figure 10.7, displays **Characteristics** and key figures (**Target value**) defined in the evaluation, and includes the comparison of the two purchasing organizations for each set of key figures. The report shows the target value for the two purchasing organizations, Germany and the UK. Although not all the characteristics are shown, they have been summarized at the currency level.

Note that for display type **1**, only one characteristic can be selected within an evaluation. When another characteristic is selected, the dialog box with the display types will not allow display type **1** to be chosen when it has already been assigned in the evaluation (see Figure 10.8).

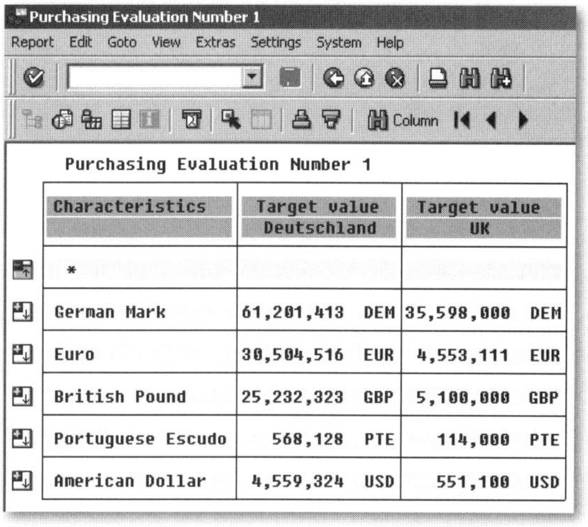

Figure 10.7 Evaluation and Comparison of the Characteristic, Purchasing Organization, with Respect to Key Figures

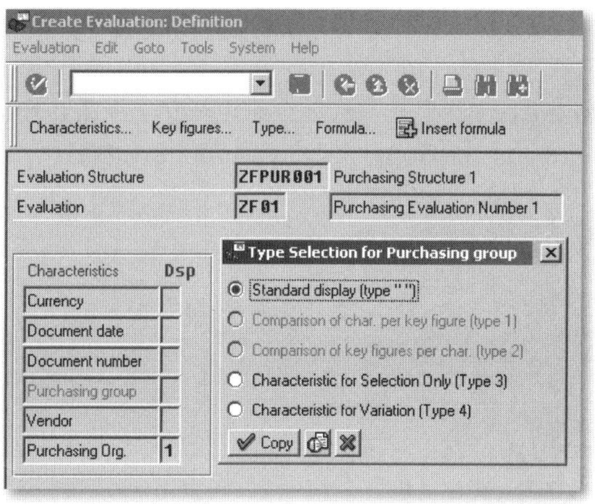

Figure 10.8 Available Display Types for Selection

Columnar Comparison of Key Figures per Characteristic (Type 2)

This display type allows the analyst to display all key figures for a characteristic and then repeat the display for however many columns are to be compared. For example, using the characteristics in Figure 10.9, the **Vendor** could be selected. The analyst can then decide on how many vendors to compare. The **Number of columns for type 1 or type 2** field in Figure 10.9 will contain the number of columns required. The default for this display type is **2**.

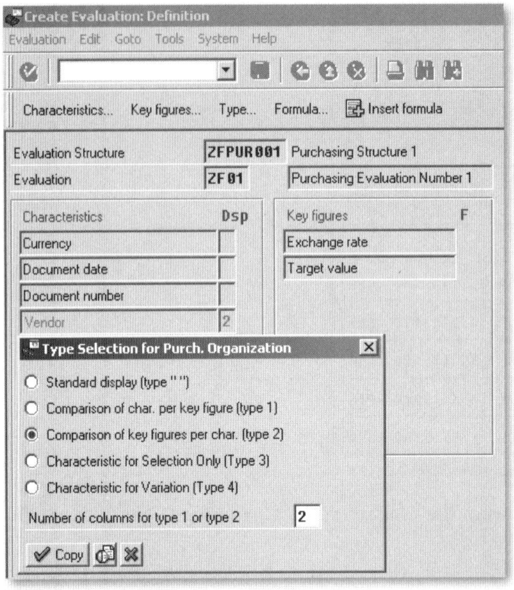

Figure 10.9 Display Type 2 Selected for Vendor Characteristic, Transaction MC11

After the evaluation is saved and executed, the evaluation requires that the vendor details are entered for the comparison, as shown in Figure 10.10.

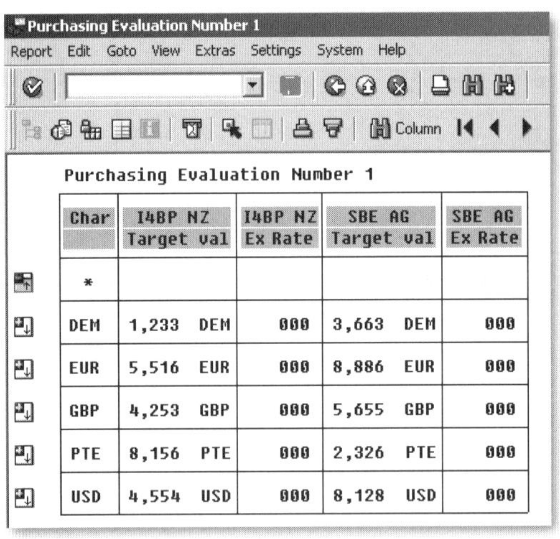

Figure 10.10 Evaluation Results of Evaluation and Comparison of Key Figures for Specified Vendors

The result shows the top level of characteristics, e.g., currency and the key figures, as well as the exchange rate and target value for each of the comparison characteristics, e.g., specified vendors.

Display in Selection Only (Type 3)

This display type indicates that the characteristic is available for selection only, but will not be displayed on the resulting report. This display type may be selected for a characteristic due to the aesthetics of the resulting report, or because the analyst does not want the characteristic to be shown for security or confidentiality reasons. The characteristic can be selected and assigned a display type **3**, as shown in Figure 10.11.

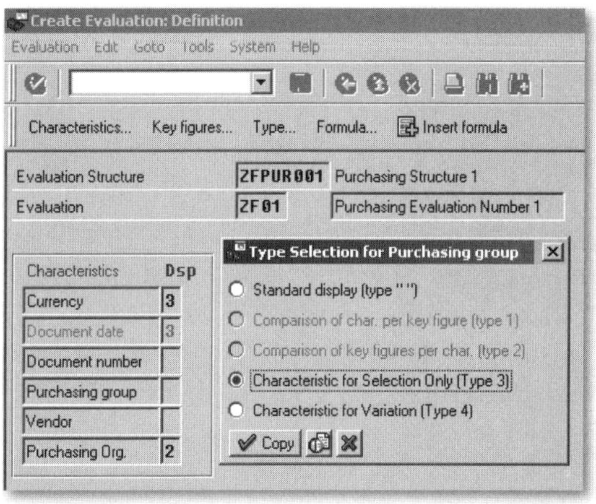

Figure 10.11 Characteristics Currency and Document Date Assigned for Display Type 3

Display in Variation Only (Type 4)

The characteristic can be assigned a display type **4**. This will allow the characteristic to be displayed only in a variation. We will discuss evaluation variables later in this chapter.

10.1.5 Layout Control

During the creation of an evaluation, the analyst might wonder how the output will be displayed. The layout control option allows the analyst to see instantly how the data report will look, and how any changes to characteristics, key figures, or display type will be reflected.

The analyst can view the layout control by using the **F8** key or using the header menu: **Edit • Layout • Layout Control**.

The layout control is useful when assigning the display type, because the analyst can immediately see how the display types affect the output. In Figure 10.12, the characteristics and their corresponding display types are shown along with the **Layout Control** box.

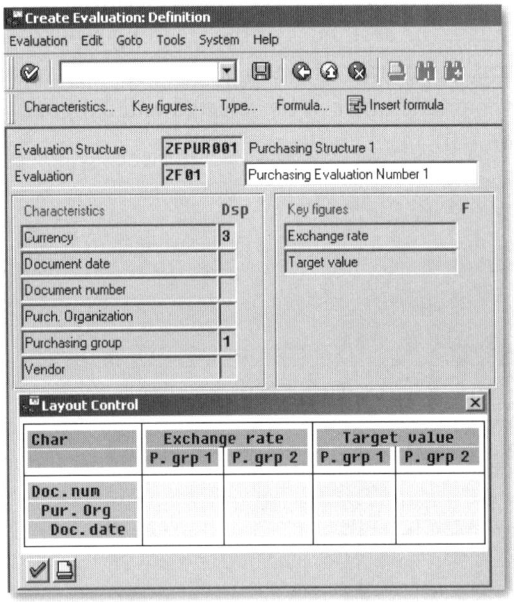

Figure 10.12 Layout Control Box with Corresponding Characteristics and Display Types

10.1.6 Entering a Formula

The flexibility of the evaluation is further enhanced by the ability to enter a formula within the evaluation. Calculations can be performed on key figures and then displayed in the results, allowing the analyst to create customized reports without any need for ABAP programming. A formula may be required to create a percentage, for example, the percentage of times that the purchase order price is exceeded per month.

In the example shown in Figure 10.13, the evaluation is using an evaluation structure from the inventory management area. This evaluation structure refers to a number of other evaluation structures in the inventory management area.

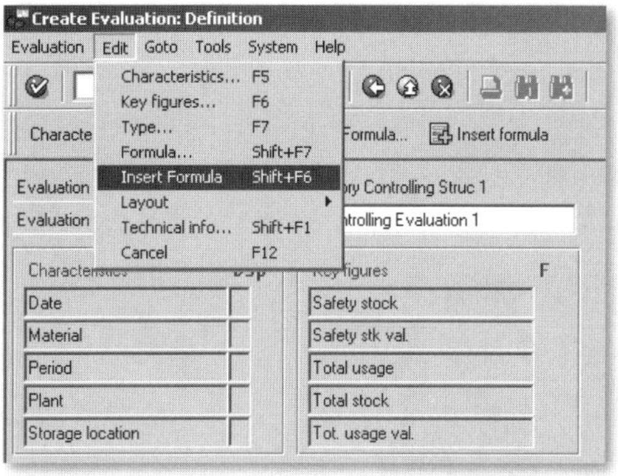

Figure 10.13 Characteristics and Key Figures for Evaluation in Which a Formula Is Entered

If the analyst requires that a formula or calculation be entered into the evaluation, then the key figure must be selected. The option from the header menu, **Edit • Insert Formula**, or the **Shift + F6** key can be used, as shown in Figure 10.13.

Once the option to enter a formula has been selected, a dialog box will appear with the available key figures and fields to enter the formula, as shown in Figure 10.14. When the key figures are displayed, they appear with their corresponding technical names, as shown in Figure 10.14.

The analyst can then create the formula by entering a name for it. The formula details can be created by selecting the key figures and using mathematical operators such as **+**, **–**, *****, **/**, and **()**. In Figure 10.14, the formula safety stock coverage has been created, which is a calculation of the total stock divided by the safety stock.

When the formula is saved, it will appear as a separate line alongside the key figures with a checkmark in the formula (**F**) column; in this example, it is **Safety Stk Cvr** as shown in Figure 10.15.

When the evaluation is executed, the formula behaves like a key figure and is displayed as a column alongside the key figures. Figure 10.16 shows the results for the evaluation created, and the calculated figure Safety Stock Coverage (**Safety Stk Cvr**) is displayed as a column next to the key figures **Safety Stk** and **Tot Stk**.

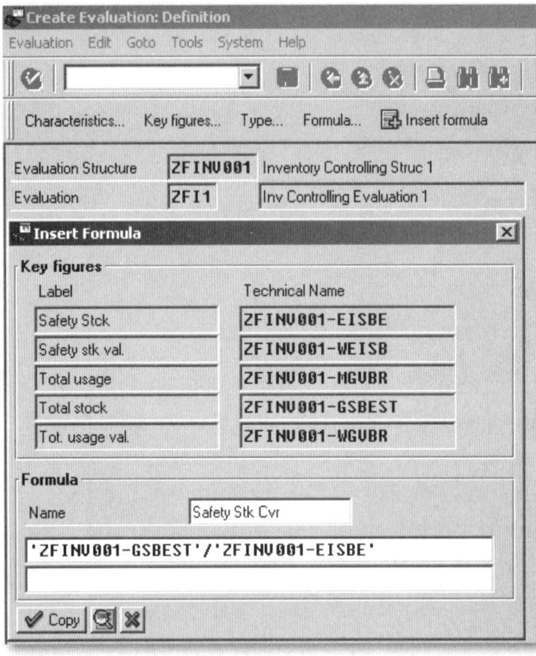

Figure 10.14 Available Key Figures to Be Used in Entry of New Formula in Evaluation

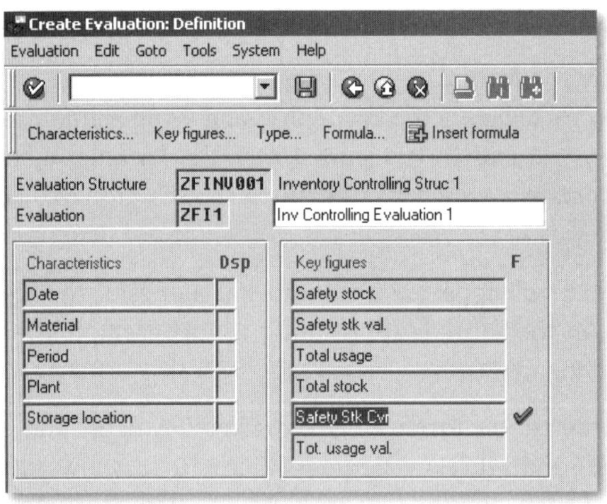

Figure 10.15 New Formula in Key Figures Section

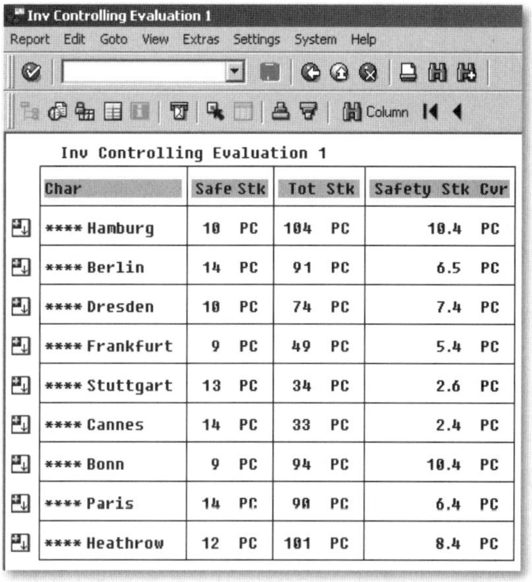

Inv Controlling Evaluation 1

Char	Safe Stk	Tot Stk	Safety Stk Cvr
**** Hamburg	10 PC	104 PC	10.4 PC
**** Berlin	14 PC	91 PC	6.5 PC
**** Dresden	10 PC	74 PC	7.4 PC
**** Frankfurt	9 PC	49 PC	5.4 PC
**** Stuttgart	13 PC	34 PC	2.6 PC
**** Cannes	14 PC	33 PC	2.4 PC
**** Bonn	9 PC	94 PC	10.4 PC
**** Paris	14 PC	90 PC	6.4 PC
**** Heathrow	12 PC	101 PC	8.4 PC

Figure 10.16 Calculated Figure Safety Stock Coverage as Column

10.2 Change an Evaluation

After an evaluation has been created and executed, the analyst may decide to either amend the characteristics or key figures, or change the display options.

The evaluation can be changed using Transaction MC12, and this can be found using the navigation path: **SAP Menu • Logistics • Logistics Controlling • Logistics Information System • Flexible Analyses • Evaluation • Change**.

10.2.1 Change Evaluation—Initial Screen

The transaction, as shown in Figure 10.17, requires the analyst to enter the **Application**, the relevant **Evaluation Structure**, and the **Evaluation**, which is the name of the evaluation.

Please note that the transaction also allows the analyst to execute the evaluation directly from this screen, and it is easy to select the Execute icon and not the Continue icon.

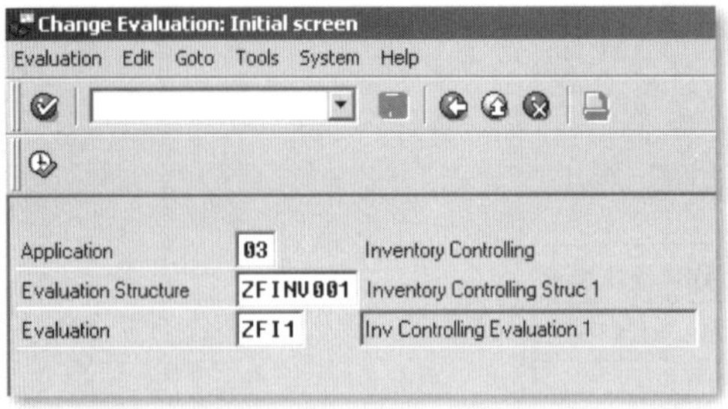

Figure 10.17 Initial Screen for Evaluation Change, Transaction MC12

10.2.2 Change Display Options

A common reason for changing evaluations is to alter the way in which the report is displayed. This may be as simple as changing the width of a column, or as complex as redesigning a report.

The display options, shown in Figure 10.18, are accessed by selecting the layout option from the header menu, and either by selecting an individual option or by selecting the display options via the path: **Edit • Layout • Display Options**.

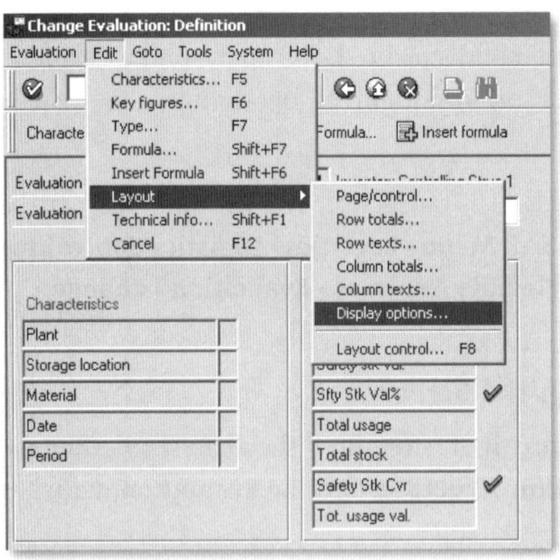

Figure 10.18 Header Menu Path for Display Options, Transaction MC12

The display options allow the analyst to use the standard layout or to define her own report layout. There is an option at the bottom of the screen to define the report layout. Once that option is selected, all the options (length, width, etc.) will become valid for modification.

In the **Change Report Layout** dialog box, the initial tab is the **Page/control** tab, as shown in Figure 10.19. The analyst can modify the page length, page width, margins, print sequence, and colors.

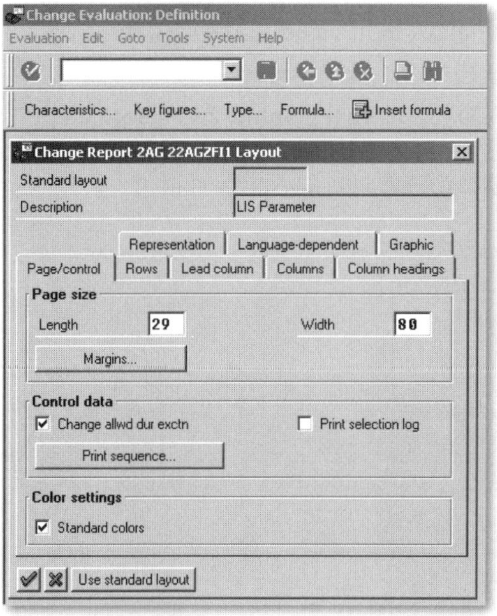

Figure 10.19 Page/Control Parameters for Display Options of Evaluation

The next tab, **Rows**, is for the modification of rows. Here, as shown in Figure 10.20, the analyst can make modifications to the total rows, suppress zero rows, and edit the way in which signage is used.

The other tabs allow the analyst to make further changes to the display output and are described below:

- **Lead Column**
  Define the contents of the lead column, define the indentation, define the width and position, and allow underscored text
- **Columns**
  Set the position of the totals, set the break character between the columns, and define column width
- **Column Headings**
  Define the contents of the column headings and define the orientation of the column headings

- **Representation**
  Define decimal places, define scaling, define zero value, and define undeterminable values
- **Language Dependent**
  Define decimal display, define debit/credit value, and date definition
- **Graphic**
  Define the graphic display for 2D, 3D, initial graphic, and color palette

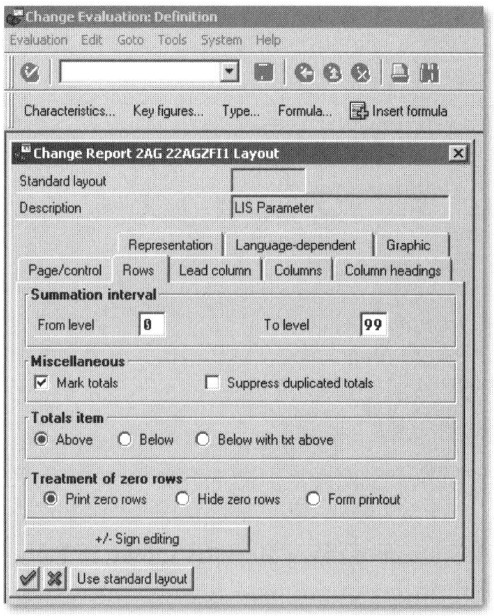

Figure 10.20 Parameters for Rows of Display Options of Evaluation

10.3 Deleting an Evaluation

If an evaluation is no longer required, it can be deleted. The analyst can delete an evaluation by selecting the evaluation change Transaction MC12, and this can be found using the navigation path: **SAP Menu • Logistics • Logistics Controlling • Logistics Information System • Flexible Analyses • Evaluation • Change**.

The application area, evaluation structure, and evaluation should be entered. The **Delete** option is found in the header menu by selecting **Evaluation • Delete** or by using the **Shift + F2** key, as shown in Figure 10.21.

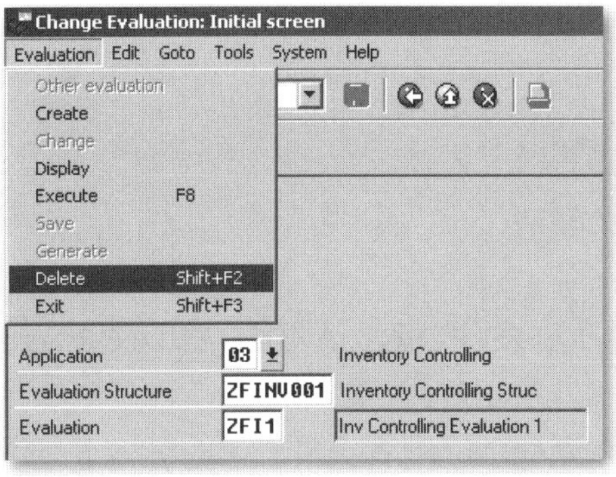

Figure 10.21 Deleting Evaluation Function, Transaction MC12

10.4 Create a Set

A set can be used to group together values or a range of values for an evaluation. The set is then referenced when an evaluation is executed. A set can be created for all of the characteristics that are defined for an evaluation structure. A set can be created using Transaction GS01, or from the header menu of the change evaluation Transaction (MC12): **Tools • Sets • Create.**

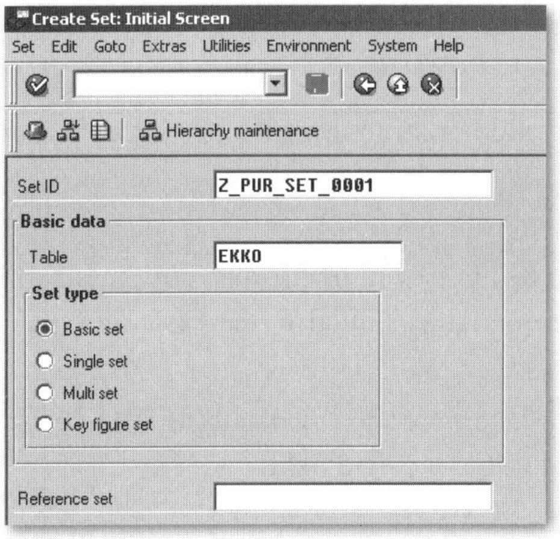

Figure 10.22 Initial Screen for Creating a Set, Transaction GS01

The initial screen for creating a set, as shown in Figure 10.22, requires the analyst to enter a Set ID. The Set ID field is a 24-character alphanumeric field, but can also contain special characters such as underscore and hyphen. For example, in Figure 10.22, the name shown is **Z_PUR_SET_0001**.

10.4.1 Naming of a Set

A number of rules apply to the naming of the Set ID:

- User-defined Set IDs should start with a letter.
- Set IDs cannot contain blank characters.
- Set IDs are not case-specific.
- Set IDs cannot be named TRUE, T, FALSE, F, NOT, AND, NAND, OR, and NOR.
- Set IDs beginning with a number are delivered with the SAP system.
- Set IDs beginning with a zero are display-only.

10.4.2 Basic Set Data

The set can refer to a table or structure. The name of the object is entered and is used to reference the field, key values, or set name in the set details screen. In Figure 10.22, the set is referencing the purchasing table EKKO.

10.4.3 Set Type

The set type determines how the data is entered into the set. There are four types of sets:

- **Basic Set**
  The set refers to one field on the table or structure, and a range of values can be entered.
- **Single Set**
  A number of subordinate sets can be entered in the details, but the set still refers to a single field on the selected table, similar to the basic set type.
- **Multi-Set**
  A number of subordinate sets can be entered in the details as a single set, but the reference is to a table and not to a single field.
- **Key Figure Set**
  Used when a set refers to an evaluation structure. The structure is entered and selected key figures can be entered into the set. The key figures are entered to determine the columns for the report.

10.4.4 Entering Set Details for a Table

The set details are entered as line items with a range of values. For example, in Figure 10.22, the set is defined as a basic set referencing one table. The details can be added for that set for a defined table field, as shown in Figure 10.23.

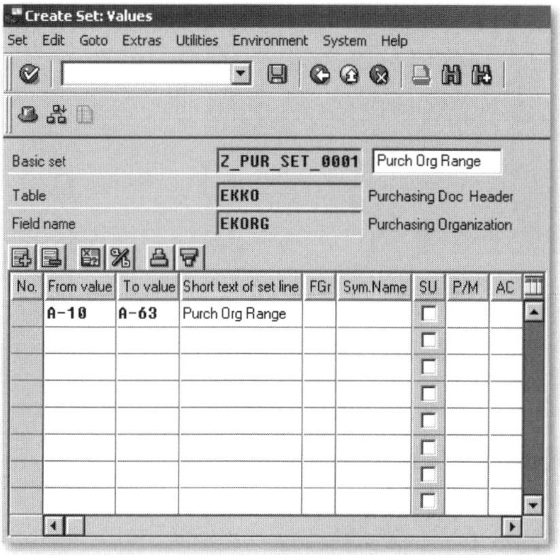

Figure 10.23 Range of Values for Table Field, EKKO-EKORG in Creation of a Set, Transaction GS01

10.4.5 Entering Set Details for an Evaluation

The set can be used by the analyst to store a set of key figures that can be run against an evaluation to determine columns for the report. Using the Transaction GS01 or selecting from the header menu of the change evaluation Transaction MC12, the analyst can create a set to store values for key figures. On the initial screen for creating a set, the set name is entered and the set is defined with the set type selected as **Key figure set**, as shown in Figure 10.24.

The detail screen, as shown in Figure 10.25, allows the analyst to select a key figure from the evaluation that was entered for the set.

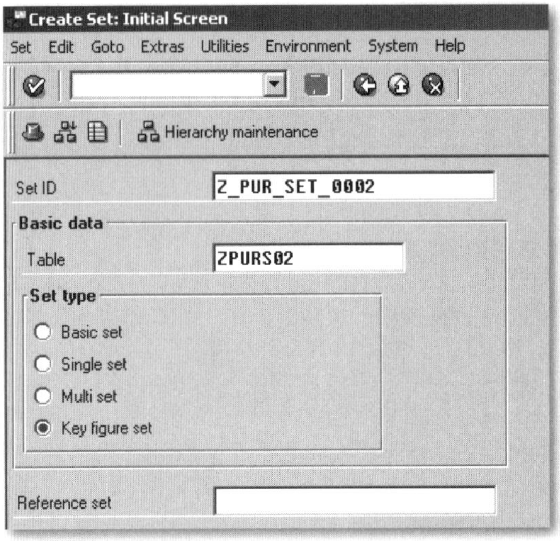

Figure 10.24 Entry Screen for Creating a Set with Set Type Defined for Key Figure Value Entry

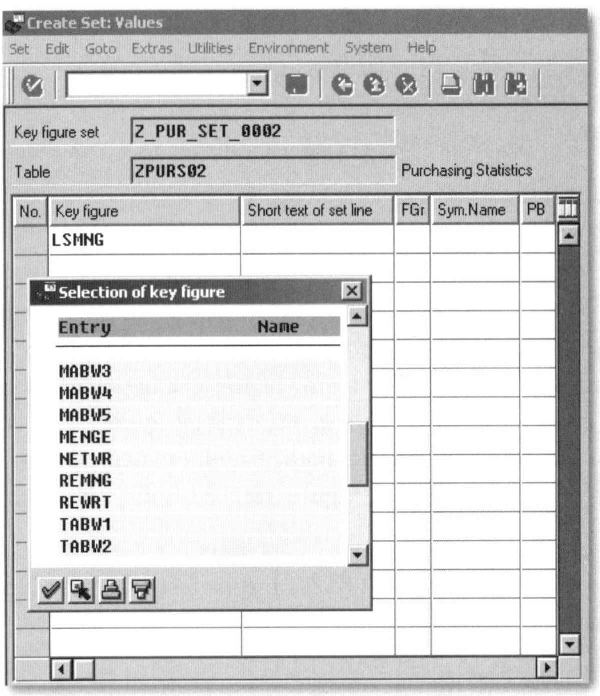

Figure 10.25 Key Fields of Evaluation Being Selected for Set

10.5 Summary

In this chapter, I have discussed the role of the evaluation, which is used to retrieve the data from the evaluation structure and display the results in a report layout. The layout is defined based on the characteristics and key figures defined in the evaluation. In addition, you can create columns for the report that allows calculations based on key figures. Along with the evaluation's ability to manipulate the report layout is that its apparent flexibility, makes it a great tool for monitoring supply chain functionality for a company.

In Chapter 11, I'll talk about hierarchies, which are commonly used in reporting where totals are required on various levels.

A hierarchy allows the analyst to create a structure in which to report on the data resulting from an analysis. The hierarchy is defined with nodes and terminates with sub-nodes displaying the characteristic values.

11 Hierarchies

The hierarchy functionality is an important tool for the analyst, because it allows him to create a defined structure where summary totals can be valued at the levels within the hierarchy, based on the nodes and sub-nodes created. Many reports can be summarized with totals at various levels; for example, in Purchasing, the levels can include Purchase Order detail, Purchase Order at Purchase Group level, and Purchase Orders at Purchase Organization level.

Similar to the definition of a structure in classification, a significant amount of planning is required by the analyst to create a hierarchy. The analyst will require information to be displayed or reviewed in a certain manner, and the design of a hierarchy should reflect this. Although information reports can be created in ABAP, the flexibility of the LIS and tools such as hierarchy creation allow the analyst, not the programmer, to create the reports needed for logistics monitoring.

11.1 Example of a Hierarchy

Once the analyst has identified an area that needs examination, he will review the objects that are in question and determine how the hierarchy needs to be created to identify any issues that are occurring.

For this example, we'll assume that the area the analyst wants to monitor revolves around a group of materials. The analyst has identified a group of 10 materials that are all components in finished goods that fail quality inspection more than 30% of the time and cause the production order to complete beyond the target time expected.

The analyst may have found that these 10 component materials are common in all the finished goods that are failing quality inspection. The analyst would like to create a hierarchy that structures the materials and then review the results at each level of the hierarchy to see if the issue is with a group of individual materials.

The analyst can use a variety of SAP functionality to aid in the structure of a hierarchy. If implemented, the classification system is a great tool for identifying hierarchies. Product groups and material hierarchies are also useful to the analyst.

In this example, the analyst believes that the supply chain problem may be due to transportation of the products or lie with the country of origin of the component material. To leverage the hierarchy tool, the analyst has designed the hierarchy to show the following:

Top Level Hierarchy

The top level of the hierarchy contains three transportation processes as seen below:

- **Material brought in by air**
  - Material from the UK
  - Material from Germany
  - Material from India
- **Material brought in by ship**
  - Material from Japan
  - Material from Brazil
- **Material brought in by truck**
  - Material from Canada
  - Material from Mexico

Once the analyst has determined how the hierarchy should be structured, it can then be created in SAP.

11.2 Creating a Hierarchy

The hierarchy can be created using Transaction MCK1, or can be found using the navigation path: **SAP Menu • Logistics • Logistics Controlling • Logistics Information System • Environment • General Hierarchy • Create**.

The initial information required for the hierarchy is a hierarchy name, a description, and the data element that the hierarchy will be used for, as shown in Figure 11.1.

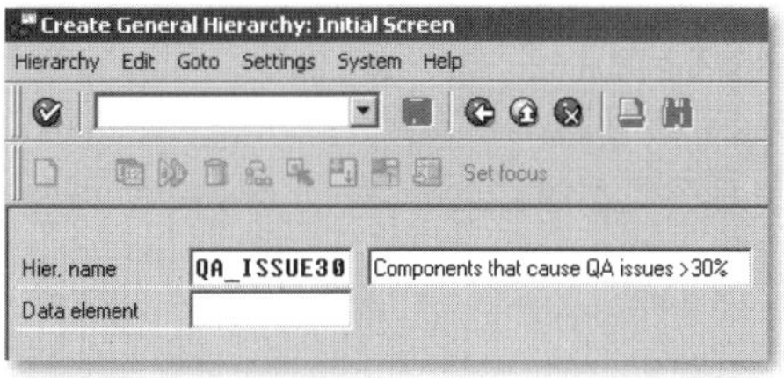

Figure 11.1 Initial Screen for Creating a Hierarchy, Transaction MCK1

11.2.1 Hierarchy Name

The hierarchy name should describe the use of the hierarchy, as various analysts may use it over time. The field is 10 characters in length and is alphanumeric. For example, a hierarchy name could be ZWM_COUNT7.

11.2.2 Hierarchy Description

The description of the hierarchy should be as detailed as possible for future reference. The field can accommodate a description of 40 characters. The description should reference the main application area and the hierarchy details. If your client uses structured descriptions, then this protocol should be followed. For example, structured descriptions usually refer to the levels of the hierarchy and for a purchasing hierarchy could be MM-PUR, Purchasing Org, Purchasing Group.

11.2.3 Data Element

The hierarchy should refer to a particular object, for example, a vendor, material, piece of equipment, etc. The data element entered in this field should reflect the chosen object. In the example described, the material is the object being analyzed, so the analyst can find the data element name by selecting the **F4** key or by clicking on the down arrow next to the field.

To select the data element, the information structure that will be used should be selected. In the example of the 10 materials causing Quality Assurance (QA) issues in finished goods, the analyst would be selecting the material data element from an information structure in the production area. Figure 11.2 shows the information structures that are displayed by using the **F4** key.

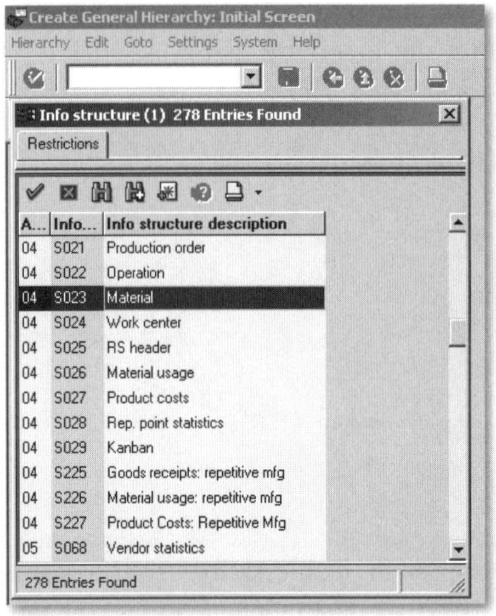

Figure 11.2 Information Structures from Which a Data Element Can Be Selected

The information structure highlighted is **S023**, as shown in Figure 11.2. Once this is selected, the available data elements are displayed for that information structure, shown in Figure 11.3.

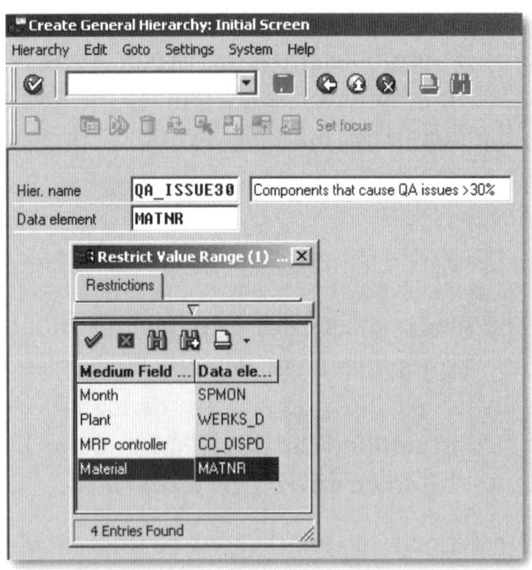

Figure 11.3 Data Elements Selected from Hierarchy

11.2.4 Hierarchy Definition

The initial screen allows the analyst to enter the name, description, and data element. Once that data has been entered, the analyst can define the hierarchy with a node and sub-nodes. In other words, the analyst can enter the layers of the hierarchy that he wants and finally define the objects that make up those layers.

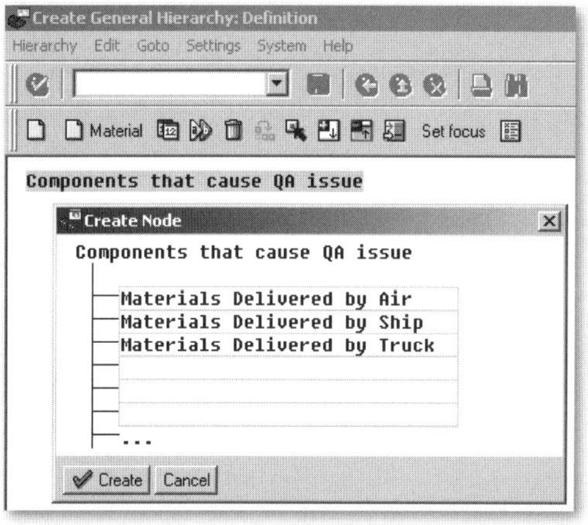

Figure 11.4 First and Second Levels of Hierarchy Entered, Transaction MCK1

The top level of the hierarchy is defined by the description that is entered into the hierarchy. The analyst can create the next level of the hierarchy, as shown in Figure 11.4, by creating nodes. This can be achieved by selecting the function keys **Ctrl + F2**, or by using the menu path: **Edit • Create Nodes.** Once all the nodes have been entered into this screen, the analyst can select **Create** and the hierarchy level will be created.

If the analyst wants to create more levels to the hierarchy, he should select a node to define further levels. He does this by placing the cursor on a node and selecting **Set Focus**, by selecting the **F5** function key, or by selecting **Edit • Set Focus** from the menu.

Once a node is selected, the analyst can enter another level of nodes or assign materials. In this example, as shown in Figure 11.5, the analyst has created another level in the hierarchy.

At a certain level, analysts will enter the objects that they want to examine. In this example, the analyst wants to examine 10 materials and will assign them to certain nodes within the hierarchy.

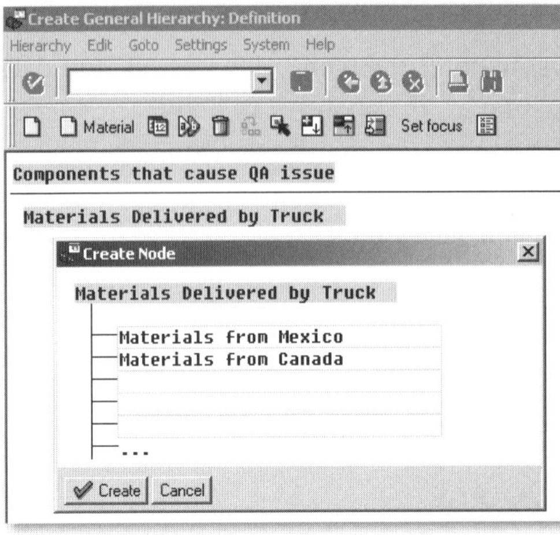

Figure 11.5 Another Level Created in Hierarchy, Transaction MCK1

The analyst can assign the objects to the node by selecting the Create Material icon, or by using the function key **Ctrl + F12**, or by using the menu path: **Edit • Material Create**.

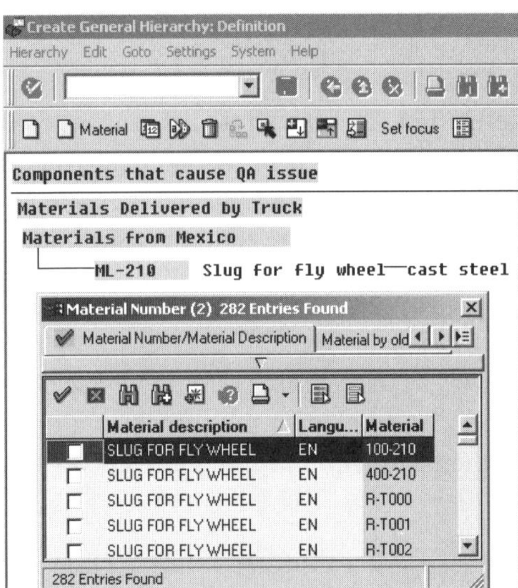

Figure 11.6 Assignment of Material to a Node within the Hierarchy Structure

The analyst can enter a number of materials to the node, as shown in Figure 11.6. The selection can be made via a matchcode if the material number is not known. A matchcode is a search for a field that provides a way of searching for values from a list of possible entries for that field. Once all the materials are assigned to the nodes, the hierarchy is complete. Figure 11.7 shows the completed hierarchy and the materials assigned to the nodes.

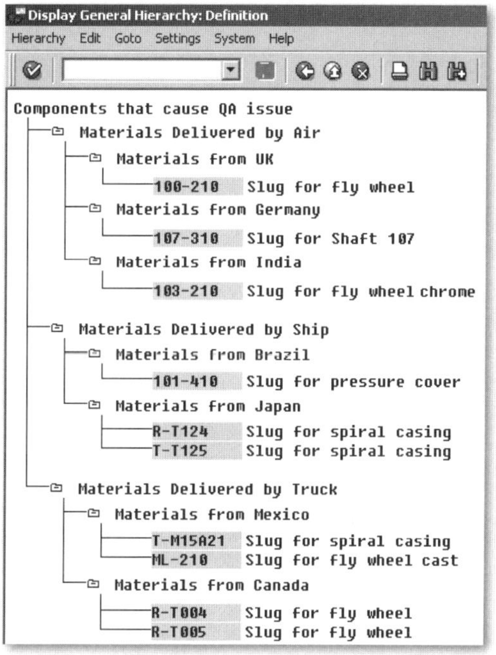

Figure 11.7 View of a Completed Hierarchy, Transaction MCK1

11.3 Hierarchy Validity Dates

The analyst can use the date functionality in the hierarchy function if there is a need to include or exclude any part of the hierarchy due to date validity. In the example we are using, the analyst may find that a certain material will no longer be transported in a certain way in the future, or that a component was being used for only a certain date period. The analyst will then want to restrict the results based on the relevant dates of each situation.

Validity dates can be used at the node or sub-node level. The functionality can be accessed by using the **Ctrl + Shift + F5** function keys, or by using the Assign Date icon, or via the header menu by selecting **Edit • Assign Date**.

The analyst can add a validity date in the process of creating a hierarchy, or via the change functionality. In this example, the analyst has discovered that the material from the UK was used only between January 1, 2006

(**01/01/2006**) and August 28, 2006 (**08/28/2006**). Consequently, the analyst can use the validity date function to assign this date to the material, as shown in Figure 11.8.

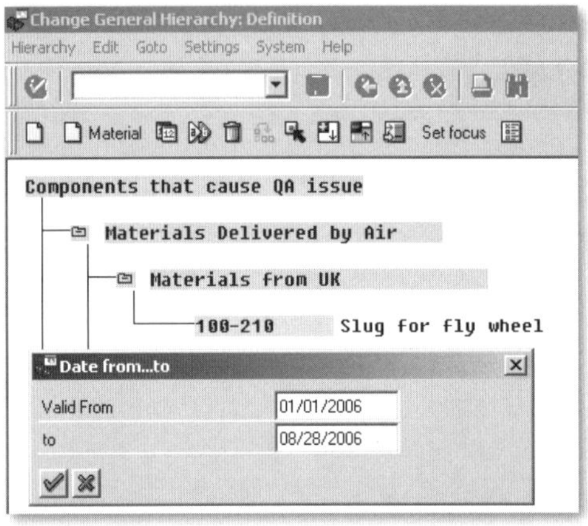

Figure 11.8 Validity Period Entered for a Certain Material in the Hierarchy

Once the material has been assigned a validity date, it is displayed on the hierarchy, as shown in Figure 11.9.

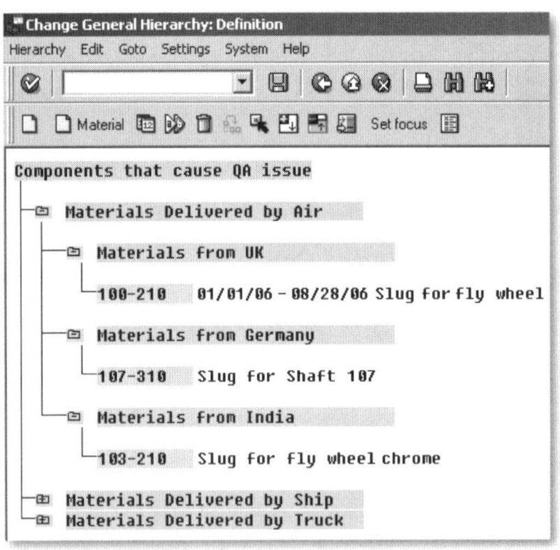

Figure 11.9 Material in Hierarchy with Validity Date Assigned

A validity date can also be assigned to a node by selecting the node and assigning a validity date. For example, the material from Japan can no longer be used after a certain date due to problems with raw materials. If the analyst knows that the date on which the shipments from Japan will cease is December 1, 2006, then the validity date can be entered into the hierarchy. The resulting hierarchy is shown in Figure 11.10. Now we can see how the hierarchy can be used.

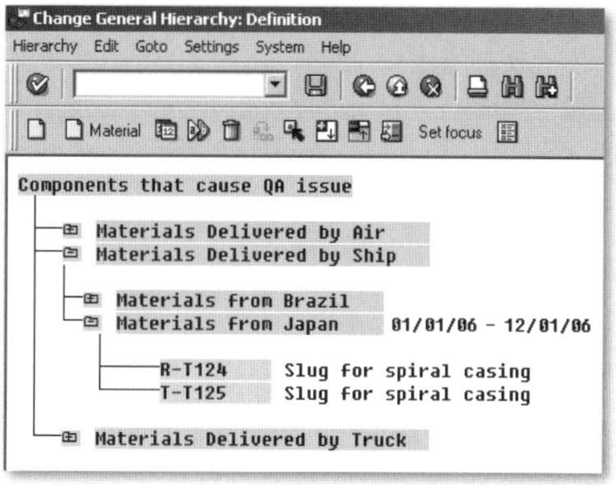

Figure 11.10 Node in Hierarchy with a Particular Validity Date Assigned

11.4 Using the Hierarchy

The user-defined hierarchy can be used when executing standard analyses. In the example that we are discussing in this chapter, the analyst is reviewing material that may be causing a problem with the quality of finished goods. The hierarchy can be run from relevant standard analyses where the material is reflected in the information structure.

For example, the standard analysis is associated with production orders and the actual time it is taking to close the order operations due to issues with quality inspection.

11.4.1 Execute a Standard Analysis

The analyst may use the standard analysis for Production Orders, transaction code MCP3, which can be found using the navigation path: **SAP Menu • Logistics • Logistics Controlling • Logistics Information System • Standard Analyses • Production • Production Order**.

The analyst will run the transaction for the plant where the error is occurring and for a period that is known to have included the issues the analyst wants to investigate. The initial screen for Transaction MCP3 is shown in Figure 11.11.

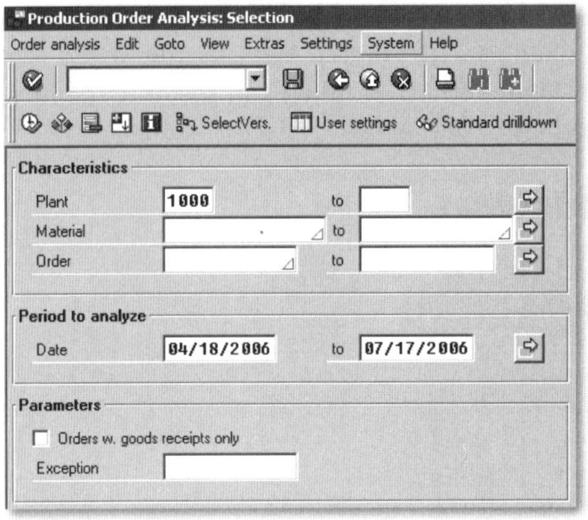

Figure 11.11 Initial Screen for Production Order Standard Analysis, Transaction MCP3

The results from the standard analysis show the plant **1000** and the key figures of target and actual operation completion times, in days are shown in Figure 11.12.

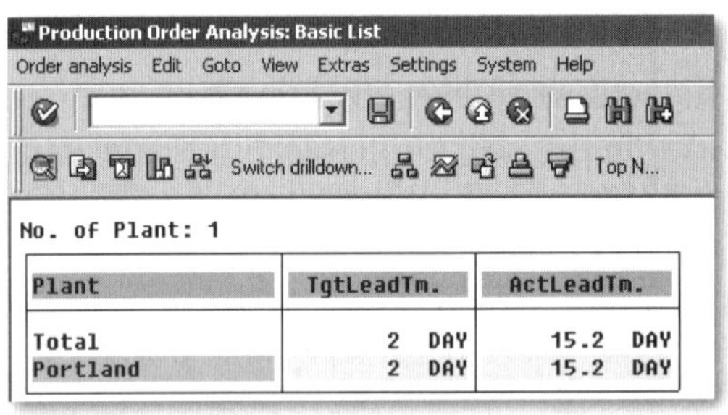

Figure 11.12 Standard Analysis for Plant 1000 Indicating an Issue with Production Order Operation Times

The result shows that for plant 1000, the target operation time is being exceeded by 13.2 days, (**ActLeadTm**. minus **TgtLeadTm.**), as shown in Figure 11.12. The analyst can now use the created hierarchy to investigate where the delays are occurring, based on the levels within the hierarchy.

11.4.2 Change to the User-Defined Hierarchy

To change to the user-defined hierarchy, the analyst should select the characteristic, in this case a plant, to be investigated and select from the menu: **View • Hierarchy Drilldown**.

A Basic List is displayed in a dialog box per Figure 11.13, enabling the analyst to choose from a number of hierarchies. The hierarchies are displayed by name in a list, from which the user-defined hierarchy can be chosen. The first hierarchy in the list, **Components that cause QA issue**, is selected.

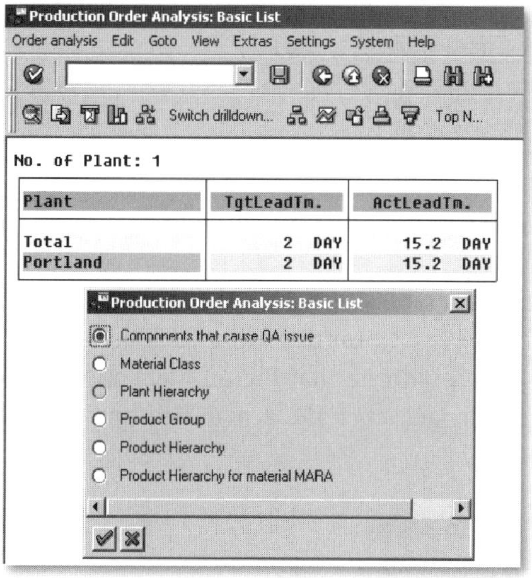

Figure 11.13 Selection of User-Defined Hierarchy Drilldown for Production Order Analysis

When the analyst has selected the hierarchy for the analysis, a dialog box opens, displaying a validity date. The default will be the current date, but depending on the analysis and the results obtained, the analyst may decide to change the validity date. If this date is changed, then part of the hierarchy may be excluded or included if any of the levels or objects were given validity date ranges. Once the validity date has been reviewed and entered, the results of the hierarchy drilldown will be displayed, as shown in Figure 11.14.

The results in Figure 11.14 show the second node of the example hierarchy. The results are defined by the node, which displays how the material is transported to the plant, for example, **Materials Delivered by Air**. The results show an obvious anomaly for the **Materials Delivered by Ship**. The other transportation methods, **Materials Delivered by Air** and **Materials Delivered by Truck**, show an actual lead time per operation close to target. However, those materials transported by ship are not within limits.

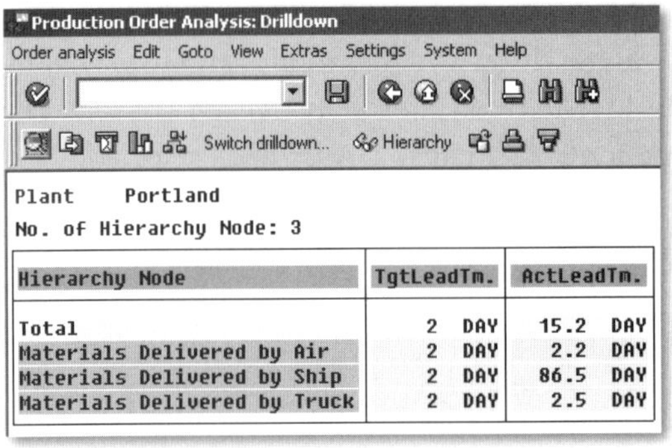

Figure 11.14 Production Order Standard Analysis Using User-Defined Hierarchy Drilldown

The analysts will then drill down the hierarchy using the **Materials Delivered by Ship** node to further investigate the reason for this variance. The results of the next level, shown in Figure 11.15, indicate that the problem appears to be with the material shipped from Japan, since the actual lead time shows the signs of the anomaly.

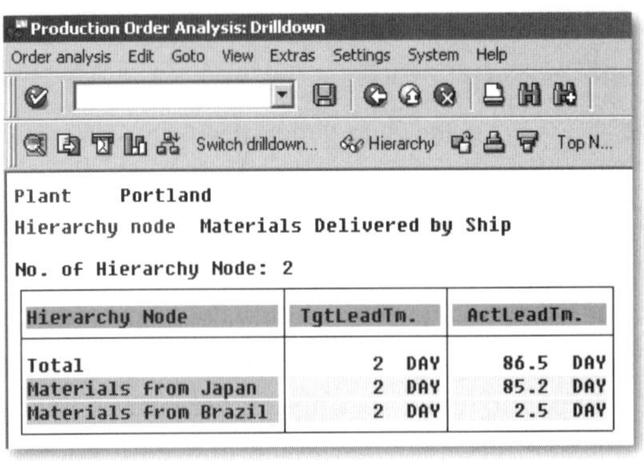

Figure 11.15 Analysis for Level in User-Defined Hierarchy Where Anomaly Is Highlighted

The analyst will then drop to the lowest level of the user-defined hierarchy where the results will show the materials that are shipped from Japan. The results will indicate whether the issue is with the individual material or the transportation method.

The lowest level of the user-defined hierarchy, as seen in Figure 11.16, shows that the issues with regards to production order operation lead times are not specific to one material but are relevant to all the materials that are shipped from one country. The hierarchy that was defined allows the analyst to hone in on the problem using the hierarchy tool. In this example, the analyst may refine the hierarchy to pinpoint specific periods, vendors, or packaging methods that may further explain the quality issues.

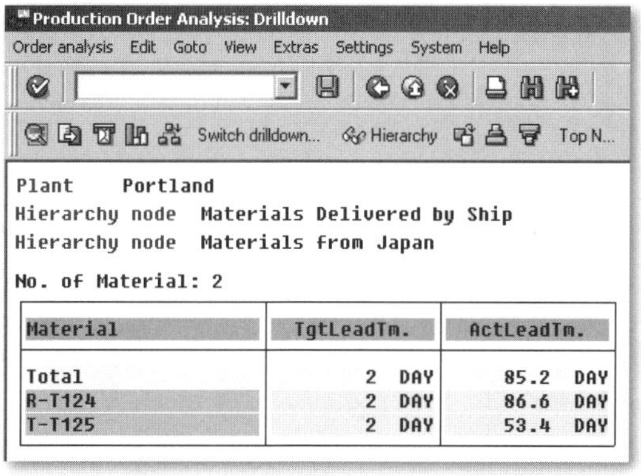

Figure 11.16 Lowest Level of User-Defined Hierarchy for Analysis of Production Orders

11.5 Changing a Hierarchy

When a hierarchy has been created and used with a standard analysis, it may require some refining. The refining may be necessary because of data skewing towards one node that creates inconclusive reporting. For example, if a hierarchy failed to show any data at a particular node, then this node is either redundant or needs to be modified. This modification can be made by using the change hierarchy Transaction MCK2, which can be accessed using the navigation path: **SAP Menu • Logistics • Logistics Controlling • Logistics Information System • Environment • General Hierarchy • Change.**

The initial screen requires that the analyst enter the hierarchy name. A matchcode is supplied if the hierarchy name is not known. After the initial screen, the hierarchy is displayed and is available for modification, as shown in Figure 11.17.

The options available in the change transaction are similar to those available in the hierarchy creation Transaction MCK1 (e.g., **Create Nodes**, **Assign Date**, **Set Focus**, etc.). In refining the hierarchy, the analyst may decide to add more materials to the selection or a new node for different delivery methods or countries.

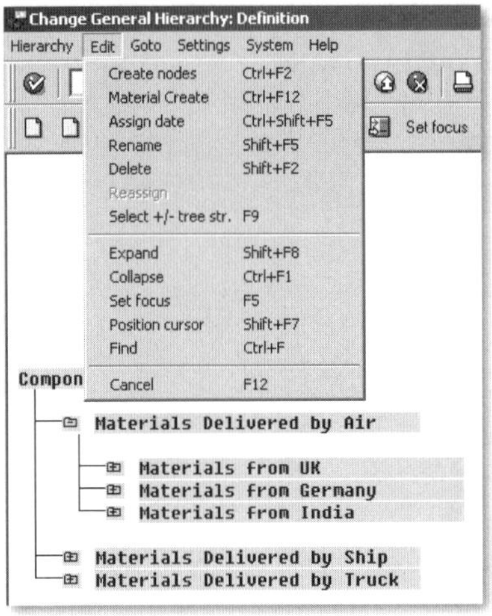

Figure 11.17 Hierarchy Change Transaction, MCK2, and Available Change Options

11.5.1 Create a Node

To create a new node, the analyst must place the cursor on the level below which he wants the new node to appear. By placing the cursor on the highest level of the hierachy, a new node will appear at the level below it.

11.5.2 Rename a Node

To rename a node, the analyst must place the cursor on the node to be changed and select **Edit • Rename** from the header menu, or use the **Shift + F5** function key. A dialog box opens, enabling her to change the node description, as shown in Figure 11.18.

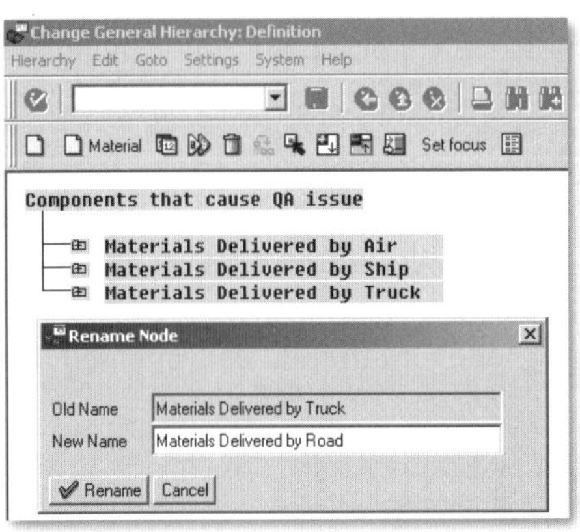

Figure 11.18 Hierarchy Change Transacton MCK2 and Renaming a Node

11.5.3 Delete a Node

To delete a node from the hierarchy, the analyst must place the cursor on that particular node and select **Edit • Delete** from the header menu, or use the **Shift + F2** function keys.

Note that all the items below the node that is to be deleted will also be deleted. Therefore, deleting a node from a high level in the hierarchy can have countless ramifications in the results obtained by using the hierarchy.

11.6 Summary

In this chapter, I have discussed the creation and use of the hierarchy for drilldown within the standard analysis. The hierarchy is a very powerful tool for the business user who needs to analyze issues that may be occurring in the supply chain. The example that we worked through here is typical of production issues that occur in manufacturing businesses every day, problems that can be resolved by using the functionality of the LIS.

In Chapter 12, I'll engage in a detailed discussion of one of the elements of the LIS, namely, the Sales Information System (SIS). For those of you who work primarily in the SD area, you will probably be familiar with the SIS and therefore may be already using some of the functionality that I will discuss.

The Sales Information System (SIS) is part of the LIS; however, it deals specifically with the SD data in SAP. The results of the evaluations can be used to identify issues, report on sales, and monitor supply chain planning.

12 Sales Information System

The SIS is probably the most used of the elements within the LIS. The Sales and Distribution consultant will usually have a reasonable understanding of the SIS, because SD users often require significant levels of reporting for sales and sales planning functionality.

Sales management deals with a number of issues that are a subset of those in the wider supply chain. Managers have to efficiently administer and monitor the sales within their enterprises. In addition, they must efficiently manage the sales plans, achieve sales targets, meet deadlines, secure new business, and beat competition. To do this, they need answers to the following questions:

- What products have key customers purchased most of the last quarter?
- What kinds of discounts have key customers enjoyed?
- What sales office has been offering the most discounts?
- What sales employee has the greatest invoiced orders last month?

The SIS can be used in the Sales and Distribution function in many different capacities, which are listed below:

- **Strategic Tool**
  To monitor trends in new products and sales opportunities, and support planning for new products and services.
- **Management Tool**
  To support market research, promotional campaigns, and pricing decisions.

- **Performance Tool**
  To analyze sales performance and the performance of the sales staff and offices.
- **Operation Tool**
  To report on customers, track sales, and provide reports that help customer service support.

This chapter will explain the foundations of the SIS, including the information structures, key figures, characteristics, and how the data is updated in the SIS.

12.1 Information Structures

As mentioned in Chapter 1, the Sales Information System comprises the following six information structures:

- **Customer (S001)**
  Analysis can be performed directly using customer information
- **Sales Office (S002)**
  Allows analysis at the sales office level
- **Sales Organization (S003)**
  Allows analysis at the sales organization level
- **Material (S004)**
  Analysis can be performed directly for a material
- **Shipping Point (S005)**
  Analysis can be performed directly for a shipping point
- **Sales Employee (S006)**
  Used for data required for employees, e.g., commission

12.2 Standard Analyses

There are seven standard analyses that can be used as part of the standard SIS functionality. Six of these analyses can be used in normal operations, while the standard analysis for Variant Configuration should be used only in operations where the company sells products that allow variant configuration.

12.2.1 Customer

The standard analysis for the customer derives its data from the information structure S001. This analysis will report on the incoming orders, invoiced sales, and credit memos given over a period of time entered in the selection screen, as shown in Figure 12.1. Selecting a range of sales organizations, materials, or customers can reduce the data retrieved from the S001 information structure. The results will be based on the period defined for the customer analysis.

The selection criteria for this analysis can be seen in Figure 12.1. This transaction can be accessed using transaction code MCTA, or using the navigation path: **SAP Menu • Logistics • Sales and Distribution • Sales Information System • Standard Analyses • Customer.**

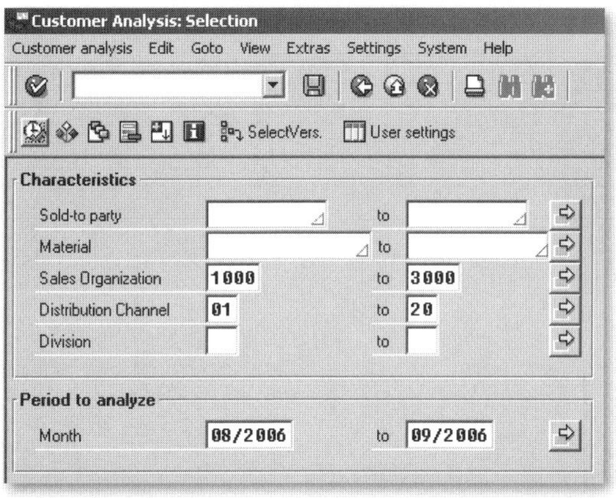

Figure 12.1 Selection Screen for Customer Analysis, Transaction MCTA

The result of the standard analysis returns the incoming orders, invoiced sales, and **Credit Memo** for customers (sold-to) based on the selection criteria entered (see Figure 12.2).

The result of the analysis allows the analyst to determine the sales and returns of customers based on the selection criteria. If the analyst needs more details, she will use the drilldown functionality for the standard analysis, as shown in Figure 12.3.

The drilldown allows the user to access the data at a lower level to answer questions about sales of a particular material to a customer, or sales in a particular period.

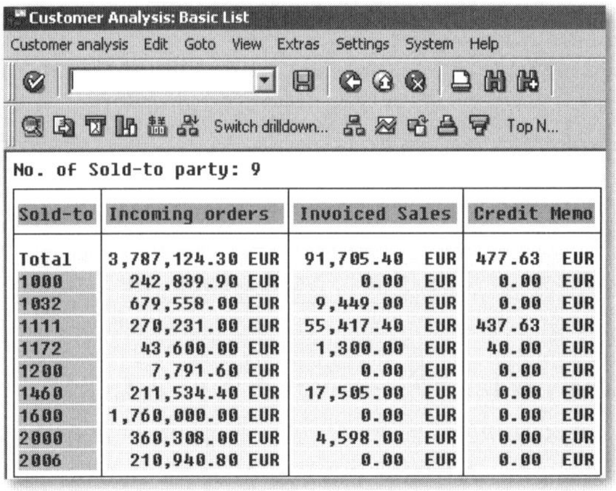

Sold-to	Incoming orders	Invoiced Sales	Credit Memo
Total	3,787,124.30 EUR	91,705.40 EUR	477.63 EUR
1000	242,839.90 EUR	0.00 EUR	0.00 EUR
1032	679,558.00 EUR	9,449.00 EUR	0.00 EUR
1111	270,231.00 EUR	55,417.40 EUR	437.63 EUR
1172	43,600.00 EUR	1,300.00 EUR	40.00 EUR
1200	7,791.60 EUR	0.00 EUR	0.00 EUR
1460	211,534.40 EUR	17,505.00 EUR	0.00 EUR
1600	1,760,000.00 EUR	0.00 EUR	0.00 EUR
2000	360,308.00 EUR	4,598.00 EUR	0.00 EUR
2006	210,940.80 EUR	0.00 EUR	0.00 EUR

Figure 12.2 Results of Customer Standard Analysis for Selection Criteria Entered, Transaction MCTA

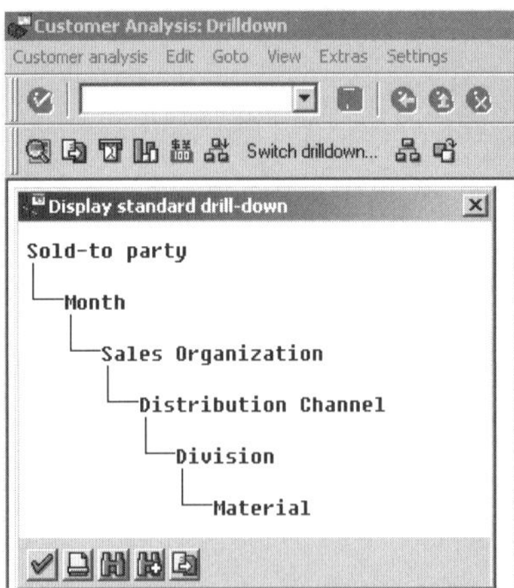

Figure 12.3 Standard Drilldown for Customer Standard Analysis, Transaction MCTA

12.2.2 Material

The material analysis is useful in finding the sales of a material during a given period, through certain distribution channels, to certain customers, etc. The standard analysis for material derives its data from the information structure S004. This analysis will report on the incoming orders, invoiced sales, open order quantity, and billing quantity over a period entered in the selection screen, as shown in Figure 12.4. Selecting a range of sales organizations, materials, or customers can reduce the data retrieved from the S001 information structure. The results will be based on the period defined for the analysis.

The selection criteria for the material standard analysis can be seen in Figure 12.4. This transaction can be accessed using transaction code MCTC, or using the navigation path: **SAP Menu • Logistics • Sales and Distribution • Sales Information System • Standard Analyses • Material.**

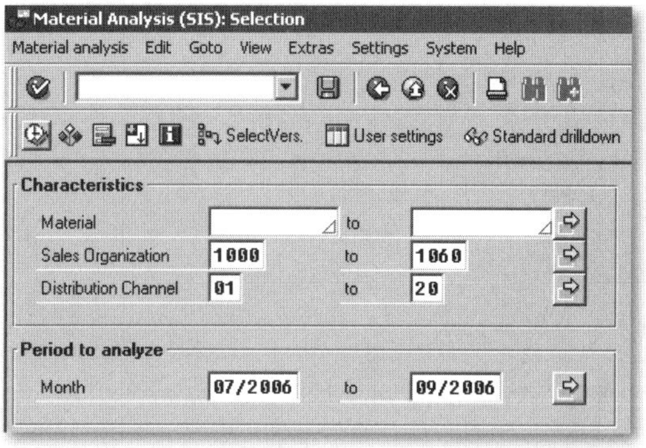

Figure 12.4 Selection Criteria for Material Standard Analysis, Transaction MCTC

The result of the materials standard analysis, displayed in Figure 12.5, shows the results based on the selection criteria entered. These are listed below:

- **Incoming ord**
  The total value of the incoming orders for the sales organization for the period entered
- **Inv. Sales**
  The value of the invoices sent to the customers
- **Open qty**
  The open order quantity
- **Bill qty**
  The quantity that has been billed to the customers

The output of the standard analysis, as shown in Figure 12.5, shows the analyst the sales of each material as well as what has been invoiced. This analysis is important for the sales team to ensure that the billing for the material is keeping up with the sales. Further analysis via drilldown may show the sales analyst what may be causing the lack of billing. The standard drilldown hierarchy for the material analysis is shown in Figure 12.6.

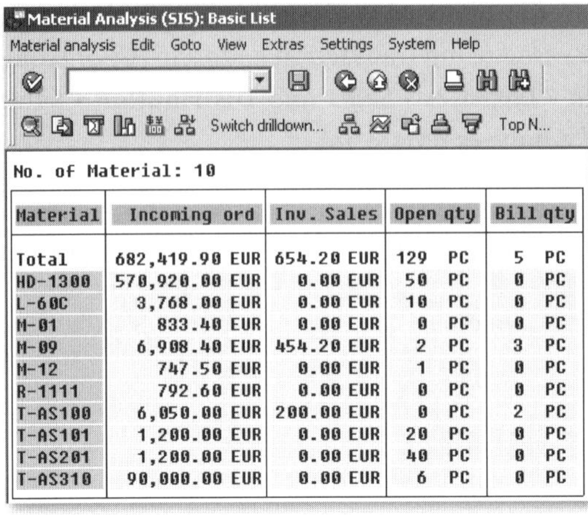

Figure 12.5 Output Results of Material Standard Analysis for Selection Criteria Entered, Transaction MCTC

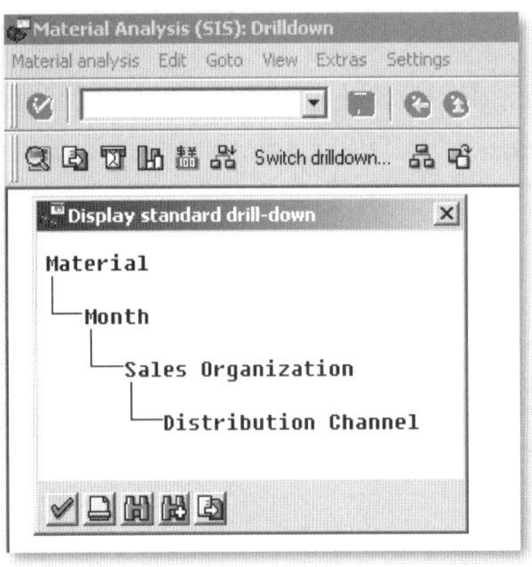

Figure 12.6 Standard Drilldown for Material Standard Analysis, Transaction MCTC

12.2.3 Sales Organization

A key metric vital for sales management is the sales figures of sales organizations. The standard analysis for sales organizations shows reports on the figures for incoming orders, total order quantity, and sales that have been invoiced.

By using the selection criteria to report on a range of sales organizations, the analyst can compare sales by sales organization either for a range of materials, a range of customers, distribution channel, etc.

The standard analysis for sales organization derives its data from the information structure S003. The selection criteria for the standard analysis are shown in Figure 12.7. This transaction can be accessed using transaction code MCTE, or by using the navigation path: **SAP Menu • Logistics • Sales and Distribution • Sales Information System • Standard Analyses • Sales Organization.**

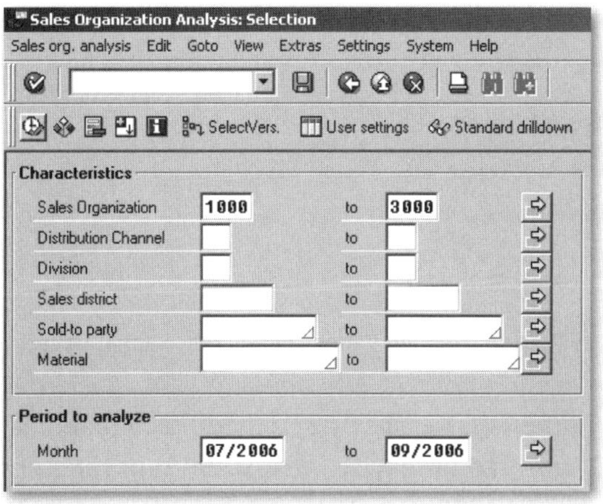

Figure 12.7 Selection Criteria Entered for Sales Organization Standard Analysis, Transaction MCTE

The result of the sales organization standard analysis returns the incoming orders, total order quantity, and total value of invoiced orders based on the selection criteria entered. This is shown in Figure 12.8.

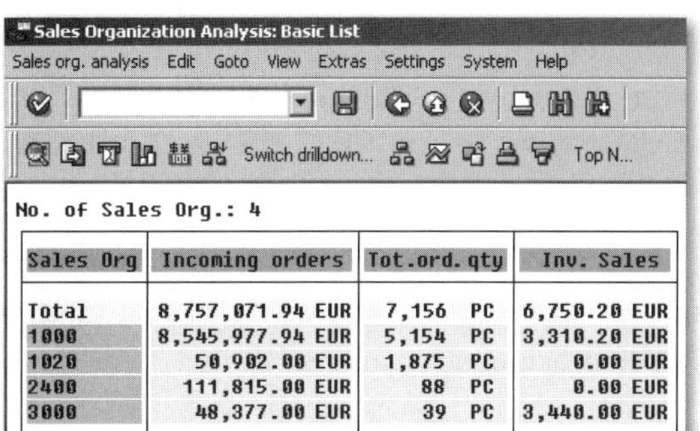

Sales Org	Incoming orders	Tot.ord.qty	Inv. Sales
Total	8,757,071.94 EUR	7,156 PC	6,750.20 EUR
1000	8,545,977.94 EUR	5,154 PC	3,310.20 EUR
1020	50,902.00 EUR	1,875 PC	0.00 EUR
2400	111,815.00 EUR	88 PC	0.00 EUR
3000	48,377.00 EUR	39 PC	3,440.00 EUR

Figure 12.8 Results of Sales Organization Standard Analysis, Transaction MCTE

The results in Figure 12.8 show the raw data for the sales organization based on the selection criteria. Sometimes it is useful for sales management to view this data in a slightly different fashion to emphasize the impact that one sales organization may have. To change the display of the figures to a percentage value, the analyst can use the option from the header menu: **Settings • Value Display • Percent.**

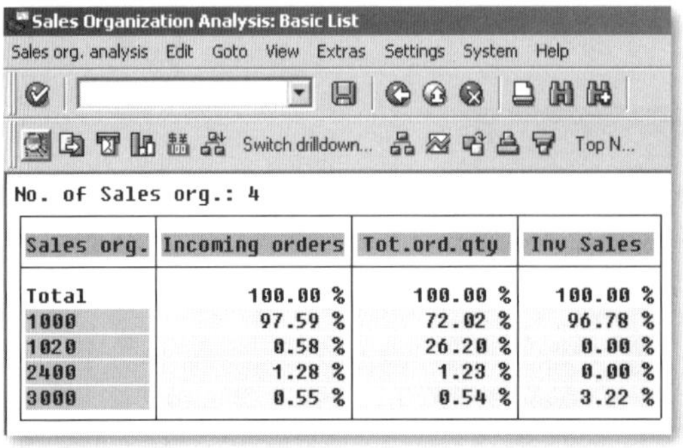

Sales org.	Incoming orders	Tot.ord.qty	Inv Sales
Total	100.00 %	100.00 %	100.00 %
1000	97.59 %	72.02 %	96.78 %
1020	0.58 %	26.20 %	0.00 %
2400	1.28 %	1.23 %	0.00 %
3000	0.55 %	0.54 %	3.22 %

Figure 12.9 Sales Organization Data in Total Percentage Values Rather Than Actual Values

The impact of the percentage values is far easier to see than the actual data. In this example, in Figure 12.9, you can clearly see that **97.59** % of the sales by value are from sales organization **1000** and that sales organization **1020** has less than one percent of sales by value, but that represents over a quarter of finished goods by quantity. The implication here is that 1020 is selling a lot of material at a very low price.

12.2.4 Shipping Point

The standard analysis for shipping point is useful because it shows the throughput of deliveries by weight and volume for a given period. The analysis can be used to try to even out the deliveries through the shipping point or to redistribute labor across the areas to ensure that the level of orders being shipped is maintained.

By using the selection criteria to report on a range of sales organizations, the analyst can compare sales by sales organization for a range of materials, a range of customers, distribution channel, etc.

The standard analysis for shipping points derives its data from the information structure S005. The selection criteria for the standard analysis can be seen in Figure 12.10. This transaction can be accessed using transaction code MCTK, or using the SAP menu and the navigation path: **SAP Menu • Logistics • Sales and Distribution • Sales Information System • Standard Analyses • Shipping Point.**

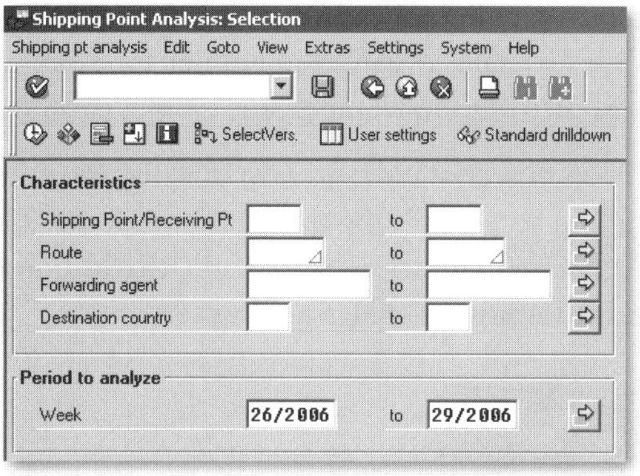

Figure 12.10 Selection Criteria for Shipping Point Standard Analysis, Transaction MCTK

The returned results for the analysis, as displayed in Figure 12.11, show the net and gross weight of the deliveries and the total volume of the items being delivered. Please note that this analysis will be valid only if the weight and volume of the material are accurately entered in the material master record, Transaction MM01. If the records are not updated, the client should be informed and a recommendation to ensure that the data is correct should be made out to him or her.

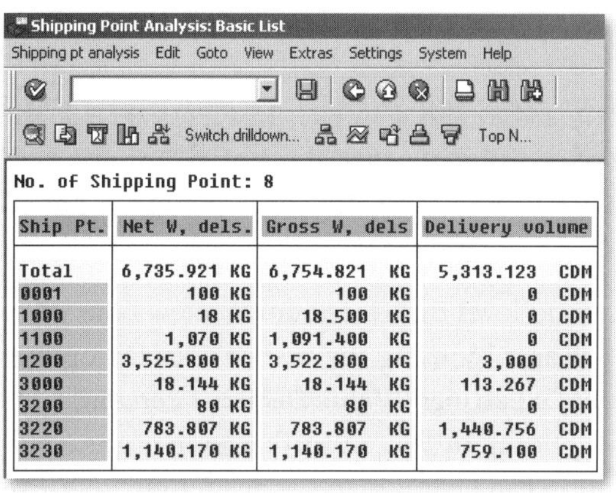

Ship Pt.	Net W, dels.	Gross W, dels	Delivery volume
Total	6,735.921 KG	6,754.821 KG	5,313.123 CDM
0001	100 KG	100 KG	0 CDM
1000	18 KG	18.500 KG	0 CDM
1100	1,070 KG	1,091.400 KG	0 CDM
1200	3,525.800 KG	3,522.800 KG	3,000 CDM
3000	18.144 KG	18.144 KG	113.267 CDM
3200	80 KG	80 KG	0 CDM
3220	783.807 KG	783.807 KG	1,440.756 CDM
3230	1,140.170 KG	1,140.170 KG	759.100 CDM

Figure 12.11 Volume and Net and Gross Weights of Deliveries Through Each Shipping Point

12.2.5 Sales Employee

The performance of sales personnel is always a key statistic that management is interested in viewing reports on. The SIS standard analysis for sales employees uses the S006 information structure and offers management a full breakdown of the sales employees' performances over a given period.

By using the selection criteria to report on a range of sales organizations, the analyst can compare employee sales by sales organization either for a range of materials, a range of customers, distribution channel, etc.

The selection criteria for the sales employee standard analysis is displayed in Figure 12.12. This transaction can be accessed using transaction code MCTI, or using the navigation path: **SAP Menu • Logistics • Sales and Distribution • Sales Information System • Standard Analyses • Sales Employee**.

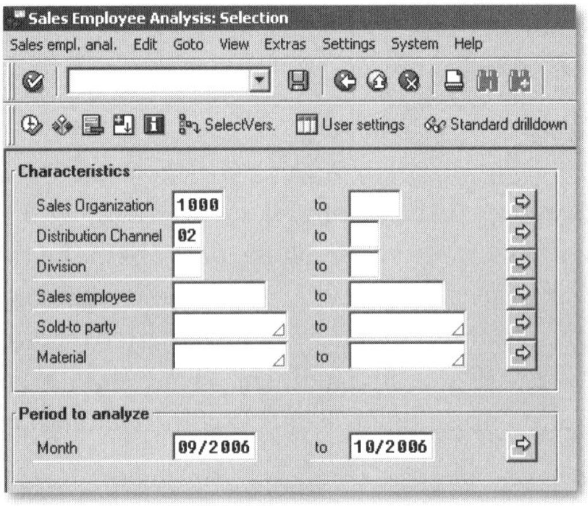

Figure 12.12 Selection Criteria for Sales Employee Standard Analysis, Transaction MCTI

The resulting data from the standard analysis shows, in Figure 12.13, the value of **Incoming orders**, total of quantity of ordered material (**Tot.ord.qty**), and total value of invoiced material (**Invoiced Sales**) over the given period entered.

The sales employee report at the top level of the drilldown shows the value of the orders and can be made clearer by using the percent display option, which is accessed via the menu path: **Settings • Value Display • Percent**. Sorting the data in ascending or descending order can further enhance the percent display option. This sort option can be found in the header menu: View-Sort in Descending Order. A dialog box will display what fields can be used to sort and in what order. The resulting data is then easier to read and gives management a clear view of the performance of the sales employees, as shown in Figure 12.14.

In Figure 12.14, it is clear from the data that employee **0001700** has the greatest value of orders, but this represents only a very small quantity. Employee **0001714** has less than six percent of total sales by value, but has over 46 % of sales by quantity. By drilling down into the data from this screen, management may discover the reasons for this anomaly, which may include the use of heavy discounting or free product to encourage sales.

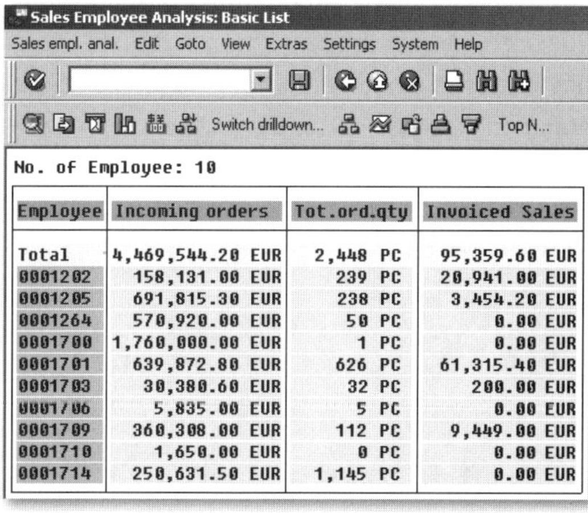

Employee	Incoming orders	Tot.ord.qty	Invoiced Sales
Total	4,469,544.20 EUR	2,448 PC	95,359.60 EUR
0001202	158,131.00 EUR	239 PC	20,941.00 EUR
0001205	691,815.30 EUR	238 PC	3,454.20 EUR
0001264	570,920.00 EUR	50 PC	0.00 EUR
0001700	1,760,000.00 EUR	1 PC	0.00 EUR
0001701	639,872.80 EUR	626 PC	61,315.40 EUR
0001703	30,380.60 EUR	32 PC	200.00 EUR
0001706	5,835.00 EUR	5 PC	0.00 EUR
0001709	360,308.00 EUR	112 PC	9,449.00 EUR
0001710	1,650.00 EUR	0 PC	0.00 EUR
0001714	250,631.50 EUR	1,145 PC	0.00 EUR

Figure 12.13 Resulting Data for Sales Employee Standard Analysis, Transaction MCTI

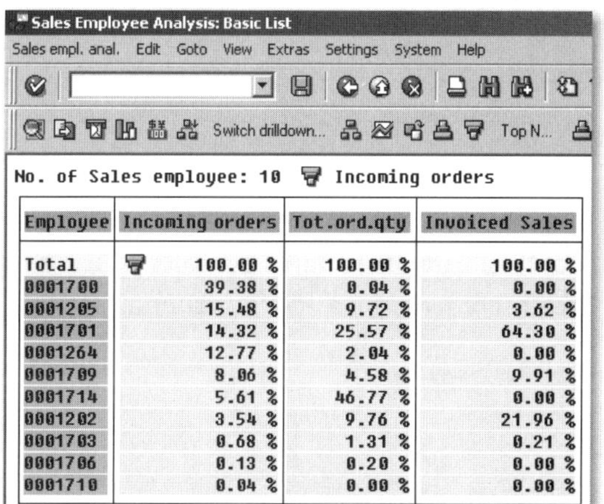

Employee	Incoming orders	Tot.ord.qty	Invoiced Sales
Total	100.00 %	100.00 %	100.00 %
0001700	39.38 %	0.04 %	0.00 %
0001205	15.48 %	9.72 %	3.62 %
0001701	14.32 %	25.57 %	64.30 %
0001264	12.77 %	2.04 %	0.00 %
0001709	8.06 %	4.58 %	9.91 %
0001714	5.61 %	46.77 %	0.00 %
0001202	3.54 %	9.76 %	21.96 %
0001703	0.68 %	1.31 %	0.21 %
0001706	0.13 %	0.20 %	0.00 %
0001710	0.04 %	0.00 %	0.00 %

Figure 12.14 Sales Employee Standard Analysis in Percent Display Option, Sorted in Descending Order for Incoming Orders

12.2.6 Sales Office

The performance of a sales office is another key metric that sales management reviews regularly. The SIS standard analysis for the sales offices uses the S002 information structure and offers management a review of the performance of sales offices over a given period.

By using the selection criteria to report on a range of sales organizations, the analyst can compare the sales office results by a range of sales organizations, materials, customers, distribution channels, etc.

The selection criteria for the sales office standard analysis can be seen in Figure 12.15. This transaction can be accessed using transaction code MCTG, or using the SAP menu and the navigation path: **SAP Menu • Logistics • Sales and Distribution • Sales Information System • Standard Analyses • Sales Office**.

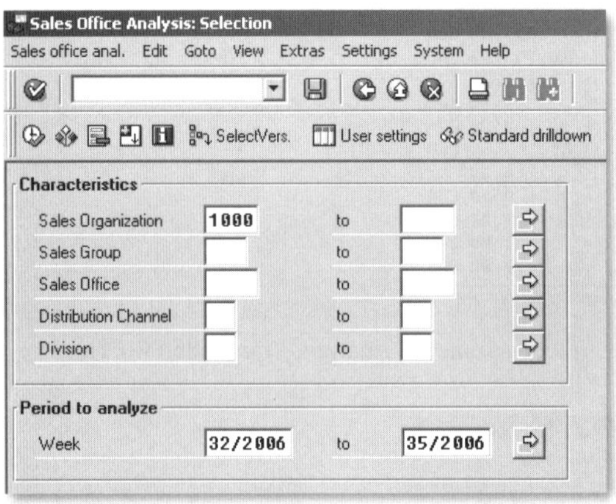

Figure 12.15 Selection Criteria for Sales Office Standard Analysis, Transaction MCTG

The result of the standard analysis (see Figure 12.16) shows the **Incoming orders**, cost of orders (**Orders: cost**) and **Invoiced Sales** per sales office over the given weekly periods that are entered via the selection criteria.

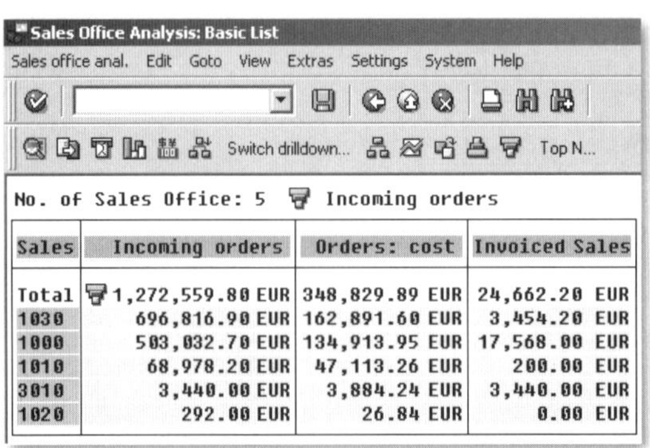

Sales	Incoming orders	Orders: cost	Invoiced Sales
Total	1,272,559.80 EUR	348,829.89 EUR	24,662.20 EUR
1030	696,816.90 EUR	162,891.60 EUR	3,454.20 EUR
1000	503,032.70 EUR	134,913.95 EUR	17,568.00 EUR
1010	68,978.20 EUR	47,113.26 EUR	200.00 EUR
3010	3,440.00 EUR	3,884.24 EUR	3,440.00 EUR
1020	292.00 EUR	26.84 EUR	0.00 EUR

Figure 12.16 Results of Sales Office Standard Analysis Sorted by Incoming Order Value

The results shown in Figure 12.16 can be drilled down to view the data at a weekly period, sales organization, distribution channel, division, and sales group.

12.3 Configuration for SIS

There are a number of configuration steps that can be made to the SIS. The following sections describe the configuration of the information structures, statistics groups, and update groups.

12.3.1 Configuration for Information Structures

Changes can be made to the way in which updates are made to the information structures in the SIS. The information structures are updated with the event data from a sales order, invoice, etc. The configuration allows the user to change the way in which these updates occur and whether any update to an information structure will occur. The changes that can be made to the information structure are the period unit of the update and the type of update to be performed.

The configuration can be found using Transaction OMO1, or by using the navigation path: **IMG • Logistics—General • Logistics Information System • Logistics Data Warehouse • Updating • Updating Control • Activate Update**.

The transaction will ask the user to select a particular function area, for example, Purchasing, Production, Retail, etc. The Sales and Distribution function area should be selected. Once the correct area has been selected, the screen will display the information structures for the SIS, as shown in Figure 12.17 on the next page.

Period Unit

The period unit is the period on which the data is updated to the structure, for example, weekly, monthly, etc. Normally the period update would be derived from the posting period of the company code; however, if it is not possible to assess a company code, then it is important to enter a period unit in the configuration.

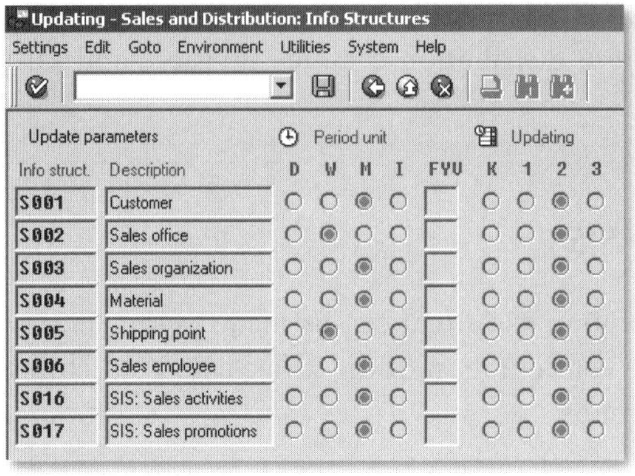

Figure 12.17 SIS Information Structures and Configuration of Period Unit and Type of Update

Type of Update

The type of update, shown in Figure 12.17, can be configured, which allows the user to choose either a method of updating or to have no updating at all. Let us look at these types in more detail below:

- **1: Synchronous Update**
  This will update the information structure at the time of the document event. The risk of using this method is that any problems during the update will cause the update not to occur and it cannot be repeated.
- **2: Asynchronous Update**
  This will not update the information structure at the time of the document event, but at a later time. This method carries no risk if the update has problems, and it can be rerun.
- **3: Collective Update**
  This is also an asynchronous update. The difference between this update and the asynchronous update is that the update is not just for a single document but for a collection of documents. The collective update job can be scheduled using Transaction MC3V.
- **K: No Update**
  This update option stops any update to the information structure.

The updates to the information structure can be made by selecting the structure and, from the header menu, EditParameters, or by using the **F2** key. The options can be changed in the dialog box, as shown in Figure 12.18.

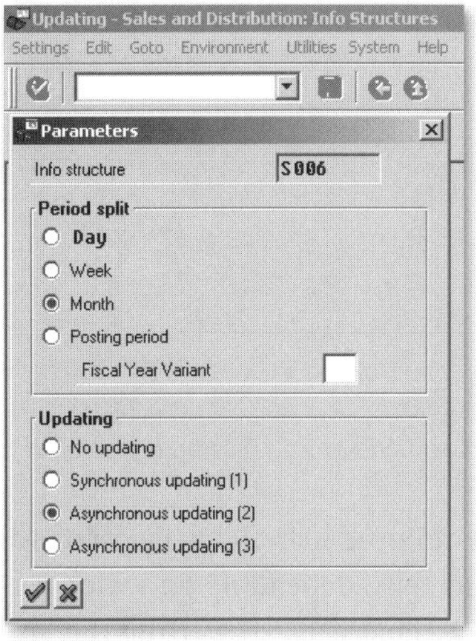

Figure 12.18 Configuration Update Screen for Information Structure, Transaction OMO1

The Sales Information System lets you restrict or allow certain data to be updated for the analysis in SIS. This modification can change the way in which the statistical data is updated in the system. The changes are configuration changes and made in the IMG. There are two definitions that we need to discuss in order to understand the configuration changes. They are:

- Statistics Groups
- Update Groups

Let's examine these in more detail now.

12.3.2 Statistics Groups

A statistics group can be defined to allow the sales analyst to group together customers, sales documents, or materials that require similar statistical updates. The creation of statistics groups is performed in the IMG. There are separate transactions for materials, customers, etc.

The example used in Figure 12.9 will show the creation of a statistics group for a material. The transaction for creating a statistics group is OVRF, or it can be found in the IMG using the navigation path: **IMG • Logistics—General • Logistics Information System • Logistics Data Warehouse • Updating • Updating Control • Setting: Sales • Statistics Groups • Maintain Statistics Groups for Material.**

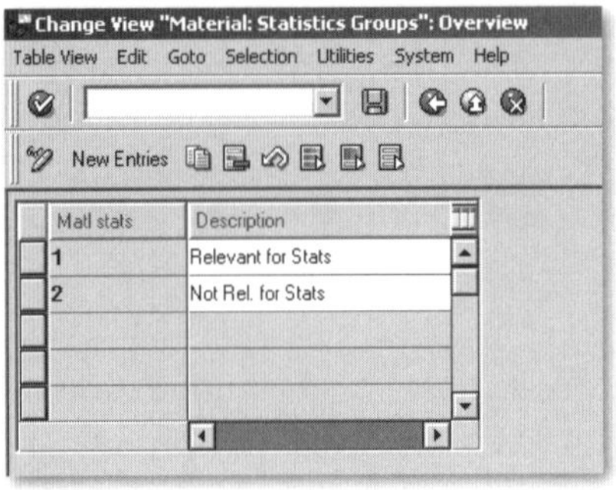

Figure 12.19 Statistics Groups for Materials, Transaction OVRF

The materials statistics group is assigned within the material master record. The field can be found on one of the sales screens, depending on which version of SAP you are using. The screen below, Figure 12.20, is from the SAP ERP Central Component (ECC) 5.0.

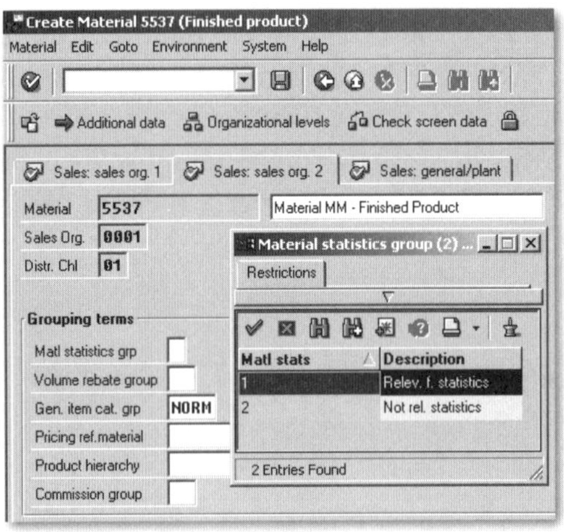

Figure 12.20 Material Statistics Group Field in Sales Screen of Material Master Record

12.3.3 Update Group

An update group is used to determine the fields, which will be created for the statistics. In a sales application, an update group is assigned to a specific business event. The number of sales elements determines the update group from the following list:

- Sales organization
- Distribution channel

- Division
- Sales document type
- Item type
- Group of customers
- Group of materials

A new update group can be created by using the IMG navigation path: **IMG • Logistics—General • Logistics Information System • Logistics Data Warehouse • Updating • Updating Definition • General Definition Using Update Groups • Maintain Update Groups.**

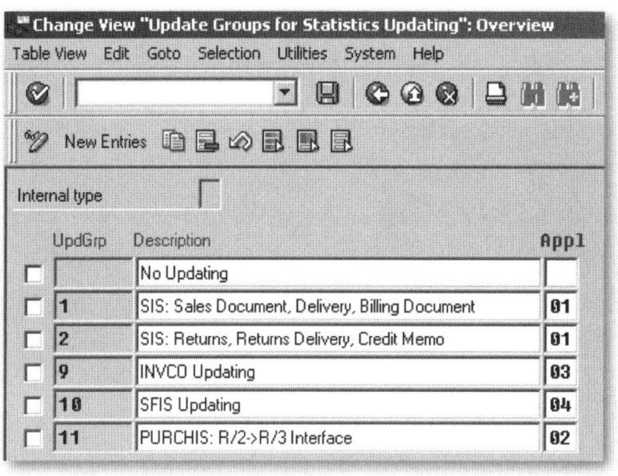

Figure 12.21 Update Groups 1 and 2 for the Sales Information System

The update groups for the SIS are shown in Figure 12.21. The application number of each update group shows which area the update group is for. In Figure 12.21, the update groups **1** and **2** are for application **01**, which represents sales and distribution.

Once the update group is created, it can be assigned to an information structure, as shown in Figure 12.22, and the specific key figure updates can be configured by using Transaction MC25 or via the IMG navigation path: **IMG • Logistics—General • Logistics Information System • Logistics Data Warehouse • Updating • Updating Definition • Specific Definition Using Update Groups • Maintain Update Rules.**

The detail screen in MC25 shows the update rules for the key figures of the information structure. Each key figure, shown in Figure 12.23, can be edited for the following:

- **Sales Event for Updating**
  Sales order (VA), delivery (VC), billing document (VD).
- **Type of Updating**
  Cumulative (A), Data Transfer (B), Counter (C).
- **Unit of Statistics**
  Weight (70), Volume (71), Time (75), etc.
- **Formula for Update**
  A formula is used when the key figure is calculated using other source fields.
- **Requirement for Update**
  A requirement is used when the key figure is updated when a combination of events occur.

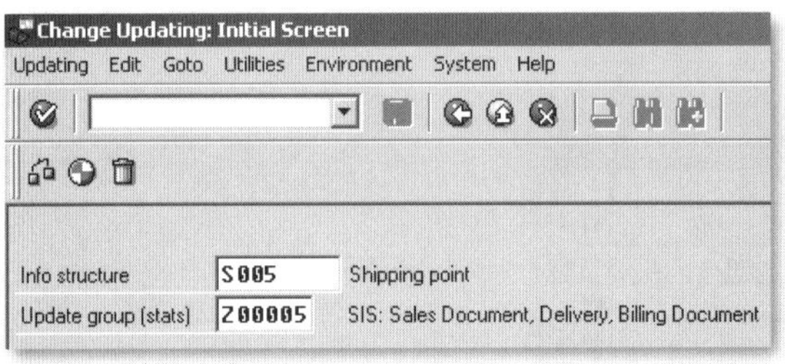

Figure 12.22 Assignment of Update Group to an Information Structure, Transaction MC25

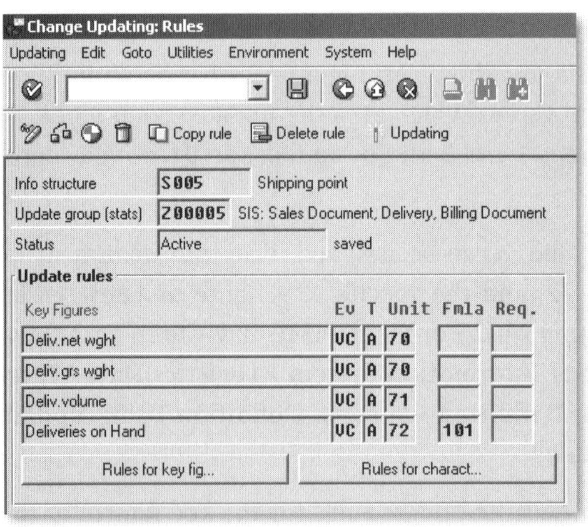

Figure 12.23 Updating Rules for Key Figures of an Information Structure, Transaction MC25

A detailed view of the update rules for a key figure, as shown in Figure 12.24, can be displayed by placing the cursor on a key figure and then selecting the options from the header menu: **Edit • Rules for Key Figures.**

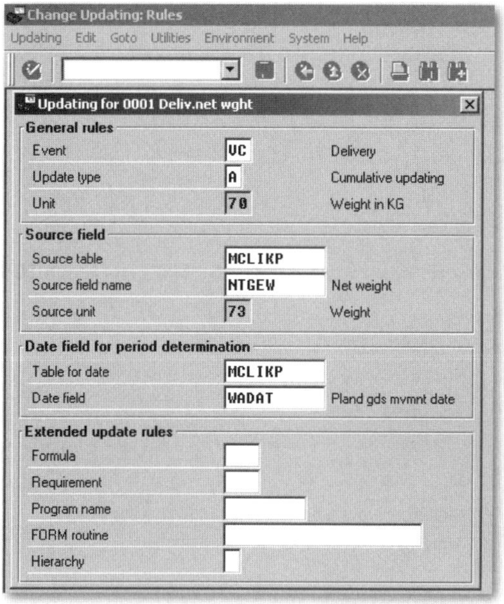

Figure 12.24 Detailed Update Components for a Key Figure, Transaction MC25

12.4 Testing the SIS Updates

Once a sales analyst has made changes to the SIS configuration, it is important to test that the data is updated when a business event is executed.

12.4.1 Switching on Update Log

To view the LIS Update Log, you must set a parameter for your own user login. The parameter to set to view the Update Log is **MCL**. This parameter can be set by selecting the user profile from any header menu, as shown in Figure 12.25. The transaction code for maintaining a user profile is **SU3**.

In Transaction SU3, shown in Figure 12.26, the **Parameter ID MCL** should be added with the **Parameter value** of **X**. After the parameter has been switched on, it is possible to review the update log in the SIS.

Figure 12.25 Menu Path to Set MCL Parameter to View Update Log for SIS, Transaction SU3

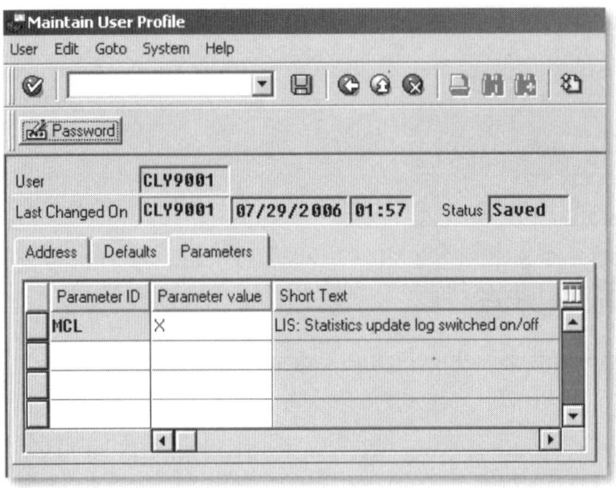

Figure 12.26 MCL Parameter Added to User Profile, Transaction SU3

12.4.2 Create a Sales Order

To test what is being updated to the information structures, the analyst should create a sales order using Transaction VA01. Then, the analyst should review the pricing data of the sales order, as shown in Figure 12.27.

12.4.3 Review the Update Log

You can view the update log by using Transaction MC30. This transaction analyzes which structures are updated for the sales event, generating a log of updates to the information structures and providing a detailed analysis. Transaction MC30 is based on the user profile and requires that the MCL parameter has been set. Figure 12.28 shows the output from this transaction and the information structures that have been updated.

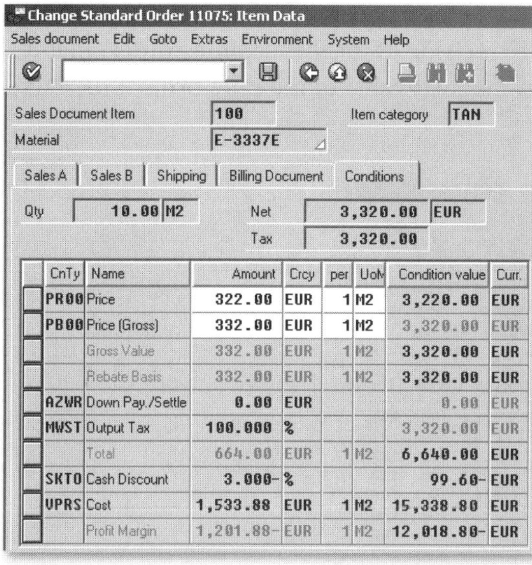

Figure 12.27 Pricing Data from a Sales Order, Transaction VA01

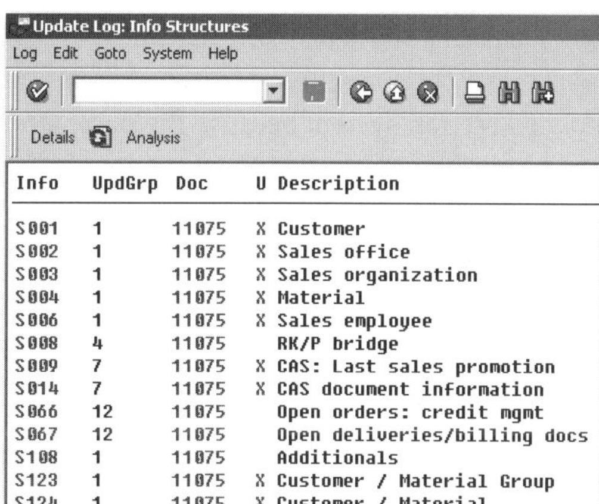

Figure 12.28 Update Log for Information Structures, Transaction MC30

The screen in Figure 12.28 also shows the information structure (**Info**), the sales document (**Doc**) that caused the information structure to be changed, and the field that was changed (**Description**).

The data analyst can further review the updates to the information structures by placing the cursor on the structure and selecting **Edit** and then **Details** from the header menu, or by selecting the **F2** function key. The detailed information on the information structure, shown in Figure 12.29, allows the user to check the data in the update log against the data on the created sales order. In this case, the figure of 3,320 Euros for the incoming orders in information structure S001 matches the total value of the sales order 11075, created in VA01 in Figure 12.27.

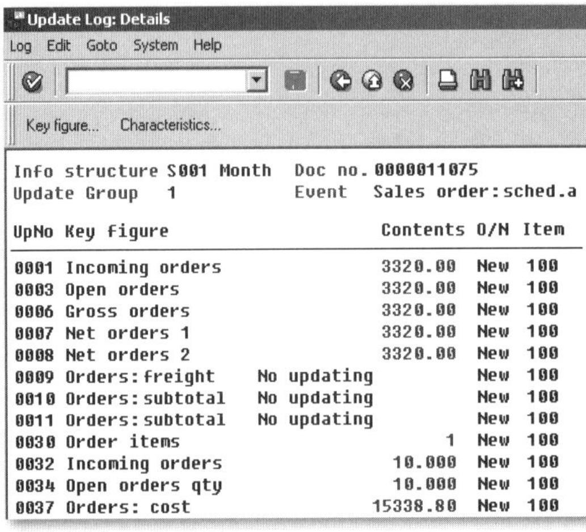

Figure 12.29 Update Log Details for S001 Information Structure, Transaction MC30

Do not set the parameter MCL in a production system because the parameter requires significant system resources and can affect system performance for users.

12.5 Summary

In this chapter, I discussed the Sales Information System. The standard analysis reporting can be effectively used by sales management to review a broad spectrum of sales activities. I also described the configuration steps that are available to analysts to ensure that the information is updated based on the requirements of sales management. Lastly, I explained the steps that analysts can take to review the updated information based on the update logs.

In Chapter 13, I will discuss the Purchase Information System (PURCHIS). This system is often overlooked, but it offers a wealth of information for supply chain management.

The Purchasing Information System, which is part of the LIS, is for purchasing data in SAP. The results can be used to identify issues and generate reports for the purchasing department, and are also used for supply chain planning.

13 Purchasing Information System

The Purchasing Information System (PURCHIS), as a part of the larger LIS, enables the purchasing analyst to produce reports relevant to decision-making for purchasing management.

Purchasing department management is concerned with a number of issues that are part of those reviewed by the overall supply chain management. Apart from salaries, purchasing accounts for a company's biggest area of expenses. Therefore, the purchasing department management is responsible for minimizing costs, since every dollar saved by purchasing is a dollar added to profit. Introducing and encouraging better buying will allow purchasing management to lower the company's purchasing costs and improve overall company revenue. To do this, management needs answers to questions such as:

- What are the price fluctuations in the supply base?
- How do they leverage purchases across the corporation?
- What demand forecasts should they communicate to the vendor?
- With what vendors should they establish long-term supply agreements, especially for products that are purchased frequently?
- Are there too many vendors in low-value added purchases and too few in the high-valued areas?

This chapter will explain the foundations of the Purchasing Information System, including the information structures, key figures, characteristics, and how the data is updated in PURCHIS.

13.1 Information Structures

The Purchasing Information System comprises four information structures, which are:

- **Purchasing Group (S011)**
  Allows analysis at the purchasing group level
- **Purchasing (S012)**
  Contains analysis for the vendor, material and material group
- **Vendor Evaluation (S013)**
  Triggered by purchase orders and goods receipt
- **Subsequent Settlement (S015)**
  Triggered by an invoice receipt or a subsequent settlement

Now we can examine key figures as they relate to information structures.

The key figures in the information structures are updated when business events take place. The key figures are updated on the following three levels:

- Header level
- Line item level
- Schedule line level

Each of the information structures updates different key figures based on the business event that takes place, such as Purchase Order creation, Vendor Evaluation updates, etc. The list below shows the updates to the key figures for the PURCHIS information structures and business events.

13.1.1 Purchasing Group (S011)

A purchasing group is a person or persons who specialize in one area of purchasing. This could be as simple as one person buying all raw materials and another buying all Maintenance, Repair, and Operating (MRO) items, or as complex as several people buying materials from one large vendor, such as Cisco or Microsoft, which is more typical of larger corporations. The Purchasing Group information structure includes the following data. Note that the updates are seen for the three previously identified levels as relevant and needed: header, line and schedule line.

- **Request for Quotation (RFQ)**
  - **Header**
    Number of RFQs

- **Line Item**
  Number of RFQ Items and Number of Quotation Items
- **Purchase Order**
  - **Header**
    Number of Purchase Orders
  - **Line Item**
    Number of Purchase Order Items
  - **Schedule Line**
    Purchase Order Value and Number of Purchase Order Schedule Lines
- **Scheduling Agreement**
  - **Header**
    Number of Scheduling Agreements
  - **Line Item**
    Number of Scheduling Agreement Line Items
  - **Schedule Line**
    Scheduling Agreement Value and Number of Delivery Schedules
- **Contract**
  - **Header**
    Number of Contracts
  - **Line Item**
    Number of Contract Line Items
- **Goods Receipt**
  - **Header**
    Number of Deliveries
- **Invoice Receipt**
  - **Line Item**
    Invoiced Amount in the Local Currency

13.1.2 Purchasing (S012)

The Purchasing information structure includes the following data.

- **Request for Quotation (RFQ)**
  - **Line Item**
    Number of RFQ Items and Number of Quotation Items

- **Purchase Order**
  - **Line Item**
    Number of Purchase Order Items and Quality Variance
  - **Schedule Line**
    Purchase Order Quantity, Required Delivery Quantity, and Purchase Order Value
- **Scheduling Agreement**
  - **Schedule Line**
    Purchase Order Quantity, Required Delivery Quantity, and Purchase Order Value
- **Contract**
  - **Line Item**
    Number of Contract Line Items
- **Goods Receipt**
  - **Line Item**
    Number of Deliveries, Quantity Delivered Variance, Delivery Date Variance, Total Delivery Time
  - **Schedule Line**
    Quantity of Goods Receipt Items
- **Invoice Receipt**
  - **Schedule Line**
    Invoice Receipt Quantity and Amount Invoiced in the Local Currency

13.1.3 Vendor Evaluation (S013)

Vendor evaluation is functionality in the purchasing area of the SAP MM module where vendors can be rated by subjective and objective criteria. The vendors are given a point score that can be weighted, depending on the criteria of the purchasing department. The Vendor Evaluation information structure includes the following elements.

- **Purchase Order**
  - **Line Item**
    Points Score Quantity Reliability
- **Goods Receipt**
  - **Line Item**
    Points Score Quantity Reliability, Points Score Date Reliability, and Shipping Instructions

13.1.4 Subsequent Settlement (S015)

Subsequent settlement refers to the practice where vendors will give their clients a discount or favorable terms if they meet some criteria that both vendors and clients agree on, such as value or quantity of goods purchased. The Subsequent Settlement information structure comprises the following elements.

- **Invoice Receipt**
  - **Line Item**
    Provision for Income, Invoiced Sales, Number of Points, Invoiced Sales Quantity, Gross Weight, Net Weight and Volume.
- **Credit Memo/Billing Document**
  - **Line Item**
    Dissolved Provision for Income, Provision Final Settlement and Provision Condition Record

Having reviewed the information structures that make up PURCHIS, we will now discuss the standard analyses in the PURCHIS that use the data from these information structures.

13.2 Standard Analyses

The standard analyses for the Purchasing Information System were described in detail in Chapter 2. Now let's get a general idea of the standard analyses.

13.2.1 Purchasing Group

The standard analysis for purchasing groups derives its data from the information structure S011. With this standard analysis, the Purchasing Organization, Purchasing Group, and Vendor are the characteristics that can be selected using the period that the purchasing analyst wants to define.

13.2.2 Vendor

The standard analysis for vendors derives its data from the information structure S012. With the vendor standard analysis, the information retrieved from the information structure allows users to analyze how much business vendors have done with certain purchase organizations, based on the period defined for the analysis.

13.2.3 Material Group

The standard analysis for material groups also derives its data from the information structure S012. The standard analysis for material groups will report on the purchase order value and quantity of the company's material groups. Selecting a range of purchasing organizations, materials, or plants can reduce the data retrieved from the information structure. The results will be based on the period defined for the analysis.

13.2.4 Material

The standard analysis for materials also derives its data from the information structure S012. The standard analysis for materials will report on the purchase order value, goods receipt totals, and order quantity of all materials or those from the selection criteria entered. The results will be based on the period defined for the analysis.

13.2.5 Vendor Evaluation

If the client uses the vendor evaluation functionality, then this particular standard analysis can aid in creating data for subjective scoring in the configured vendor evaluation calculations. The standard analysis for vendor evaluation derives its data from the information structure S013.

13.2.6 Subsequent Settlement

Subsequent settlement is functionality that allows rebate arrangements with vendors that are paid or settled at arranged dates, for example, end of a quarter or one per year. The rebates will be agreed upon for some business volume, value, quantity, or point structure. To verify the vendor's calculations, it is possible to use the standard analysis with the S015 information structure.

13.3 Long-Term Planning

In addition to the standard analyses in the Purchasing Information System, three standard analyses are available to the purchasing analyst, specifically for long-term planning. These standard analyses are based on the Purchasing information structure (S012).

The long-term planning analyses are essential for purchasing management as they prepare for contract negotiations with vendors, or are about to participate in vendor rationalization for certain items. There are three long-term planning analyses:

- Vendor
- Material Group
- Material

Before we describe these planning analyses, we need to address the preparation required to perform long-term planning.

13.3.1 Preparing for Long-Term Planning

To ensure that the analyses will execute correctly, the purchasing analyst needs some preparation. The transactions required for the setup of the long-term analyses are in the Production Planning module.

Create a Planning Scenario

The preparation for long-term planning does not have to include creating a new planning scenario. However, if you review the existing planning scenarios that have been created in your system, you may require a new scenario to fulfill the requirements of your analysis.

The planning scenario is required, as it contains the control parameters for long-term planning. These parameters include the planning period, the plant where long-term planning is to be carried out, and the independent requirements versions to be planned.

The planning scenario is created using Transaction MS31, or using the navigation path: **SAP Menu • Logistics • Production • Production Planning • Long-Term Planning • Planning Scenario • Create**. A three-character field and a 40-character description, as shown in Figure 13.1, define the planning scenario.

The planning scenario allows the analyst to produce the control parameters for a number of plants, and to determine whether sales orders should be considered, whether to include purchase requisitions, and whether to include planned orders, etc. The detailed control data can be seen in Figure 13.2.

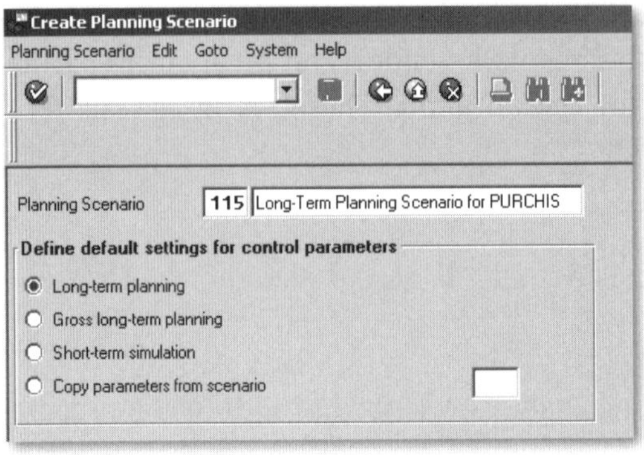

Figure 13.1 Initial Screen for Creating a Planning Scenario, Transaction MS31

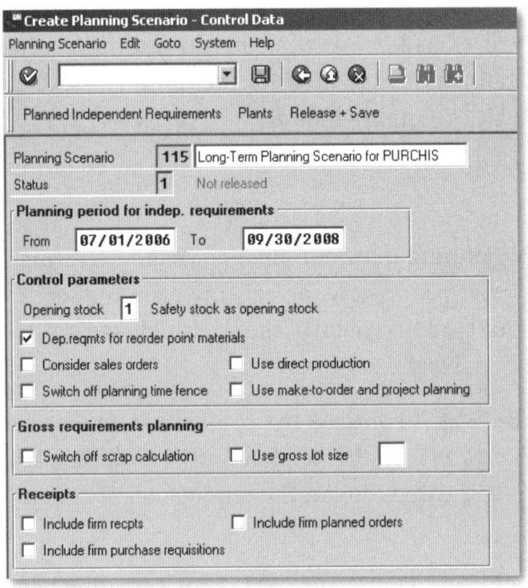

Figure 13.2 Control Data Configured for Creating a Planning Scenario, Transaction MS31

Creating Planning Data

Once the planning scenario has been created, the setup data can be created in the Production Planning area for the Purchasing Information System. The setup data can be created in Transaction MS70, or using the navigation path: **SAP Menu • Logistics • Production • Production Planning • Long-Term Planning • Evaluations • Purchasing Information System • Set Up Data**.

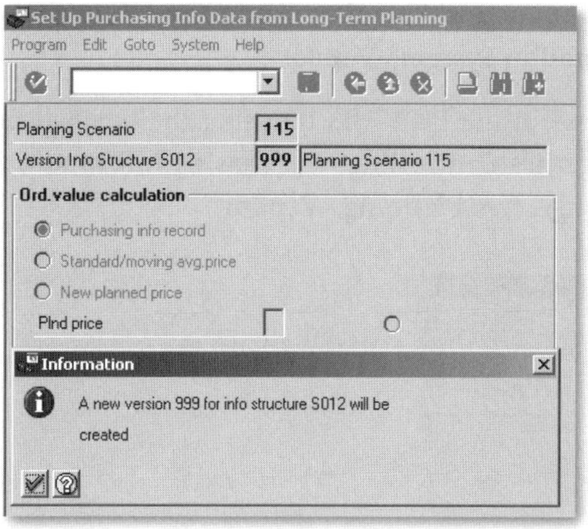

Figure 13.3 Entry Screen to Allow Data Setup for Long-Term Planning in PURCHIS

The setup data screen, as shown in Figure 13.3, requires that the user enter a planning scenario. The version information number can be added and, as the information box describes, a new version will be created. The transaction will return with information messages, warning messages, or error messages. Information messages are shown in Figure 13.4. Now let's look at our long-term planning analyses.

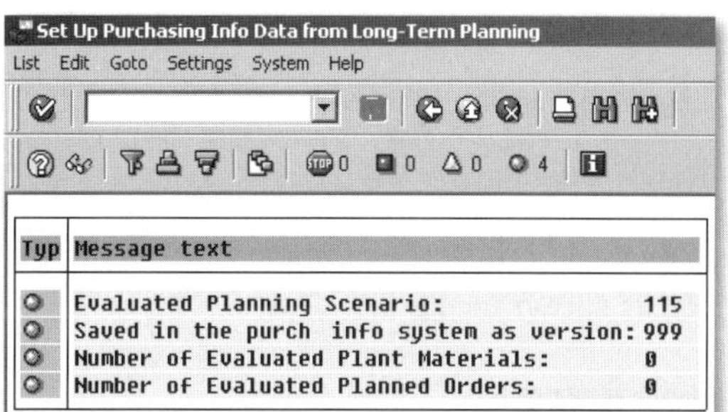

Figure 13.4 Information Messages in Results Screen, Transaction MS70

13.3.2 Long-Term Planning for Vendors

Once all the preparation has been made to run the long-term planning standard analyses, the analyst can run the required transaction.

Using Transaction MCEA, as shown in Figure 13.5, the long-term planning for vendors is executed. It is located in different areas of the SAP menu. It can be found in Production Planning by using the navigation path: **SAP**

Menu • Logistics • Production • Production Planning • Long-Term Planning • Evaluations • Purchasing Information System • Vendor.

The transaction can also be found in the PURCHIS by using the navigation path: **SAP Menu • Logistics • Logistics Controlling • Purchasing Information System • Standard Analyses • Long-Term Planning • Vendor**.

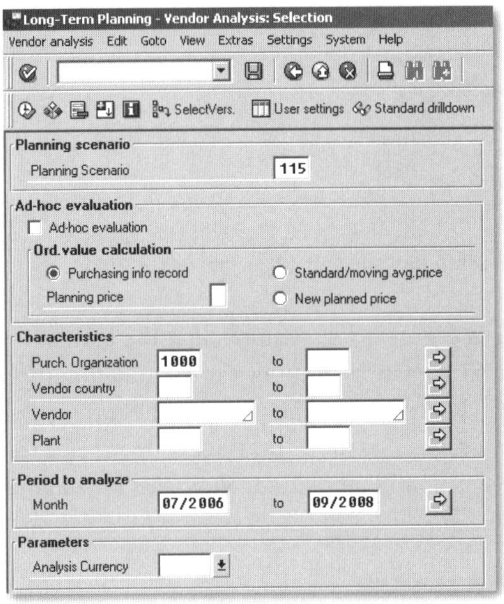

Figure 13.5 Initial Screen for Vendor Long-Term Planning Analysis, Transaction MCEA

The results of the transaction show the information for the key figures by vendor. The version, which described the criteria for the planning scenario, has returned data for five vendors, as shown in Figure 13.6.

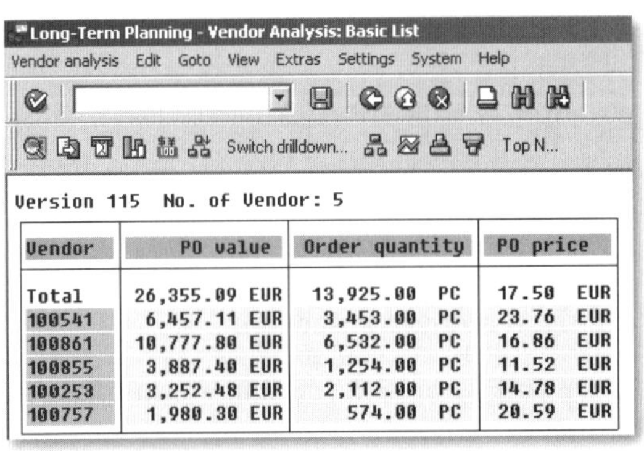

Figure 13.6 Highest Level of Results for Vendor Analysis for Long-Term Planning

The data shown in Figure 13.6 shows the planned order quantity for the five vendors. If the analyst wants to see how the planned totals are reflected per material or by month, then she will use the drilldown functionality that is part of any standard analysis.

The long-term planning of a particular purchased material is shown in Figure 13.7. The data shows the material sold by a vendor six periods into the future. This analysis can aid the purchasing department to assess if this vendor can obtain the material or whether another vendor could be used.

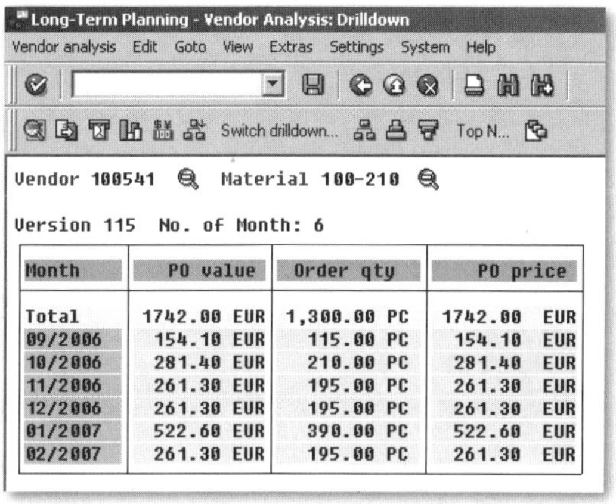

Month	PO value	Order qty	PO price
Total	1742.00 EUR	1,300.00 PC	1742.00 EUR
09/2006	154.10 EUR	115.00 PC	154.10 EUR
10/2006	281.40 EUR	210.00 PC	281.40 EUR
11/2006	261.30 EUR	195.00 PC	261.30 EUR
12/2006	261.30 EUR	195.00 PC	261.30 EUR
01/2007	522.60 EUR	390.00 PC	522.60 EUR
02/2007	261.30 EUR	195.00 PC	261.30 EUR

Figure 13.7 Long-Term Planning for a Particular Material for Six Periods into the Future

The data displayed in Figure 13.6 and Figure 13.7 is derived for the planning version 115. But, there may be other planning scenarios that have been created, which vary in the criteria used. Therefore, purchasing analysts would like to compare one version against another to see how criteria change the overall planning of purchasing objects.

Planned/Actual Comparison

A planned against actual comparison can be made from the header menu in any of the results screens. The analyst must decide on a key figure to compare and place the cursor on that key figure. Then, he can select the comparison from the header menu: **Edit • Comparisons • Planned/Actual** (see Figure 13.8).

The analyst has to select a previously created version to compare against. In this case, **Version 100** has been chosen to compare order quantity totals. The comparison will contrast the periods of planned material for both versions and show the analyst the quantity and percentage variance, as displayed in Figure 13.9.

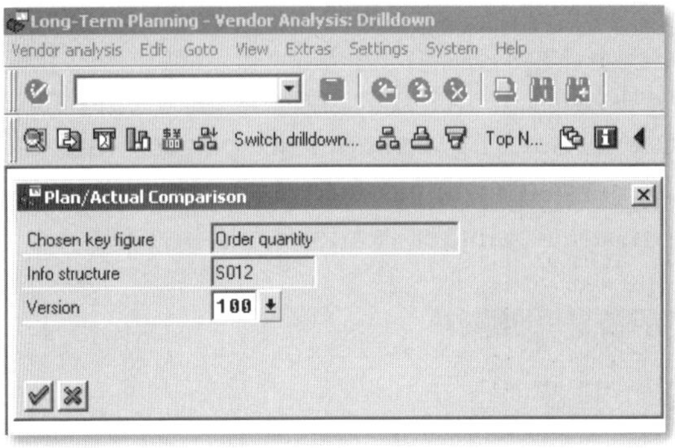

Figure 13.8 Comparison Selection for Planned Versus Actual Order Quantity

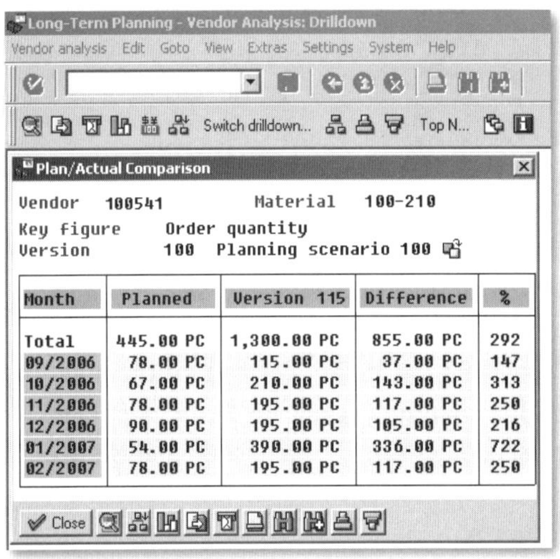

Month	Planned	Version 115	Difference	%
Total	445.00 PC	1,300.00 PC	855.00 PC	292
09/2006	78.00 PC	115.00 PC	37.00 PC	147
10/2006	67.00 PC	210.00 PC	143.00 PC	313
11/2006	78.00 PC	195.00 PC	117.00 PC	250
12/2006	90.00 PC	195.00 PC	105.00 PC	216
01/2007	54.00 PC	390.00 PC	336.00 PC	722
02/2007	78.00 PC	195.00 PC	117.00 PC	250

Figure 13.9 Planned/Actual Comparison of Two Planning Versions in the Vendor Long-Term Planning Standard Analysis

Previous/Current Comparison

A previous against current comparison can be made from the header menu of any of the results screens. The analyst must decide on a key figure to compare and place the cursor on the key figure. The analyst can select the comparison from the header menu: **Edit • Comparisons • Previous/Current.** The result of the comparison is shown in Figure 13.10.

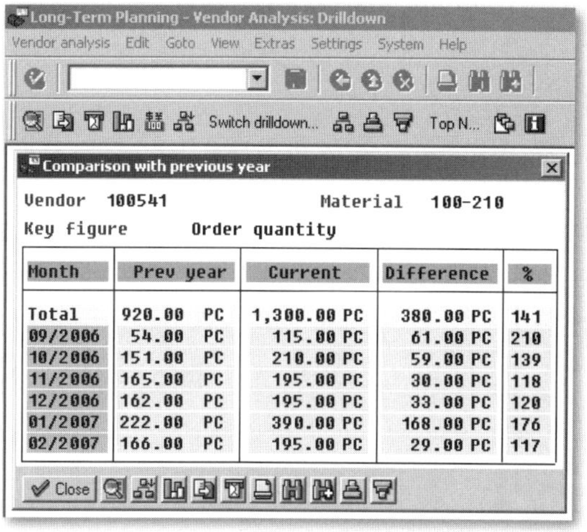

Figure 13.10 Previous/Current Comparison of Current Planning Version Against Actual from Previous Year

The comparison shows the order quantity from the figures generated by the current planned version 115. These key figures are compared against the actual figures for the same periods as the planned version, but for the previous year. The comparison shows the actual difference, if any, and the percentage difference.

This comparison is very useful for the purchasing department, as it shows how the version of the plan compares against actual figures for the previous years, and this can validate or invalidate the planning version that the department is using. In this example, seen in Figure 13.10, the planned quantities are much greater than the actual data for the previous year, which may lead the purchasing department to revise the planning scenario.

Key Figure Comparison

A key figure comparison can be made from the header menu of any of the results screens. The analyst must decide on a key figure to compare and place the cursor on the key figure. The analyst can then select the comparison key figure from the header menu: **Edit • Comparisons • Two Key Figures.** The choice of the other available key figures for the key figure comparison is shown in Figure 13.11.

The resulting comparison, depicted in Figure 13.12, shows the order quantity and the return quantity for the periods derived from the original analysis.

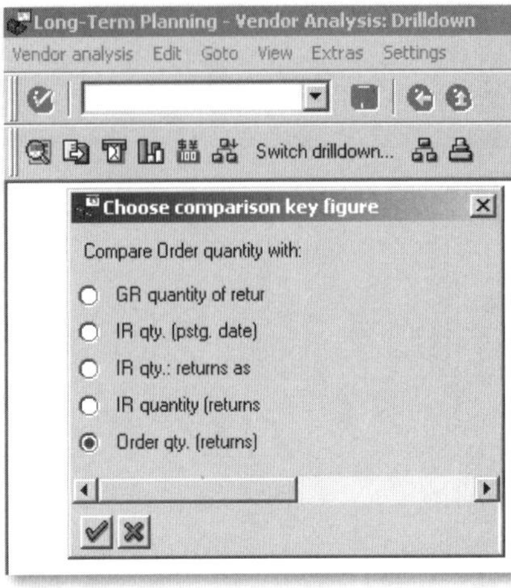

Figure 13.11 Choice of Key Figures Available to Purchasing Analyst for Two Key Figures Comparison

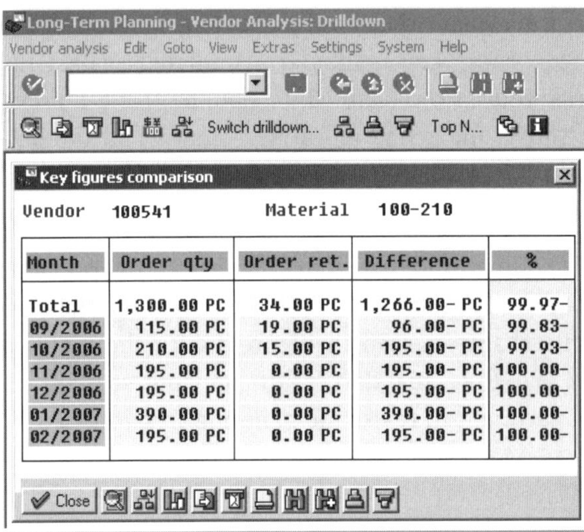

Figure 13.12 Order Quantity Compared Against Return Quantity for Key Figure Comparison

13.3.3 Long-Term Planning for Material Group

The long-term planning for material groups is executed using Transaction MCEB, as shown in Figure 13.13. It is located in different areas of the SAP menu. It can be found in Production Planning by using the navigation path: **SAP Menu • Logistics • Production • Production Planning • Long-Term Planning • Evaluations • Purchasing Information System • Material Group**.

The transaction can also be found in the PURCHIS by using the navigation path: **SAP Menu • Logistics • Logistics Controlling • Purchasing Information System • Standard Analyses • Long-Term Planning • Material Group.**

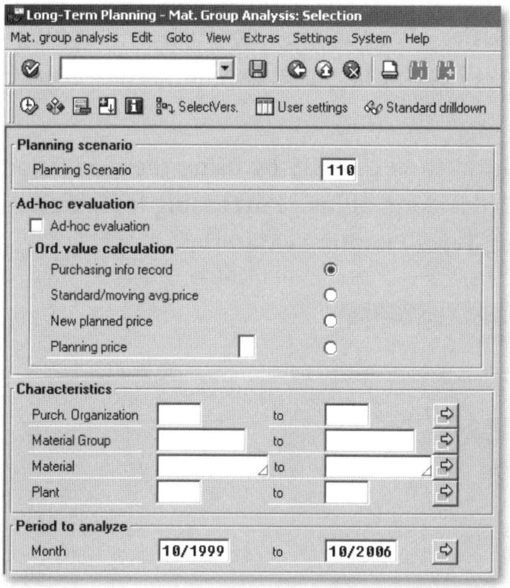

Figure 13.13 Initial Screen for Material Group Long-Term Planning Analysis, Transaction MCEB

The resulting data for long-term planning, Figure 13.14, shows the purchasing requirements for the material group and the materials that are part of that material group for the period defined in the planning scenario. This analysis is helpful to the purchasing department to analyze the purchasing requirements for the particular material groups.

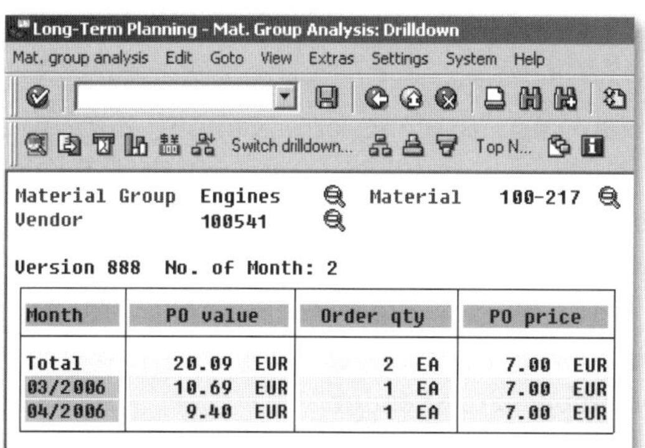

Figure 13.14 Results for Material Group Long-Term Planning Analysis, Transaction MCEB

13.3.4 Long-Term Planning for Material

The long-term planning for individual purchased materials can be performed using Transaction MCEC, as shown in Figure 13.15. It is located in different areas of the SAP menu. It can be found in Production Planning by using the navigation path: **SAP Menu • Logistics • Production • Production Planning • Long-Term Planning • Evaluations • Purchasing Information System • Material.**

The transaction can also be found in the PURCHIS by using the navigation path: **SAP Menu • Logistics • Logistics Controlling • Purchasing Information System • Standard Analyses • Long-Term Planning • Material.**

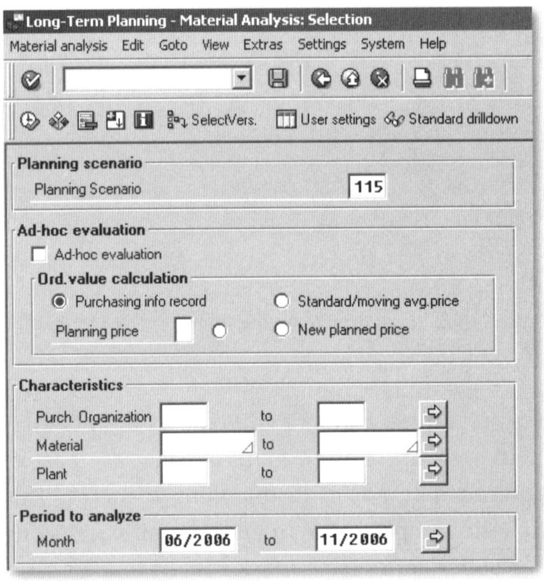

Figure 13.15 Initial Screen for Individual Material Long-Term Planning Analysis, Transaction MCEC

The resulting data for the individual material long-term planning, displayed in Figure 13.16, shows the purchasing requirements for the materials for the period defined in the planning scenario. This analysis is helpful to the purchasing department to analyze the purchasing requirements for the particular materials that will be needed. The drilldown to vendor will show the purchasing analyst where the materials will be purchased from and whether any issues may occur due to lack of supply at the vendor.

The importance of the long-term planning analyses cannot be stressed enough. Supply chain management spends significant time and effort on planning and adapting the plan to be as accurate as possible. It is important therefore to assist in the planning procedure by producing clear and relevant planning data.

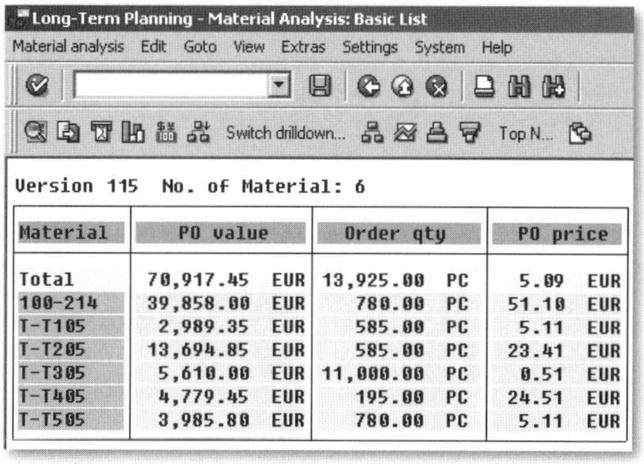

Material	PO value		Order qty		PO price	
Total	70,917.45	EUR	13,925.00	PC	5.09	EUR
100-214	39,858.00	EUR	780.00	PC	51.10	EUR
T-T105	2,989.35	EUR	585.00	PC	5.11	EUR
T-T205	13,694.85	EUR	585.00	PC	23.41	EUR
T-T305	5,610.00	EUR	11,000.00	PC	0.51	EUR
T-T405	4,779.45	EUR	195.00	PC	24.51	EUR
T-T505	3,985.80	EUR	780.00	PC	5.11	EUR

Figure 13.16 Results of Analysis for Long-Term Planning for Materials, Transaction MCEC

13.4 Summary

In this chapter, I have discussed the standard analyses that are used in PURCHIS and the long-term planning analyses that are integral to the purchasing department's decision-making. The purchasing department has to make key decisions on purchasing the right material at the right price at the right time. Any mistakes can lead to either a lack of material needed to create finished goods, for example, a stock-out, or, an excess of material purchased, resulting in warehouse charges or interest payments incurred by the company. The reports in PURCHIS are the first line of defense for the purchasing department and the purchasing analyst must use the planning scenarios to develop the best purchasing plan for the purchasing department management.

In Chapter 14, the focus of our discussion will be the Inventory Controlling information system. This also includes information on Warehouse Management.

Inventory Controlling is the subsection of the LIS that reports on the materials within the plant, the movements of material, and the planning of those materials within Inventory Management and Warehouse Management.

14 Inventory Controlling

The Inventory Controlling Information System (INVCO) is a part of the LIS that is specific to Inventory Management and Warehouse Management (WM). The analyst has a wide range of analyses to help with the investigation of issues that can arise with inventory management, for example, such reported issues as occurrences of poor physical inventory, damage to goods in the warehouse, and a lack of inventory procedures.

14.1 Information Structures

The information structures of the INVCO are based on the events that occur in the transactions of Inventory and Warehouse Management.

As mentioned in Chapter 1, Inventory Controlling is made up of seven information structures for Inventory Management two for Warehouse Management. These are briefly described below:

- **Movements (S031)**
  Contains material movement data (e.g., current valuated stock and vendor consignment stock) and is updated monthly
- **Stocks (S032)**
  For each goods movement, the current valuated and vendor consignment stocks are updated
- **Individual Movement Records (S033)**
  Based on the S031, but updated daily
- **Batch Movements (S034)**
  Pertains to all movements recorded at the batch level

- **Stocks, as related to Batches (S035)**
  Similar to the Stocks (S032) information structure, but includes information on batches
- **Planning (S039)**
  Used for flexible planning and contains no data unless the RMCBS039 report is run
- **Stock/Requirements Analysis (S094)**
  Contains all of the data for the current stock and requirements
- **WM Stock Putaway/Removal (S090)**
  Contains the data for movements of stock putaway and removal
- **WM Quantity Flow (S091)**
  Contains the data for material flow between locations

14.2 Basic Standard Analyses

We'll now discuss the standard analyses delivered with the INVCO. These relate to the following:

- Plant
- Storage Location
- Material
- Batches

All four of these are discussed in the subsections that follow.

14.2.1 Plant

The standard analysis for a plant derives its data from the information structures S031 and S032. This transaction can be accessed using transaction code MCBA, or using the navigation path: **SAP Menu • Logistics • Logistics Controlling • Logistics Information System • Inventory Controlling • Standard Analyses • Plant.**

The selection criteria are shown in Figure 14.1. The analyst can select the plant or plants to be analyzed and can further restrict this by a number of selection fields such as storage location, material, material type, etc. The analyst may want to review data specific to a plant, but also specific to a particular material group, so she would restrict that in this screen.

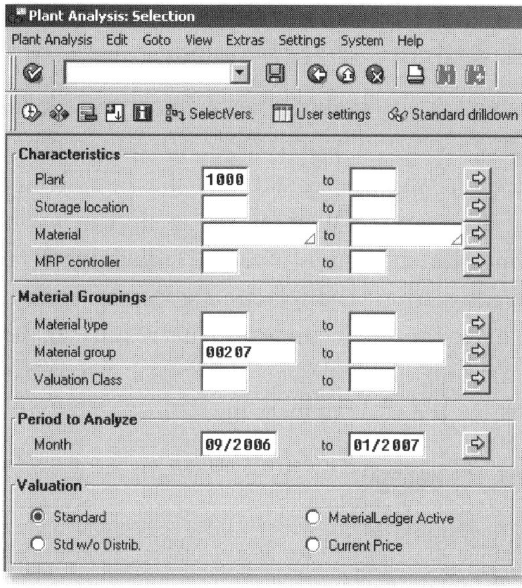

Figure 14.1 Selection Screen for Plant Analysis, Transaction MCBA

The criteria entered into the selection screen, Figure 14.1, will produce the results for one particular material group for the months specified.

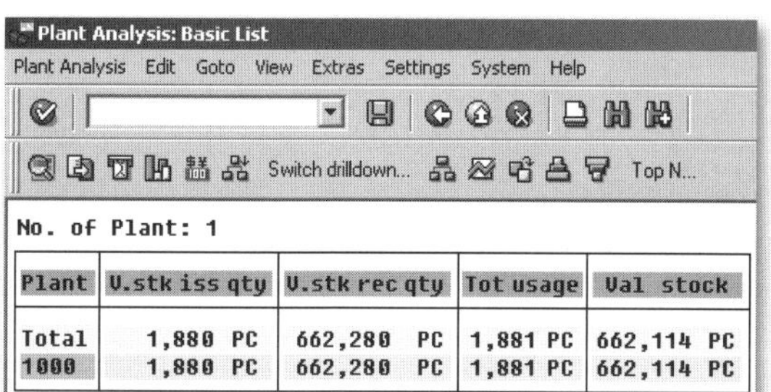

Figure 14.2 Basic List for Plant Standard Analysis, Transaction MCBA

The basic list for the plant analysis, Figure 14.2, shows the valuated stock issued from and received into the plant for the specified material group. The analyst can specify a greater number of material groups to compare figures.

14.2.2 Storage Location

The standard analysis for a storage location derives its data from the information structures S031 and S032 similar to the plant analysis. This transaction can be accessed using transaction code MCBC, or using the navigation path:

SAP Menu • Logistics • Logistics Controlling • Logistics Information System • Inventory Controlling • Standard Analyses • Storage Location.

The storage location analysis is useful to the analyst to evaluate storage location performance. Often, one storage location is used more often than other storage locations, and consequently, warehouse staff can have difficulty locating material in a busy area. This report will show the analyst if this is occurring and whether the inventory management needs to move material to other storage locations to ease congestion. The selection screen, as shown in Figure 14.3, is similar to that for the plant analysis. The result can be restricted by the selection criteria, and, in this case, a material group has been chosen to restrict the results for the storage location.

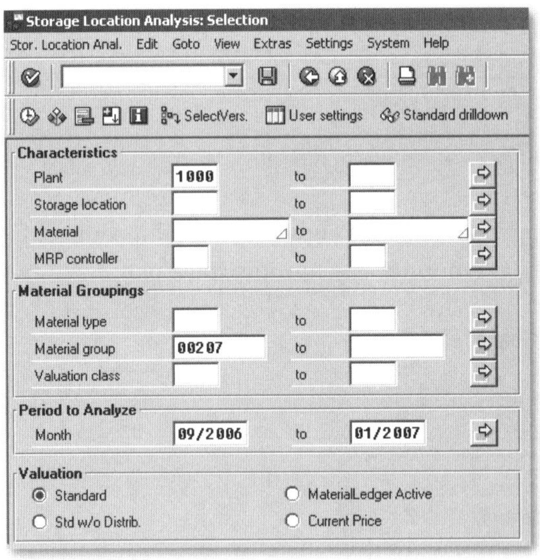

Figure 14.3 Selection Criteria for Storage Location Analysis, Transaction MCBC

The criteria entered into the selection screen, Figure 14.3, will produce the storage location results for one particular material group for the months specified.

The results of the standard analysis, as displayed in Figure 14.4, shows the issues and receipts for the individual storage locations that are specific to the material group entered in the selection criteria. The information may be useful to the analyst who wants to see whether the material is being evenly distributed between storage locations, or whether specific storage locations, which should not have been used, were used.

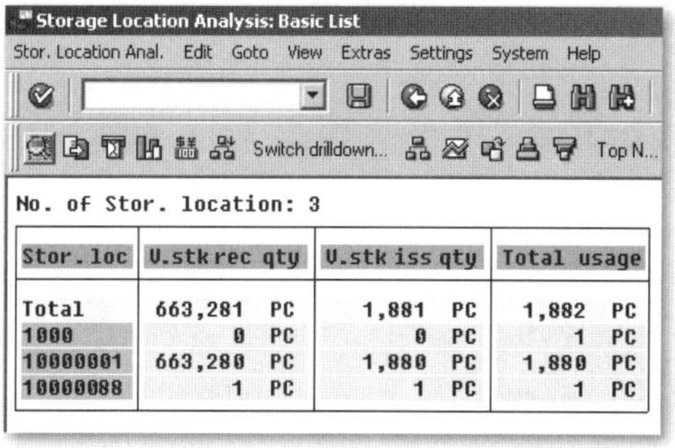

Figure 14.4 Results of Storage Location Standard Analysis, Transaction MCBC

14.2.3 Material

The standard analysis for material derives its data from the information structures S031 and S032, similar to the plant and storage location analyses. This transaction can be accessed using transaction code MCBE, or using the SAP menu and the navigation path: **SAP Menu • Logistics • Logistics Controlling • Logistics Information System • Inventory Controlling • Standard Analyses • Material.**

The material analysis is useful to the analyst to evaluate material location and the locations where the material has been placed and issued from for the period entered in the selection criteria. The selection screen, as shown in Figure 14.5, is similar to that for the plant and storage location analysis. The result can be restricted by the selection criteria, and in this case a plant and a material group have been chosen to restrict the results for the storage location.

The standard analysis for materials will allow the analyst to see where the material has been received and issued. This is useful for analysts when they are considering consolidation of material into a smaller number of locations. Consolidating the number of locations used for a particular material can reduce the work the warehouse staff has to do to place and retrieve stock. Shorter moves can mean a more efficient warehouse.

The results of the standard analysis, as displayed in Figure 14.6, show the issues and receipts for the materials that are specific to the material group entered in the selection criteria. The information is restricted by the period entered and is useful to the analyst who wants to see movements of the materials during that period. The report is useful to monitor slow-moving material.

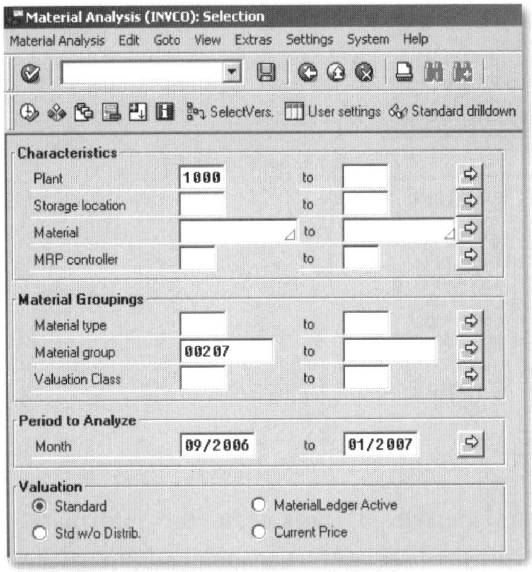

Figure 14.5 Selection Criteria for Material Standard Analysis, Transaction MCBE

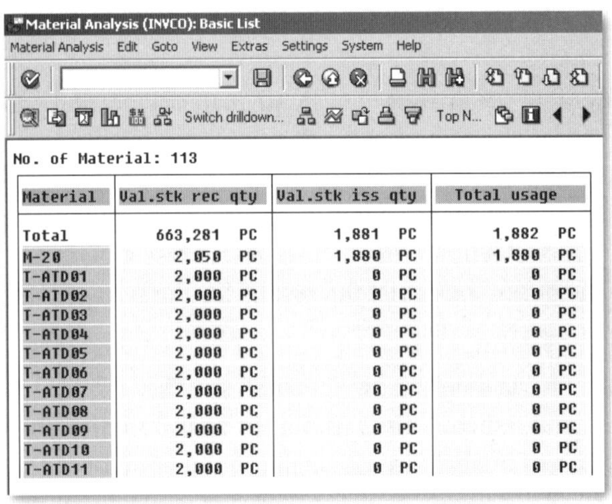

Figure 14.6 Results of Material Standard Analysis, Transaction MCBE

14.2.4 Batches

The standard analysis for batches derives its data from the information structures S034 and S035. The results can be based on a period of time defined for the analysis.

The selection criteria for the batch analysis can be seen in Figure 14.7. This transaction can be accessed using transaction code MCBR, or using the navigation path: **SAP Menu • Logistics • Logistics Controlling • Logistics Information System • Inventory Controlling • Standard Analyses • Batches**.

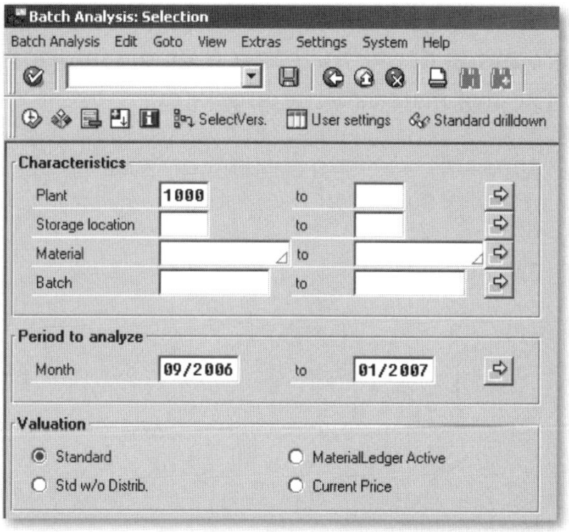

Figure 14.7 Selection Criteria for Batch Standard Analysis, Transaction MCBR

The selection criteria are vital to obtain specific results for batches. The analyst may require an analysis of all batches in a plant or just for a specific material.

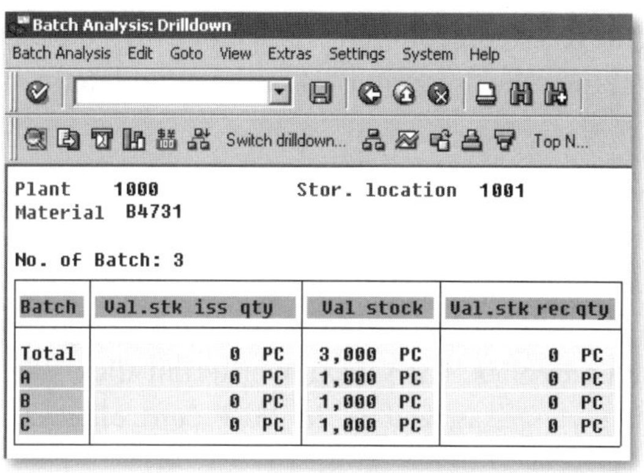

Figure 14.8 Results of Batch Standard Analysis, Transaction MCBR

The results of the analysis, shown in Figure 14.8, are useful to the analyst, as they monitor what batches are not being selected for production or sale. Further analysis, for example, looking at the batch characteristics, may be required to determine whether the batch is no longer valid for use.

14.3 Material Groupings Standard Analyses

There are five standard analyses that are part of the material groupings heading (in some versions of SAP, this is called Material Pricing Groups). The standard analyses for material groupings derive their data from the information structures S031 and S032. The five material groupings are:

- **MRP Controller**
  Transaction MCBG
- **Business Area**
  Transaction MCBI
- **Material Groups**
  Transaction MCBK
- **Division**
  Transaction MCBM
- **Material Type**
  Transaction MCBO

Let's examine these material groupings in more detail.

14.3.1 MRP Controller

The standard analysis for the MRP controller lets the analyst review the materials that fall under a specific MRP controller or a range of MRP controllers. The results can be based on the selection criteria and the period defined for the analysis.

The selection criteria for the MRP controller analysis are displayed in Figure 14.9. This transaction can be accessed using transaction code MCBG, or using the navigation path: **SAP Menu • Logistics • Logistics Controlling • Logistics Information System • Inventory Controlling • Standard Analyses • Material Pricing Groups • MRP Controller**. The selection criterion allows the analyst to enter a **Plant**, or plant range, as well as the **MRP Controller** and specific period range.

The results of the analysis, shown in Figure 14.10, are useful to the analyst who monitors material usage. The review of the material via MRP controller can be useful, depending on how the division of production material is performed in your company. It is a useful report, as it shows the production materials rather than purchased materials.

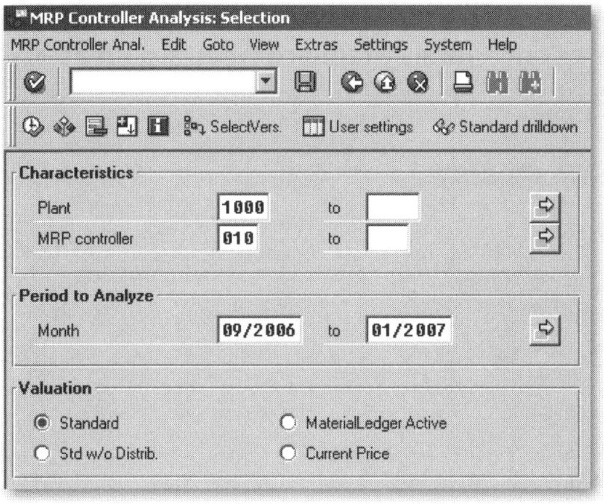

Figure 14.9 Selection Criteria for MRP Controller Standard Analysis, Transaction MCBG

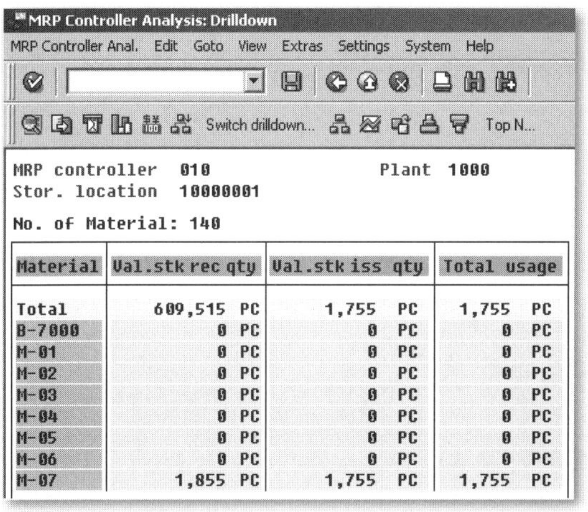

Figure 14.10 Results of MRP Controller Standard Analysis, Transaction MCBG

14.3.2 Business Area

A business area is more familiar to those with a financial background than to those in inventory management; however, the analyst is frequently expected to produce reports with regard to operations, which may be defined in some companies as a business area. In SAP a business area is defined as an organizational unit of financial accounting that has a separate area of operations, and value changes recorded in financial accounting are allocated.

The selection criteria for business area analysis are displayed in Figure 14.11. This transaction can be accessed using transaction code MCBI, or by using the navigation path: **SAP Menu • Logistics • Logistics Controlling • Logistics Information System • Inventory Controlling • Standard Analyses • Material Pricing Groups • Business Area**.

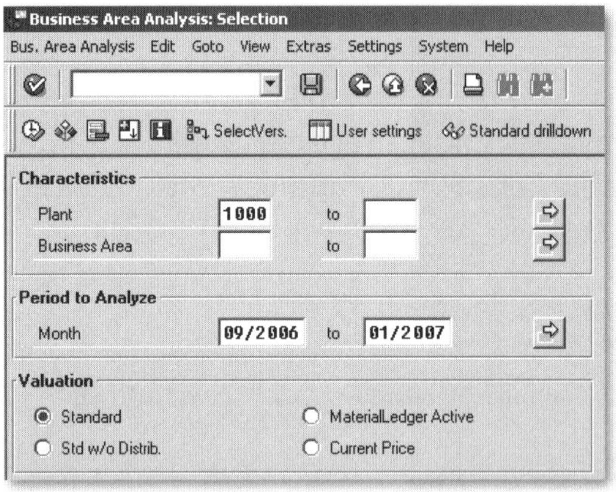

Figure 14.11 Business Area Standard Analysis Selection Screen, Transaction MCBI

For this transaction, there are limited selection criteria. The analyst can either select a particular business area to review or select by plant.

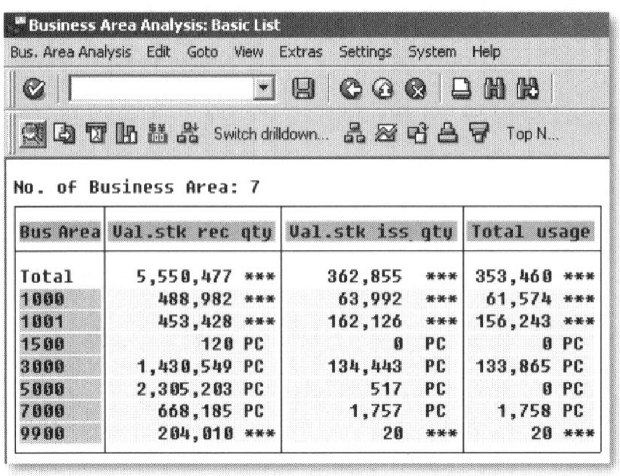

Figure 14.12 Results for Business Area Standard Analysis, Transaction MCBI

The results for the business area analysis, in Figure 14.12, show that there are seven business areas that have transactions within a single plant, in this case plant **1000**. Using the drilldown functionality, the analyst can further review the information regarding the individual business area.

14.3.3 Material Group

Depending on how material groups have been designed for use in your company, inventory analysts may be required to retrieve information on material groups rather than specific materials.

The selection criteria for material group analysis can be seen in Figure 14.13. This transaction can be accessed using transaction code MCBK, or using the SAP menu and the navigation path: **SAP Menu • Logistics • Logistics Controlling • Logistics Information System • Inventory Controlling • Standard Analyses • Material Pricing Groups • Material Groups.**

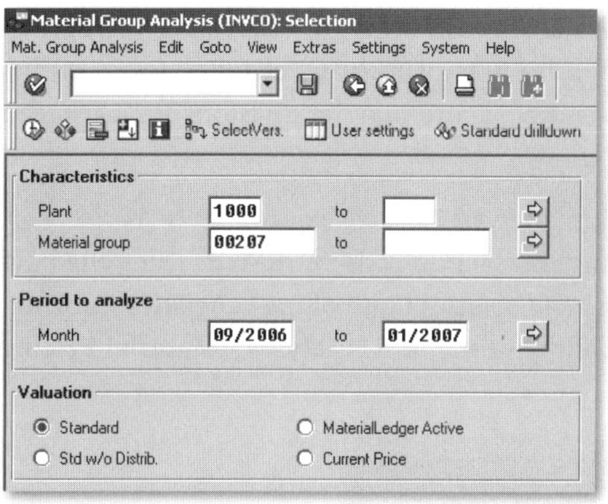

Figure 14.13 Selection Screen for Material Group Standard Analysis, Transaction MCBK

The analysis can be for a single material group or for a range. The results can be restricted further by selecting a specific plant or range of plants.

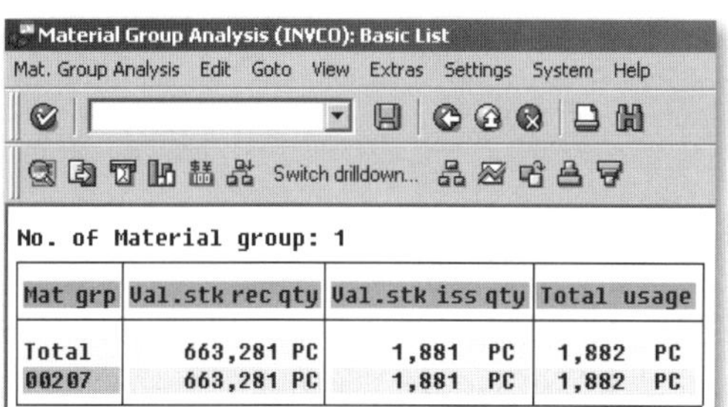

Figure 14.14 Results for Material Group Standard Analysis, Transaction MCBK

The selection criteria entered in Figure 14.13 has resulted in the data in Figure 14.14. This data shows the inventory issues and receipts for the materials that are included in the particular material group entered (00207). The inventory analyst could use this analysis with different time periods to compare the usage for the material group. Differences in usage or issues could indicate a seasonal trend that would be useful in determining forecasting models.

14.3.4 Division

Standard analysis by division can be performed for materials that have been assigned to that division. A division is a particular grouping in the sales function. Material and services are sold by a sales organization through distribution channels, such as retail, wholesale, mail order, Internet sales, etc. A division can then group the type of sales in a distribution channel, for example, under the retail distribution channel. There may be divisions for packaged foods, drinks, bulk food, etc.

The selection criteria for division analysis can be seen in Figure 14.15. This transaction can be accessed using transaction code MCBM, or using the navigation path: **SAP Menu • Logistics • Logistics Controlling • Logistics Information System • Inventory Controlling • Standard Analyses • Material Pricing Groups • Division**.

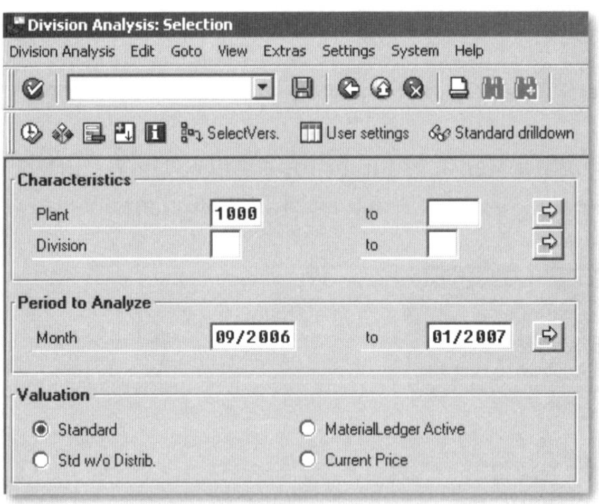

Figure 14.15 Standard Analysis for a Division, Transaction MCBM

The analyst can select single division for analysis or analysis for all divisions within a plant or range of plants.

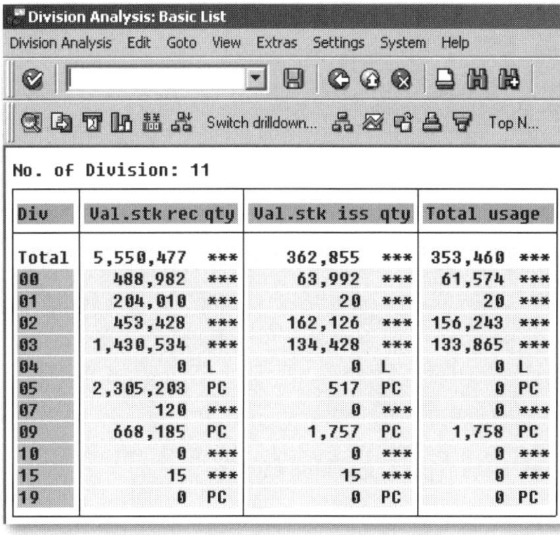

Div	Val.stk rec qty		Val.stk iss qty		Total usage	
Total	5,550,477	***	362,855	***	353,460	***
00	488,982	***	63,992	***	61,574	***
01	204,010	***	20	***	20	***
02	453,428	***	162,126	***	156,243	***
03	1,430,534	***	134,428	***	133,865	***
04	0	L	0	L	0	L
05	2,305,203	PC	517	PC	0	PC
07	120	***	0	***	0	***
09	668,185	PC	1,757	PC	1,758	PC
10	0	***	0	***	0	***
15	15	***	15	***	0	***
19	0	PC	0	PC	0	PC

Figure 14.16 Standard Analysis for Divisions Within a Single Plant, Transaction MCBM

The selection criteria shown in Figure 14.15 resulted in the data shown in Figure 14.16. The division standard analysis displays the figures for each division with material movements in the plant that was specified in this example.

14.3.5 Material Type

Analysts will often require data on the performance of material types, e.g., finished goods, trading goods, raw materials, etc. The standard analysis for material groups allows the analyst to select a single material type or a range of material types for comparison.

The selection criteria for material type analysis can be seen in Figure 14.17. This transaction can be accessed using transaction code MCBO, or by using the navigation path: **SAP Menu • Logistics • Logistics Controlling • Logistics Information System • Inventory Controlling • Standard Analyses • Material Pricing Groups • Material Type**.

In this example, the analyst wants to review all of the material type movements for the **Plant** designated as **1000** in a given period. More often the analyst would review just one material type and drill down to see more specific data on that material type.

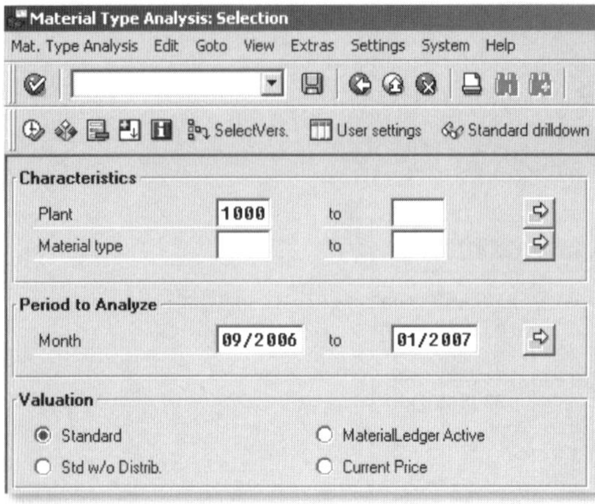

Figure 14.17 Standard Analysis for Material Type, Transaction MCBO

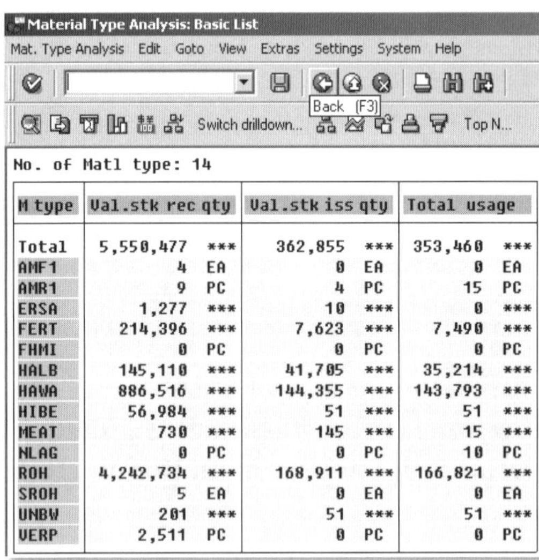

Figure 14.18 Resulting Data for Material Type Standard Analysis, Transaction MCBO

The data shown in Figure 14.18 is for all material types in plant 1000. The information shows that the receipts for raw materials and trading goods far outweigh the issues, which would imply that there are very high stock levels in the warehouse. By using the drilldown function, further analysis can be performed on the material types that are of most interest. If there is a concern about high stock levels, then the analyst can use the parameter controlling functionality, which I'll explain in the next section.

14.4 Parameter Controlling

The parameter controlling functionality lets the analyst review issues that may be occurring and causing unnaturally high levels of stock. Parameter controlling uses standard analyses to allow analysts to find the materials that require attention.

The standard analysis contains five predefined dual characteristics that allow the analyst to refine his search on why certain inventory issues are occurring. We'll discuss these classifications next.

14.4.1 Standard Analysis

Before the analyst can use the dual classifications, the standard analysis must be run and the area that the analyst wants to focus on is used in the selection criteria.

The selection criteria for standard analysis are shown in Figure 14.19. This transaction can be accessed using transaction code MCBV, or using the navigation path: **SAP Menu • Logistics • Logistics Controlling • Logistics Information System • Inventory Controlling • Standard Analyses • Parameter Controlling • Evaluation.**

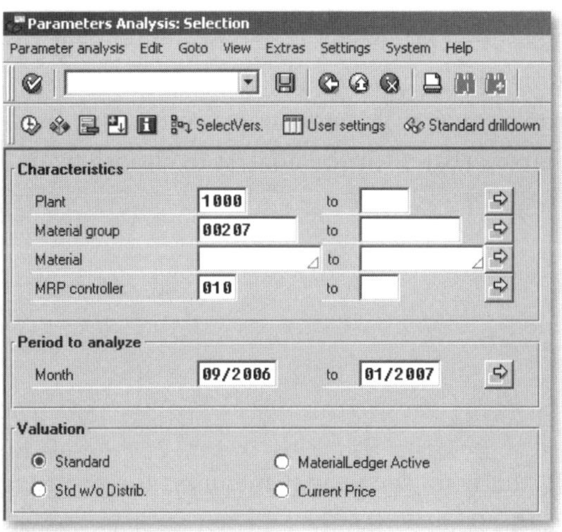

Figure 14.19 Selection Screen for Parameter Controlling Standard Analysis, Transaction MCBV

In the selection criteria, the analyst should enter as much data as possible if the data that is returned can help to pinpoint inventory issues. In the example in Figure 14.19, the analyst has entered plant, material group, and MRP controller information.

Once the data is returned, the analyst can use the dual classifications to further examine the resulting data, as shown in Figure 14.20.

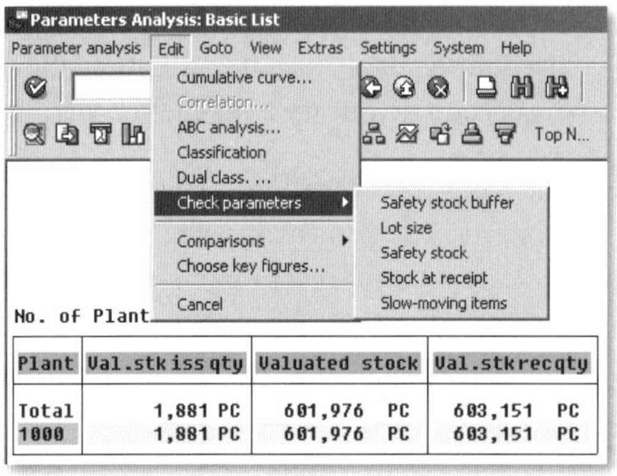

Figure 14.20 Resulting Data for Standard Analysis and Header Menu Options for Dual Classifications

14.4.2 Dual Classifications

Earlier we described the dual classification feature. This is where the analyst can divide the characteristic values into classes with reference to two key figures. However, the system automatically divides the data into six classes, which can then be changed by the analyst. The parameter controlling function has five predefined dual characteristics for the analyst to choose from:

- Safety Stock Buffer
- Lot Size
- Safety Stock
- Stock at Receipt
- Slow-Moving Items

These characteristics can be selected from the header menu on the resulting data screen, as shown in Figure 14.20.

14.4.3 Safety Stock Buffer

The safety stock buffer dual classification can be executed from the results screen by selecting **Edit • Check parameters • Safety stock buffer**. The dual classification is performed with the two key figures: **range of coverage of the average receipt** and **range of coverage of the average stock at receipt**.

A high safety stock buffer will help companies avoid stock-out situations; however, the safety stock should not be so large that the cost to store it exceeds its value. A high safety stock is reflected by a large average stock at receipt key figure.

14.4.4 Lot Size

The lot size dual classification can be executed from the results screen by selecting **Edit • Check parameters • Lot size**. The key figures, range of coverage of the average receipt, and value of the average receipt are compared for this dual classification.

Lot size is a difficult classification to use, because if a lot size is too high, it will produce too much inventory in stock. Depending on the consumption of the material, however, a small lot size may not be appropriate.

14.4.5 Safety Stock

The safety stock dual classification can be executed from the results screen by selecting **Edit • Check parameters • Safety stock**. The key figures of value of the average stock at receipt and stock factor are compared for this dual classification.

The key figure stock factor can be calculated by dividing the average stock at receipt by safety stock, and the optimum figure should be as close to one as possible. Analysts looking at this figure will check to ensure that this number does not creep up and out of control, indicating a buildup of stock in the warehouse.

14.4.6 Stock at Receipt

The stock at receipt dual classification can be executed from the results screen by selecting **Edit • Check parameters • Stock at receipt**. The key figures of the range of coverage of the average stock at receipt and value of the average stock at receipt are compared.

Analysts look at the stock at receipt to ensure that the material does not arrive at the plant from a vendor or production too early, as it will cost money to store material.

14.4.7 Slow-Moving Items

The slow-moving items dual classification can be executed from the results screen by selecting **Edit • Check parameters • Slow-moving items**. The key figures of the value of the last consumption and days without consumption are compared for this dual classification. The analyst will review items that have a large number of days without consumption. There may already be a company policy that determines how many days without any consumption constitute a slow-moving item. The logistics management needs to know what materials are slow-moving as soon as they reach a certain threshold. Reducing the amount of slow-moving material, especially finished goods, will reduce inventory-holding costs.

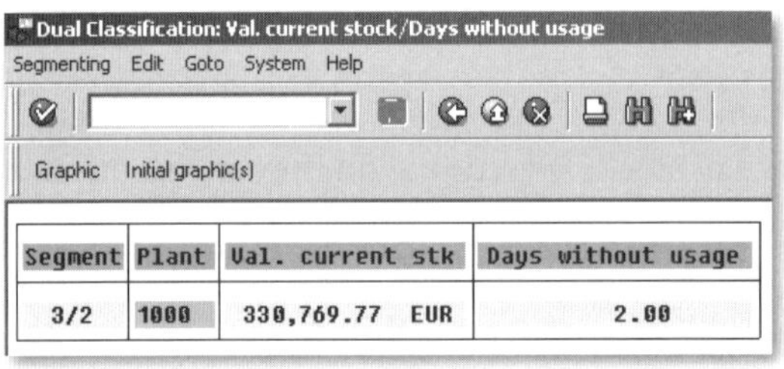

Figure 14.21 Dual Classification for Slow-Moving Items, Transaction MCBV

In this example, illustrated in Figure 14.21, the **Days without usage** figure is **2.00** days. That figure is meaningless unless the analyst knows how many days it should be. If the company is a fast-moving consumer goods manufacturer, two days may be 20 times slower than it requires and this would be an issue. However, in a company that has large project-based manufacturing, such as aircraft or buildings, two days may be perfectly acceptable.

14.5 Stock/Requirements

There are two standard analyses that the user can execute for the stock/requirements situation:

- Current Situation—Transaction MCBZ
- Long-Term Planning—Transaction MCB

Let's take a closer look at these analyses.

14.5.1 Current Situation

This standard analysis is used to review the current stock and requirements data from the MRP data. This standard analysis enables the analyst to choose where the information for the analysis is derived from. In Figure 14.22, you can see the selection criteria for Transaction MCBZ. The transaction has the option to allow data on an ad-hoc basis, which means directly for the current MRP run or from the information structure S094. The **Ad-hoc evaluation** indicator must be set for the data to be taken from current MRP data. If the indicator is not set, the information structure is used.

However, to update the information structure S094 with the correct data, a program must first be executed. This program is called RMCBDISP, which can be executed via Transaction SE38.

The Transaction MCBZ can be found by using the navigation path: **SAP Menu • Logistics • Logistics Controlling • Logistics Information System • Inventory Controlling • Standard Analyses • Stock/Requirements • Evaluation.**

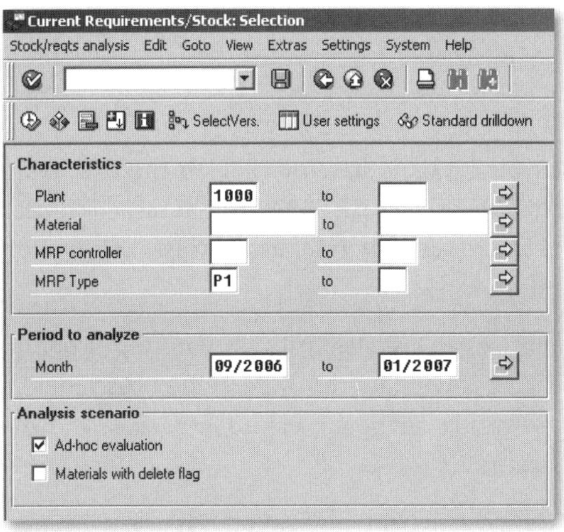

Figure 14.22 Selection Screen for Standard Analysis for the Current Situation for Stock/Requirements, Transaction MCBZ

The example in Figure 14.22 shows that the analyst has requested that the standard analysis report on only materials with an **MRP Type** of **P1**, which is the MRP type for event-based planning. This means that the MRP will generate firm planned orders for materials as part of an MRP run.

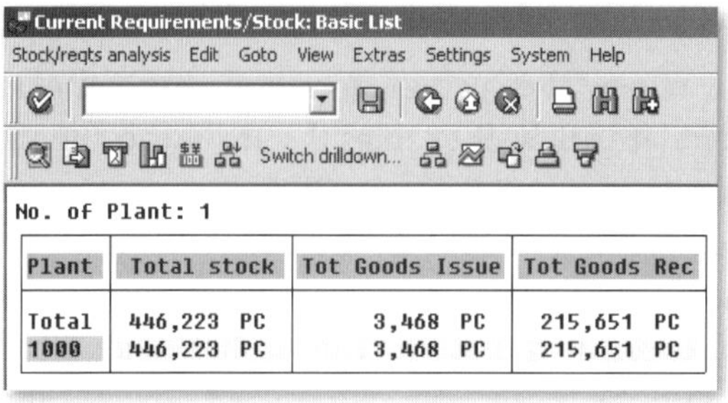

Figure 14.23 Results of Standard Analysis for Current Stock/Requirements Situation, Transaction MCBZ

For the analyst, the information shown in Figure 14.23 indicates that the stock levels for materials with an MRP type of P1 are very high when compared with the amount of material that has been issued from the plant in the period of the analysis. Information like this can help the analyst to identify what types of material can cause stock issues. In this example, the analyst may decide to review materials with a P1 MRP type to identify potential issues.

14.5.2 Long-Term Planning

The long-term planning standard analysis is based either on the data from the latest MRP run or the information structure S094. This transaction uses the **Ad-hoc evaluation** indicator in the same manner as the Current Situation standard analysis.

The long-term planning standard analysis also uses a planning scenario (explained in Chapter 13), as shown in Figure 14.24. Other parameters include the plant used in long-term planning, the planning period, and the requirements versions to be planned.

You can access Transaction MCB by using the navigation path: **SAP Menu • Logistics • Logistics Controlling • Inventory Controlling • Standard Analyses • Stock/Requirements • Long-term Planning**.

In Chapter 13, we explained the importance of using planning scenarios in long-term planning analyses. The result of the long-term planning analysis is shown in Figure 14.25.

We can now move to our discussion of Warehouse Management.

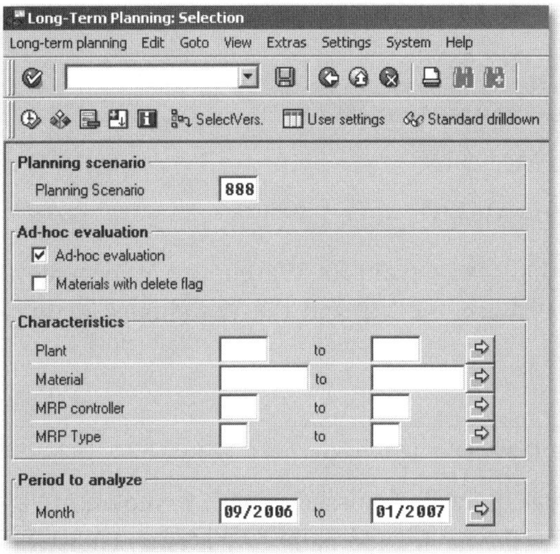

Figure 14.24 Selection Criteria for Long-Term Planning Analysis for Stock/Requirements, Transaction MCB

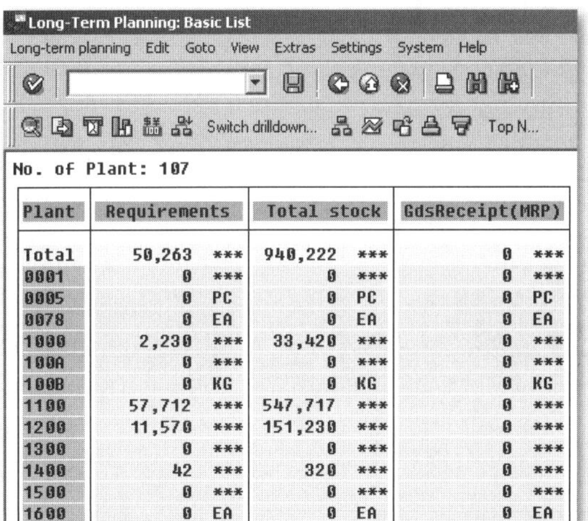

Figure 14.25 Results from Long-Term Planning Standard Analysis for Stock/Requirements, Transaction MCB

14.6 Warehouse Management

If your client has implemented Warehouse Management (WM), the standard analyses in this section are relevant. The standard analyses for WM use the information structure S091. The five standard analyses for WM are:

- Stock Placement/Removal—Transaction MCL1
- Quantity Flows—Transaction MCL5
- Material Placement/Removal—Transaction MCL9
- Material Flows—Transaction MCLD
- Movement Types—Transaction MCLH

There are a number of reports that are relevant for Warehouse Management that can be found within the WM area of SAP and the Warehouse Activity Monitor.

14.6.1 Stock Placement/Removal

The stock placement and removal analysis, Transaction MCL1, shown in Figure 14.26, can be found by using the navigation path: **SAP Menu • Logistics • Logistics Controlling • Logistics Information System • Inventory Controlling • Standard Analyses • Warehouse Management • Stock Placement/Removal**.

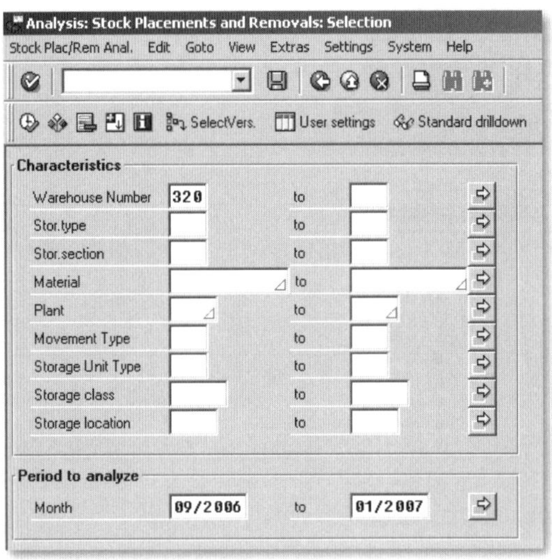

Figure 14.26 Selection Criteria for Stock Placement/Removal Analysis, Transaction MCL1

The selection criteria screen allows the analyst to select information for a specific warehouse or a specific storage type, as shown in Figure 14.26. Depending on the issues that the analyst is trying to highlight, she can use a large number of criteria to narrow down the focus of the analysis results.

Further analysis can be achieved by using the drilldown functionality on the data as seen in Figure 14.27.

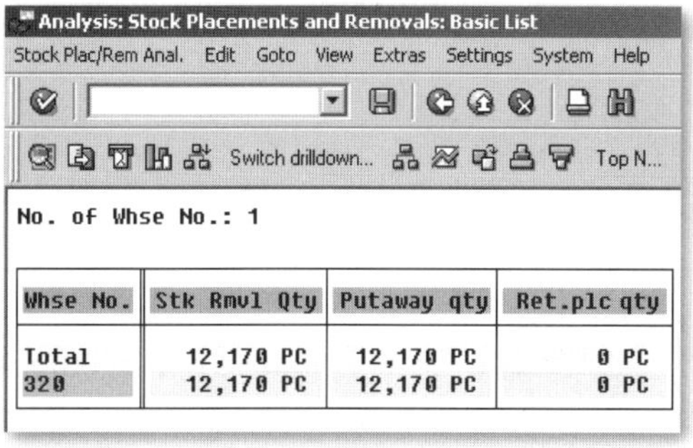

Figure 14.27 Results for WM Stock Placement/Removal Analysis, Transaction MCL1

14.6.2 Quantity Flows

The quantity flows transaction shows the analyst the flow of material between warehouse locations. The Transaction MCL5, shown in Figure 14.28, can be found using the navigation path: **SAP Menu • Logistics • Logistics Controlling • Logistics Information System • Inventory Controlling • Standard Analyses • Warehouse Management • Quantity Flows**.

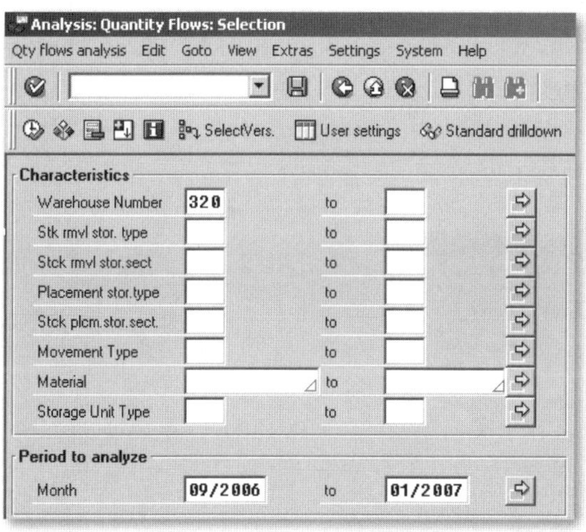

Figure 14.28 Selection Screen for Quantity Flows Analysis, Transaction MCL5

The resulting data shows the quantity of movements by warehouse. To access the information regarding individual material, the drilldown function is used. The resulting data, shown in Figure 14.29, is obtained by drilling down from the **Warehouse No.**, placement storage type (**Plcmnt stor.ty**), and removal storage type (**Rmvl stor. type**).

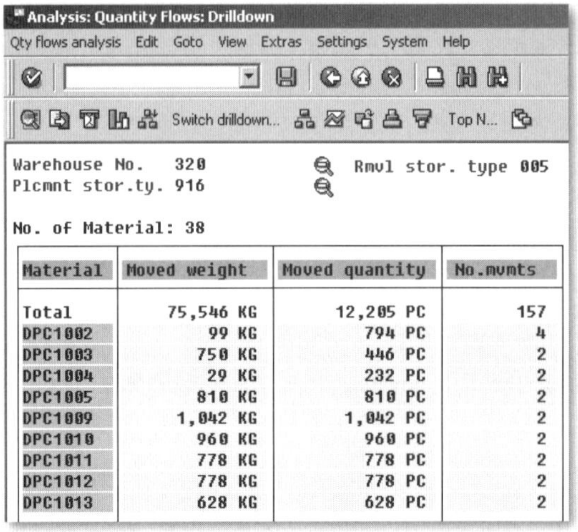

Figure 14.29 Resulting Data for Quality Flows Analysis After Using the Drilldown Functionality

14.6.3 Material Placement/Removal

The material placement and removal analysis, Transaction MCL9, shown in Figure 14.30, can be found by using the navigation path: **SAP Menu • Logistics • Logistics Controlling • Logistics Information System • Inventory Controlling • Standard Analyses • Warehouse Management • Material Placement/Removal**.

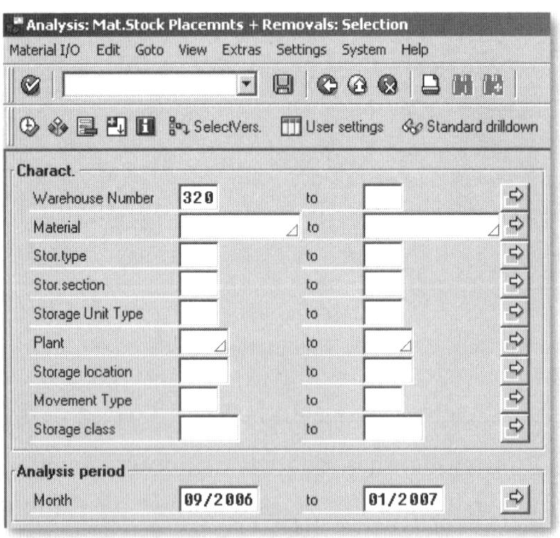

Figure 14.30 Selection Screen for Material Placement/Removal Analysis, Transaction MCL9

The results data, as shown in Figure 14.31, displays the drilldown of the warehouse level to the material level. The drilldown shows the quantity placed and removed per material for the warehouse selected.

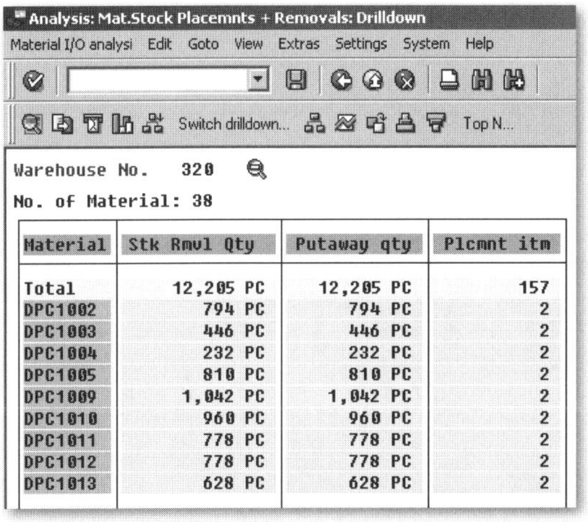

Material	Stk Rmvl Qty	Putaway qty	Plcmnt itm
Total	12,205 PC	12,205 PC	157
DPC1002	794 PC	794 PC	2
DPC1003	446 PC	446 PC	2
DPC1004	232 PC	232 PC	2
DPC1005	810 PC	810 PC	2
DPC1009	1,042 PC	1,042 PC	2
DPC1010	960 PC	960 PC	2
DPC1011	778 PC	778 PC	2
DPC1012	778 PC	778 PC	2
DPC1013	628 PC	628 PC	2

Figure 14.31 Material Data for Material Placement/Removal Analysis, Transaction MCL9

14.6.4 Material Flows

The material flows analysis is useful to the warehouse analyst to review the flow of material from one event to the next. The resulting data will report on the average time from one event to the next.

The material flows analysis, Transaction MCLD, shown in Figure 14.32, can be found by using the navigation path: **SAP Menu • Logistics • Logistics Controlling • Logistics Information System • Inventory Controlling • Standard Analyses • Warehouse Management • Material Flows.**

The resulting data for this analysis is interesting, as it calculates the time between the creation of one event and the creation of the next, for example, the time between the creation of a Transfer Request and the creation of the corresponding Transfer Order. The resulting data, as shown in Figure 14.33, displays the quantity of material used and the average time between certain warehouse events. The analyst can review the data and investigate further if there are large time delays between certain warehouse events.

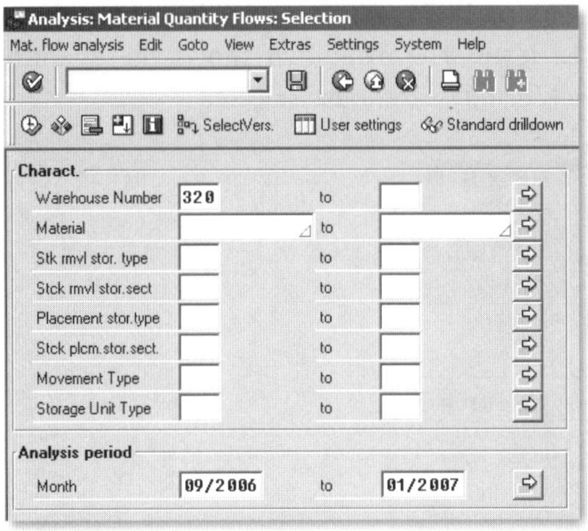

Figure 14.32 Material Flows Analysis for Warehouse Management, Transaction MCLD

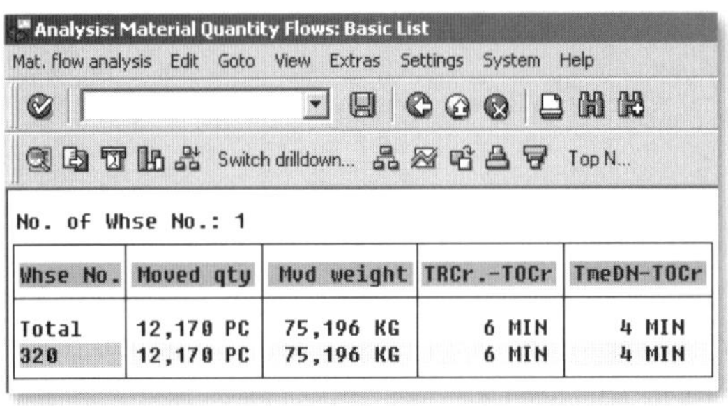

Figure 14.33 Results of Material Flows Analysis, Transaction MCLD

14.6.5 Movement Types

The movement types analysis lets the analyst investigate movements in and out of the warehouse and pinpoint any issues by selecting just one or a range of movement types, for example, movement type 101 for goods receipt of Purchase Orders, or movement type 551 for goods issue to scrap, etc.

The movement types analysis, Transaction MCLH, shown in Figure 14.34, can be found by using the navigation path: **SAP Menu • Logistics • Logistics Controlling • Logistics Information System • Inventory Controlling • Standard Analyses • Warehouse Management • Movement Types**.

The resulting data, as shown in Figure 14.35, displays the number of movements for a certain movement type per warehouse. The analyst can use the drilldown functionality to review the movements.

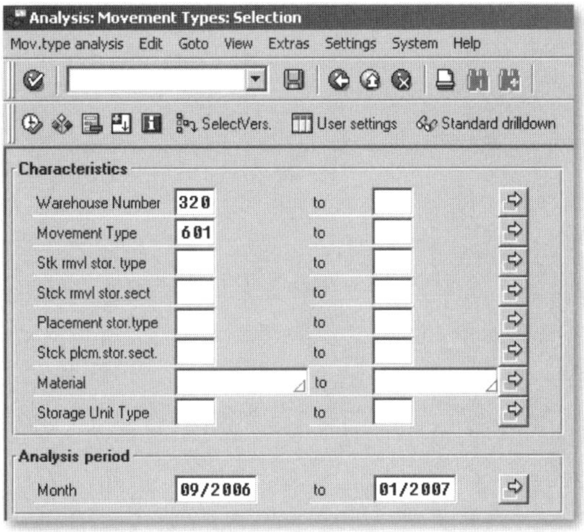

Figure 14.34 Selection Screen for Movement Types Analysis, Transaction MCLH

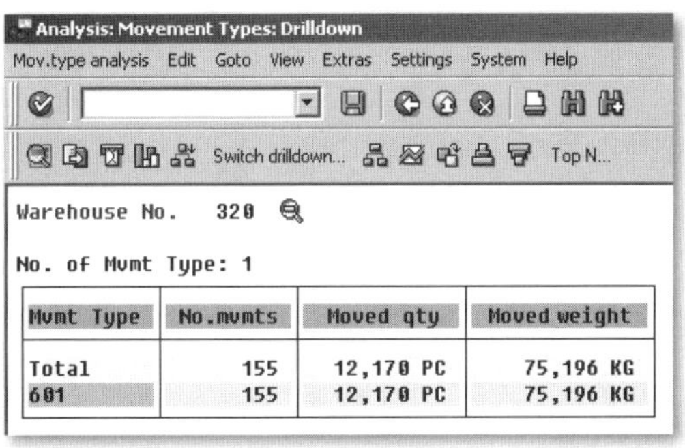

Figure 14.35 Results of Movement Type Analysis, Transaction MCLH

14.7 Summary

In this chapter, I discussed the elements of the Inventory Controlling information system. The analyst has a large number of standard analyses from which to investigate any issues that arise in the either Inventory Management or Warehouse Management. In addition to the standard analyses, the analyst can create reports based on flexible analysis, which was examined in Chapter 8.

In Chapter 15, I will discuss the Shop Floor Information System, which focuses on the production procedures and the reporting of that data.

The Shop Floor Information System (SFIS) provides analysts with data collected from the events that occur as part of the company's manufacturing process. Data is collected from Production Orders, Operations, Goods Receipts, Goods Issues, and the Kanban process.

15 Shop Floor Information System

Shop Floor Information Systems have become very important to manufacturers, especially in industries with rigid controls and regulations. Companies may need to ensure that their processes and shop floor reporting adheres to certain contractual or legal obligations from customers or governments.

In addition, companies are striving to reduce waste in the production process, be it waste of materials, time, or labor. The reports from the SFIS can help the management fine-tune the manufacturing operation to achieve a quality product in the most cost-efficient manner.

The standard analyses described in this chapter form the basis of how the production analyst can investigate production issues that will help the company to achieve its manufacturing goals.

15.1 Information Structures

The SFIS contains information structures for the following:

- Production Orders
- Kanban
- All Orders—Process Orders
- Run Schedule Headers, used in Repetitive Manufacturing

Let's look at these in more detail.

Production Order Information Structures

The four structures related to Production Orders are shown below:

- **Production Order (S021)**
  Contains the material data for the line item on an order
- **Operation (S022)**
  Contains the operation data from a production order
- **Material (S023)**
  Contains the aggregated data for materials at the order level
- **Work center (S024)**
  Contains the totals records for work center for the order level

Kanban Information Structure

Only one information structure is used for Kanban information, as seen below:

- **Kanban Information Structure (S029)**
  Contains data for Kanban transactions

Order Information Structures

The structures listed below are used for process and production orders:

- **Material Consumption (S026)**
  Contains the data for the material usage of orders
- **Product Costs (S027)**
  For production and process orders; SAP updates both planned and actual costs for the product costs

Run Schedule Header Information Structures

Two information scheduler structures relate to repetitive manufacturing, as listed below:

- **Run Schedule Header (S025)**
  Contains the goods receipt statistics for repetitive manufacturing
- **Reporting Point Statistics (S028)**
  Provides the reporting point statistics from the Run Schedule Header

15.2 Standard Analyses

A number of standard analyses are used for reviewing data in the Production area. These standard analyses review the data in the information structures related to Work Centers, Operations, Material, Production Orders, etc., and are described in more detail below. The relevant information structures are S021 through S029.

15.2.1 Work Center

The standard analysis for work centers will produce results that report on the target lead time and the actual lead times for the plant, work center, and planner group, based on the time period entered.

The target lead time is calculated in an operation as the period between the scheduled input time at the work center and the time of the latest scheduled finish of the operation. For an order, it is the time between the start and finish of the operation.

The actual lead time is defined at the operation level as the period between the input time at the work center and the completion confirmation time. The total time is from queue time, execution time, and move time.

At order level, actual lead time is defined as the period between the reported start time and the finish time. This total is from the execution times and transit times of the operations, in addition to the order floats before and after production.

Figure 15.1 shows the selection screen for the work center standard analysis, Transaction MCP7, and can be found using the navigation path: **SAP Menu • Logistics • Logistics Controlling • Logistics Information System • Shop Floor Information System • Standard Analyses • Work Center**.

Production management is always concerned when the operations scheduled for a particular work center exceed the target times. The analyst would use this standard analysis to review the target and actual operation times over a particular period to establish if there is an issue with a specific work center.

After the initial selection criteria is entered into the selection screen, as shown in Figure 15.1, the result will be returned for the plant, as shown in Figure 15.2. To review just the work centers, the production analyst can select Switch drilldown and switch the analysis to the planner group, period, or work center. In this case, the **Work center** option has been selected (see Figure 15.2).

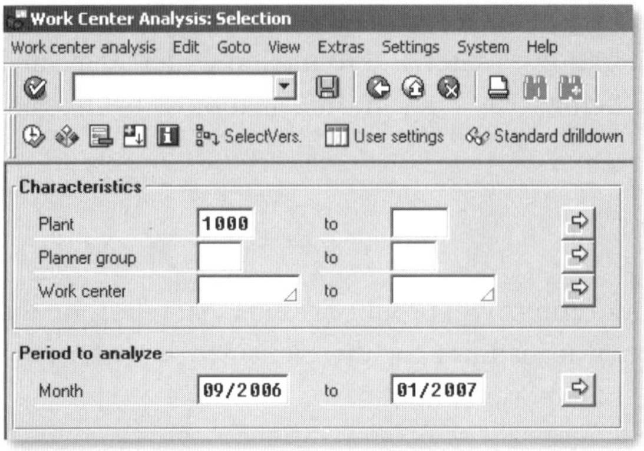

Figure 15.1 Selection Screen for Work Center Standard Analysis, Transaction MCP7

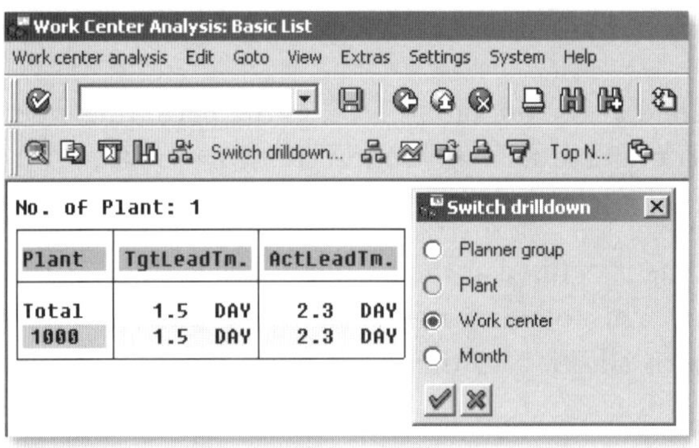

Figure 15.2 Results of Work Center Standard Analysis for Specified Plant, Transaction MCP7

By switching the drilldown to work center, the analyst can get a total view of all the work centers rather than just those work centers for a specific planner group. The analyst can then pinpoint the issue to a specific work center or work centers, as shown in Figure 15.3.

In Figure 15.3, the resulting data for the plant shows that two work centers have actual lead times far in excess of the target lead times. The analyst therefore has identified the two work centers causing this problem and can further investigate the causes for these excessive lead times.

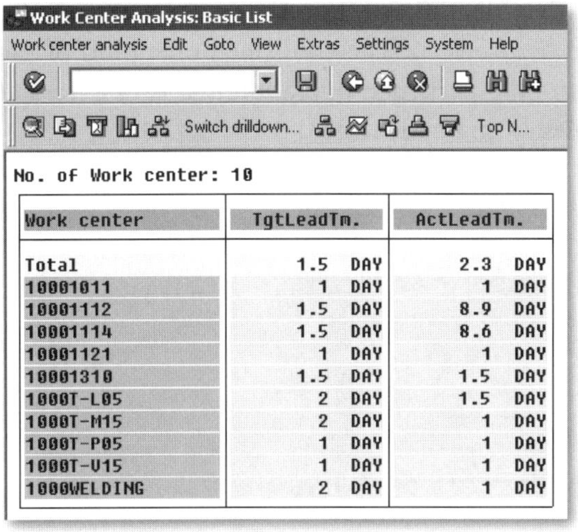

Work Center Analysis: Basic List

No. of Work center: 10

Work center	TgtLeadTm.	ActLeadTm.
Total	1.5 DAY	2.3 DAY
10001011	1 DAY	1 DAY
10001112	1.5 DAY	8.9 DAY
10001114	1.5 DAY	8.6 DAY
10001121	1 DAY	1 DAY
10001310	1.5 DAY	1.5 DAY
1000T-L05	2 DAY	1.5 DAY
1000T-M15	2 DAY	1 DAY
1000T-P05	1 DAY	1 DAY
1000T-V15	1 DAY	1 DAY
1000WELDING	2 DAY	1 DAY

Figure 15.3 Results of Work Center Analysis for all Work Centers for Selected Plant

15.2.2 Operation

An operation is an activity in a production order where something is performed, for example, a manufacturing action such as painting, heating, etc. The sequence of operations performed in a production order adds up to make the lead time for the finished material to be completed.

The analyst can use this analysis to review the operations of production orders of a plant or those for a particular work center. In the previous example of a work center that had issues with lead time, the analyst may then use this analysis to try to identify any specific operation that is causing delays in the operation time.

Figure 15.4 shows the selection criteria for the operation standard analysis, Transaction MCP1, which can be found by using the navigation path: **SAP Menu • Logistics • Logistics Controlling • Logistics Information System • Shop Floor Information System • Standard Analyses • Operation**.

The resulting data shows the operational lead time for the plant, similar to the resulting data in the work center analysis. This time, to view the operation data, the drilldown needs to switch to the work center, as shown in Figure 15.5.

Once the drilldown has switched to the work center, the drilldown can be completed to view the work center identified (**10001112**) as causing an issue in the previous section, then the material, production order, and date. The drilldown gets down to the operations for the production order (**000060002207**), as shown in Figure 15.6. The confirmed operation of the production order is shown, and the particular operation that is in excess of the target lead time (**TgtLeadTm.**) can be identified.

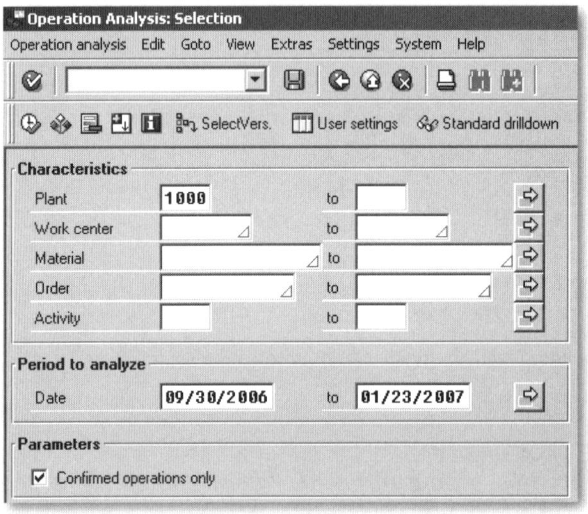

Figure 15.4 Selection Screen for Operation Standard Analysis, Transaction MCP1

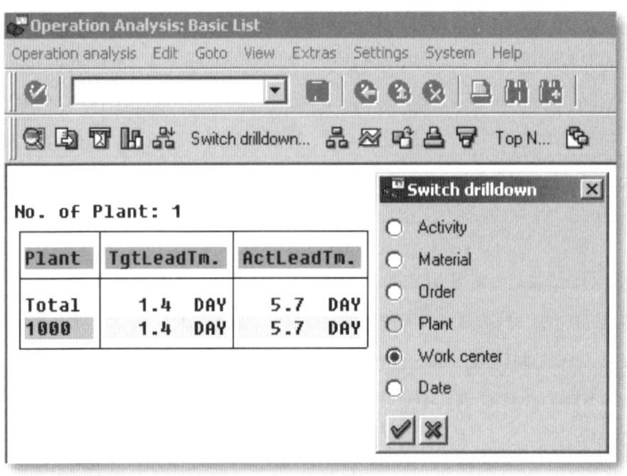

Figure 15.5 Results of Operation Standard Analysis for Specified Plant, Transaction MCP1

From this example, it is clear that the analyst can use the standard analyses in combination with the drilldown functionality to investigate issues in the production area.

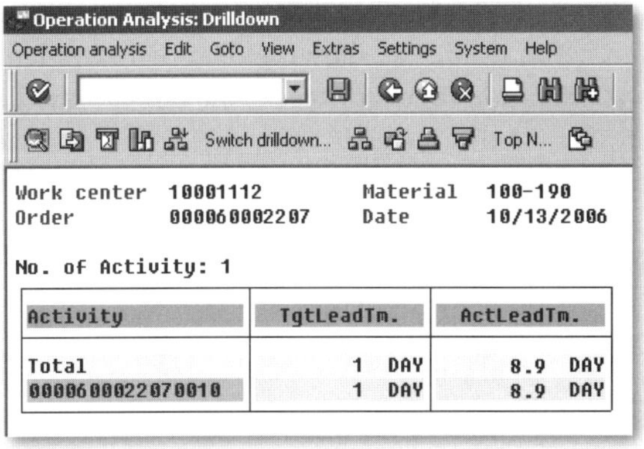

Figure 15.6 Drilldown for Operations Standard Analysis, Transaction MCP1

15.2.3 Material

The material standard analysis in the Shop Floor Information System reports on the target and actual time of the operations, as in the other standard analyses in this section. However, this analysis is integral to examining production issues with a particular material. In the example we shall show here, a material has been identified as having production issues. The material analysis should therefore focus on the single material, but the analysis should include all plants.

The material standard analysis queries the data in the information structure S023. Figure 15.7 shows the selection criteria for the material standard analysis, Transaction MCP5, which can be found by using the navigation path: **SAP Menu • Logistics • Logistics Controlling • Logistics Information System • Shop Floor Information System • Standard Analyses • Material.**

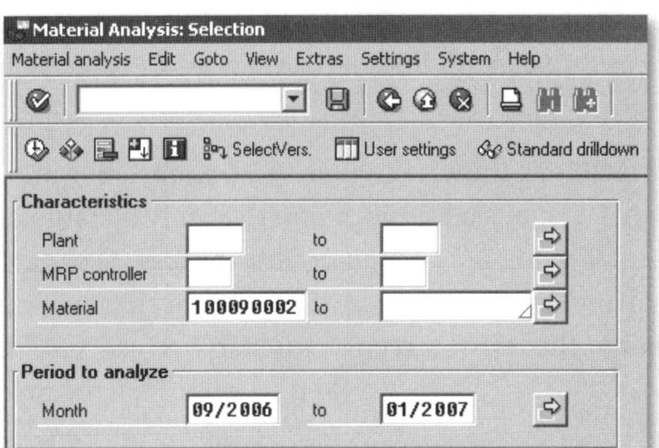

Figure 15.7 Selection Criteria for Material Standard Analysis, Transaction MCP5

The analysis returns the results for the plants that manufacture the material entered in the selection criteria. The results, as shown in Figure 15.8, identify one plant where the actual operation time far exceeds the target time for the material. The analyst can then further investigate to determine what at that plant is causing these issues.

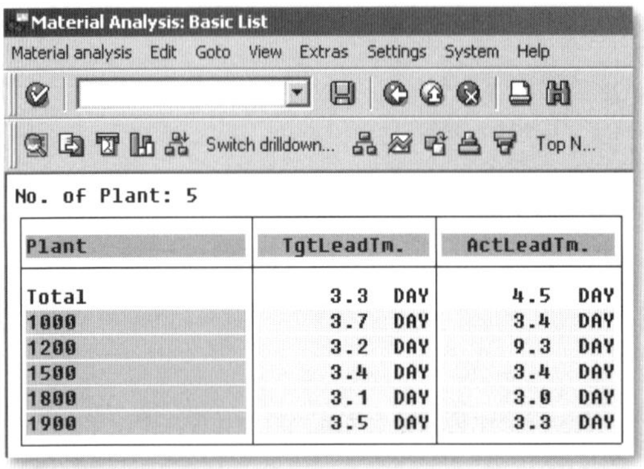

Figure 15.8 Resulting Data for Material Standard Analysis, Transaction MCP5

15.2.4 Production Order

The production order standard analysis allows the production analyst to monitor production orders for any issues that may have occurred. Any issue may be visible due to the excessive lead time. The more time the production order takes to complete over the target time, the less effective the company is at getting product to the customer.

Figure 15.9 shows the selection criteria for the production order standard analysis, Transaction MCP3, which can be found by using the navigation path: **SAP Menu • Logistics • Logistics Controlling • Logistics Information System • Shop Floor Information System • Standard Analyses • Production Order**.

The resulting data for **Plant 1000**, as shown in Figure 15.10, does not indicate that there is any issue with actual lead times, as there is only a marginal variance in time. However, to view the production orders, the analyst should switch drilldown, as shown in Figure 15.10, and display the production orders for the period entered in the initial screen.

By switching the drilldown to the production order, the results will highlight any issues for an individual order, as shown in Figure 15.11.

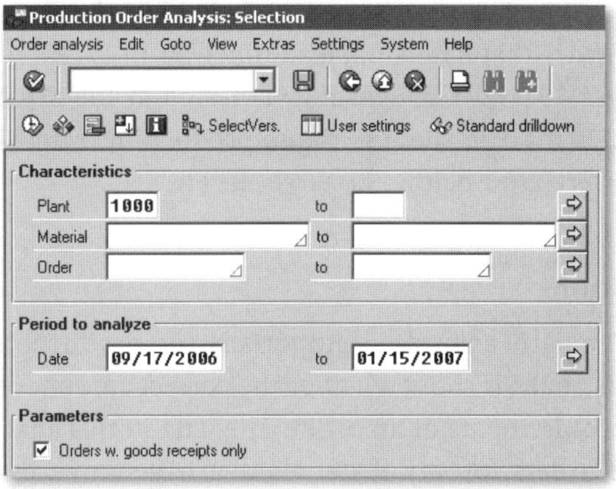

Figure 15.9 Selection Screen for Production Order Standard Analysis, Transaction MCP3

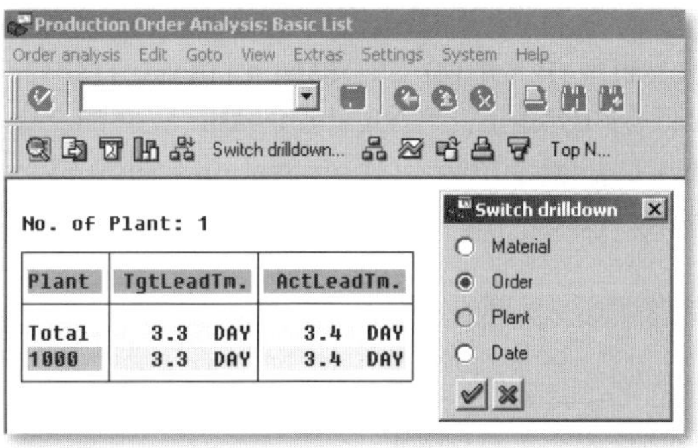

Figure 15.10 Detailed Results for Transaction MCP3 and Switch Drilldown Screen

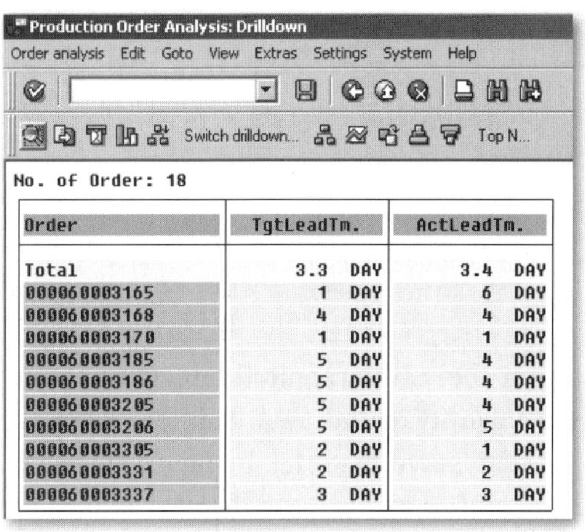

Figure 15.11 Drilldown for Production Order Standard Analysis, Transaction MCP3

The initial results don't indicate any issues; however, switching the drill-down shows one production order that has actual lead times far in excess of the target lead time (see Figure 15.11). This was not indicated at the plant level—as the average lead times masked the one rogue production order—because the other lead times were at or below the target levels.

15.2.5 Material Consumption

The material consumption standard analysis is important for production staff, because the results of this analysis show whether the correct amount of materials was issued for the requirements of an order. The data in this analysis can help to pinpoint the orders for any materials that have an excess issued above the required quantity for that order. This may indicate that operations within the production order are causing excessive scrap, or that the Bill of Materials (BOM) for the finished good is not correct.

Figure 15.12 shows the selection criteria for the standard analysis, Transaction MCRE, which can be found by using the navigation path: **SAP Menu • Logistics • Logistics Controlling • Logistics Information System • Shop Floor Information System • Standard Analyses • Material Consumption**.

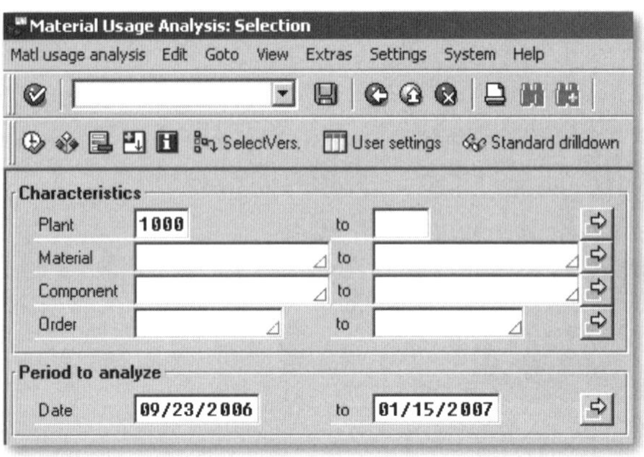

Figure 15.12 Selection Screen for Material Consumption Standard Analysis, Transaction MCRE

The resulting data for this transaction shows the required quantity of material for the production orders, the quantity withdrawn from stock for the production orders, and the value of that issued material. In Figure 15.13, the data is aggregated at the **Plant** level and to analyze the data for issues; the resulting data should be switched to **Material**.

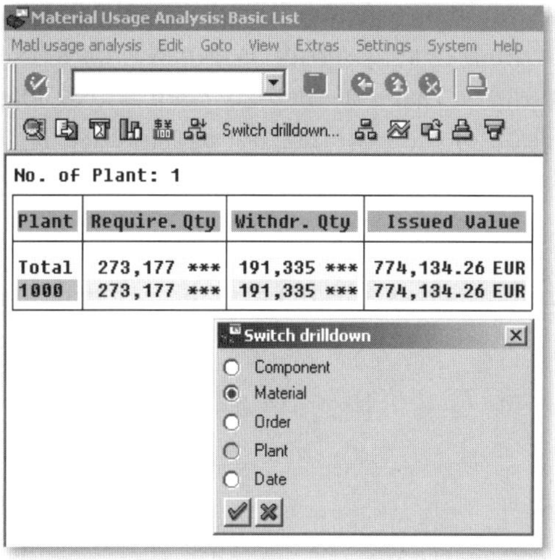

Figure 15.13 Initial Data Result for Material Consumption Standard Analysis, Transaction MCRE

By switching the drilldown to the material, the analyst can see what material has been issued more material than required. The value of the material issued may influence whether the analyst will investigate further. Management wants to reduce costs and a slight wastage of expensive component material is more important to investigate than the large wastage of low-cost items.

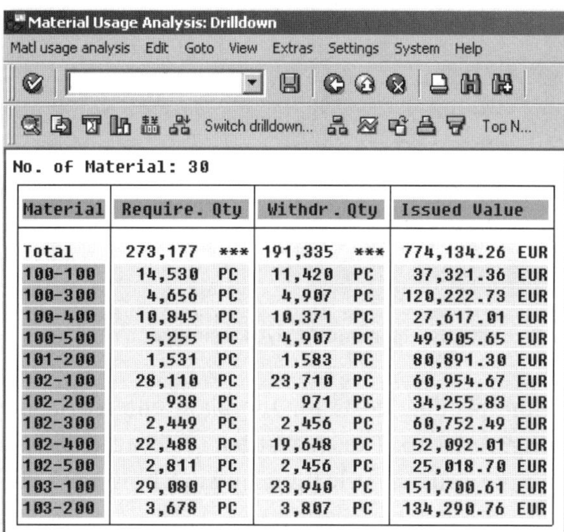

Figure 15.14 Material Data for Material Consumption Analysis, Transaction MCRE

The analyst can review the results, shown in Figure 15.14, and determine that, for several materials, the withdrawal quantity is greater than the requirements. Based on the value of the material that has been issued, the analyst can prioritize the investigation of the materials out of tolerance.

15.2.6 Product Costs

The product costs standard analysis reviews the data in the information structure S027. The results of the analysis show the following three items:

- Value of Total Product, which is the total of fixed costs and variable costs for materials
- Value of Fixed Price Product
- Value of Variable Price Product

Figure 15.15 shows the selection criteria for the product costs standard analysis, Transaction MCRI, which can be found by using the navigation path: **SAP Menu • Logistics • Logistics Controlling • Logistics Information System • Shop Floor Information System • Standard Analyses • Product Costs**.

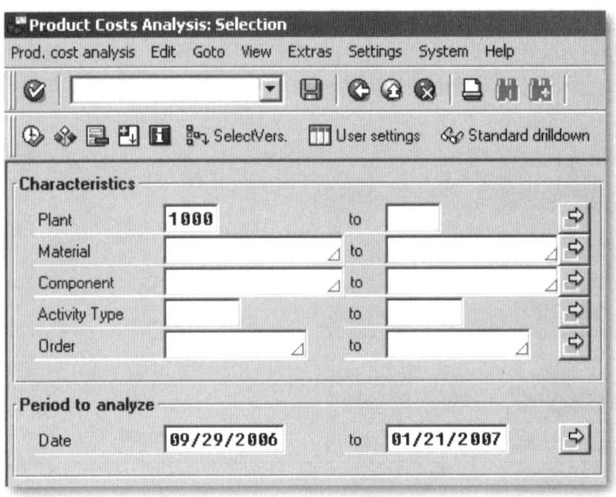

Figure 15.15 Selection Screen for Product Costs Standard Analysis, Transaction MCRI

The resulting screen shows the product costs for the plant entered in the selection criteria, as seen in Figure 15.16. The analyst can review the data on a day-by-day basis to review the product valuation by switching the drill-down to **Date**.

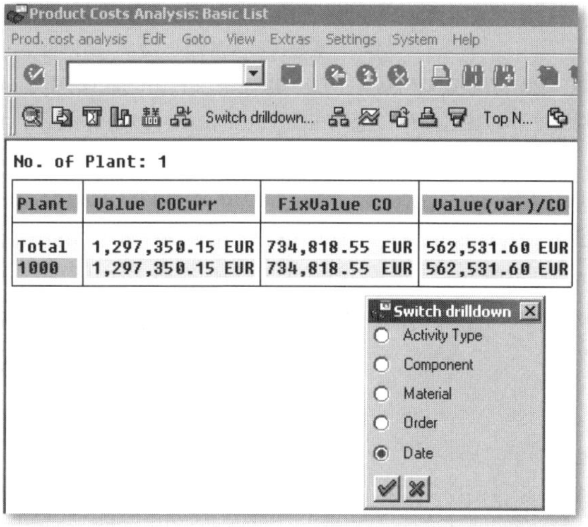

Figure 15.16 Resulting Data for Plant Level for Product Costs Standard Analysis, Transaction MCRI

After the drilldown has been changed and the resulting data is in date format, the analyst can review the value of the material at any given date within the period entered in the selection screen (see Figure 15.17).

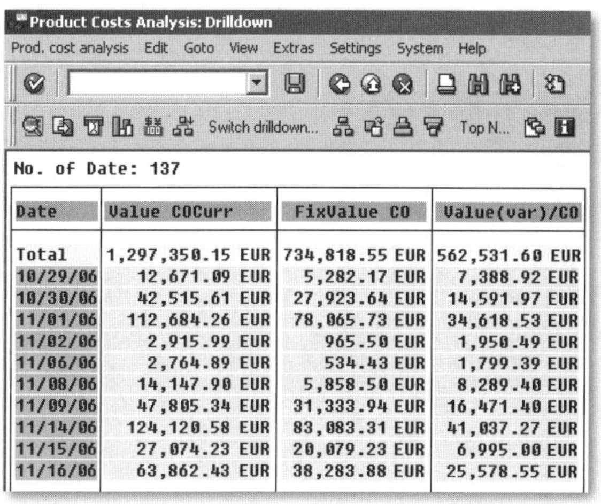

Figure 15.17 Part of Product Costs Analysis Displaying Daily Product Values for Selected Plant, Transaction MCRI

15.3 Repetitive Manufacturing

Repetitive manufacturing is identified by the production of discrete units, often at high speeds and large quantities. The materials tend to move in a continuous flow during the production process. The materials flow continuously along a direct route until they are complete. There is no need for in-process inventory as the components are continuously moving. For costing, a calculation for an individual unit cost is not needed. Examples of repetitive manufacturing include injection molding, high-speed consumer products, packaging, and medical devices.

15.3.1 Goods Receipt

The goods receipt analysis for repetitive manufacturing allows the analyst to review the goods receipts for a period of time and identify any scrap anomalies. The resulting data will show the scrap quantity for different characteristics. The analyst can enter a selection of characteristics in the selection screen, as shown in Figure 15.18.

The goods receipt analysis transaction is MCP6, and it can be found using the navigation path: **SAP Menu • Logistics • Logistics Controlling • Logistics Information System • Shop Floor Information System • Standard Analyses • Repetitive Manufacturing • Goods Receipt**.

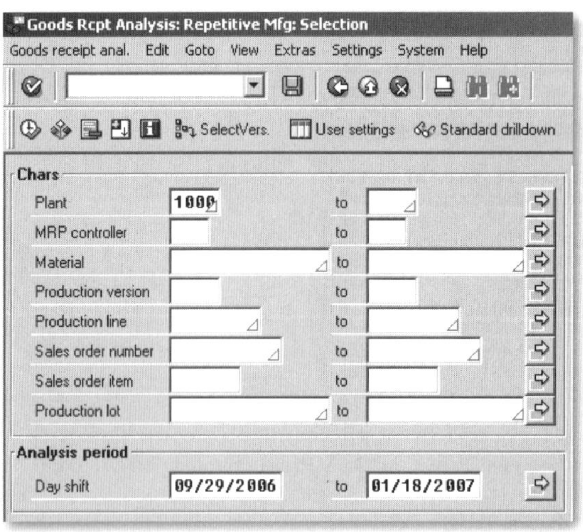

Figure 15.18 Selection Screen for Goods Receipt Analysis Run for Repetitive Manufacturing, Transaction MCP6

The results screen shows the goods receipt quantity for the period defined in the selection screen for the plant entered. The analyst may gain more insight into the repetitive manufacturing process by switching the drilldown to show the goods receipt and scrap quantity for the **Material**, as shown in Figure 15.19.

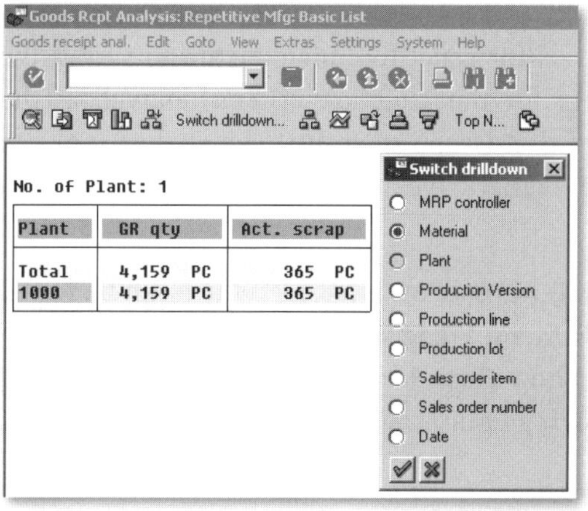

Figure 15.19 Results for Goods Receipt Analysis for Plant Level and Switch Drilldown Option, Transaction MCP6

To analyze the data at the material level, the analyst would need to switch the drilldown to **Material**, as shown in Figure 15.19. The resulting data shows what material has levels of scrap that are particularly high, as shown in Figure 15.20. The analyst can then investigate the issue with scrap in the repetitive manufacturing process for the errant material.

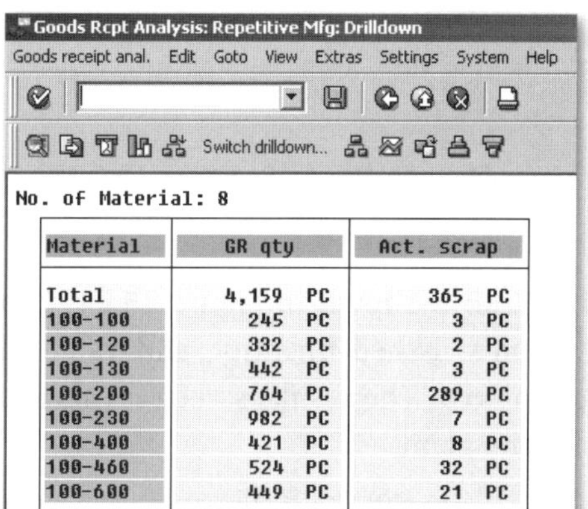

Figure 15.20 Goods Receipt and Actual Scrap Material for Each Material in Repetitive Manufacturing, Transaction MCP6

The analyst would examine this report, seen in Figure 15.20, and find that it indicates that one particular material has an issue with scrap, while another two may have problems also. The analyst can then investigate those materials in further detail.

15.3.2 Material Consumption

The material consumption analysis for repetitive manufacturing shows the analyst the requirement quantity for the selection criteria, as well as the quantity issued and the value of that issued quantity. The analyst looks to ensure that there are no line items that have a greater issued quantity than the requirement value.

The material consumption analysis transaction is MCRP, which can be found using the navigation path: **SAP Menu • Logistics • Logistics Controlling • Logistics Information System • Shop Floor Information System • Standard Analyses • Repetitive Manufacturing • Material Consumption**.

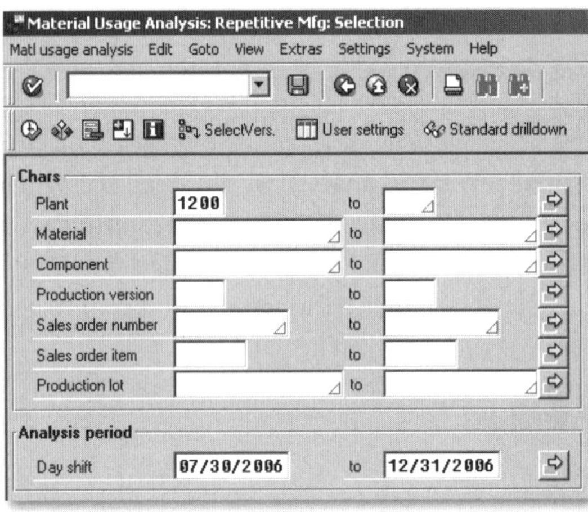

Figure 15.21 Selection Criteria for Material Consumption Analysis for Repetitive Manufacturing, Transaction MCRP

The selection screen for Transaction MCRP is shown in Figure 15.21. The resulting data will show the requirements, issued quantity, and value of issued quantity for the characteristics entered. The results screen, as shown in Figure 15.22, displays the values for the plant.

The analyst would usually be more interested in the data for the material or the production order. By using the drilldown, the material is the next level of the hierarchy and the results are shown in Figure 15.23.

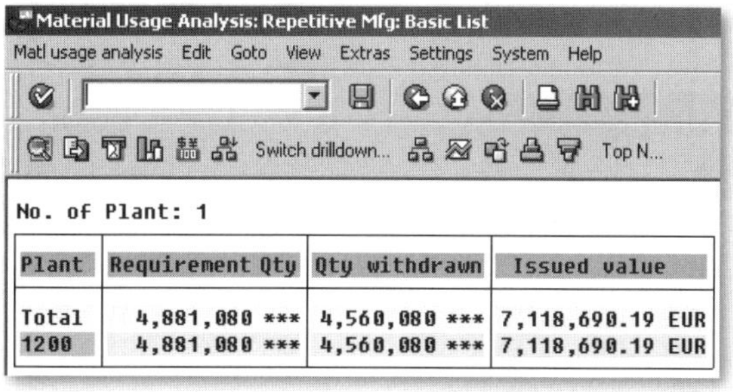

Figure 15.22 Results Screen for Material Consumption Analysis for Repetitive Manufacturing, Transaction MCRP

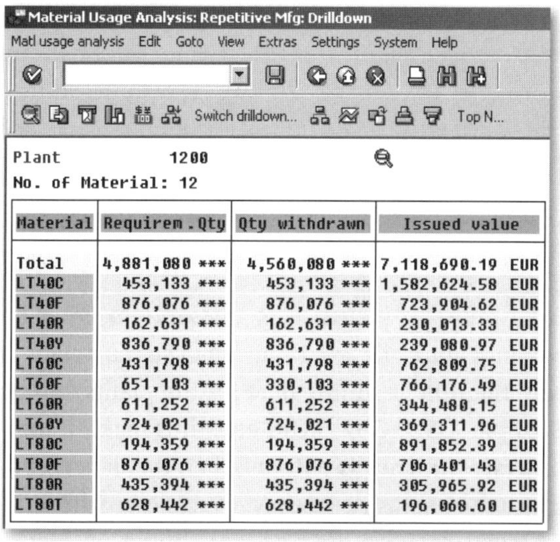

Figure 15.23 Material Data for Material Consumption Analysis for Repetitive Manufacturing, Transaction MCRP

15.3.3 Product Costs

The product costs analysis is useful in comparing the material valuation at several plants for repetitive manufacturing. The transaction code for this analysis is MCRK. This transaction is very similar to the standard analysis for product costs, MCRI, and can be easily confused.

The product costs analysis transaction can be found using the navigation path: **SAP Menu • Logistics • Logistics Controlling • Logistics Information System • Shop Floor Information System • Standard Analyses • Repetitive Manufacturing • Product Costs.**

The selection screen for Transaction MCRK is shown in Figure 15.24.

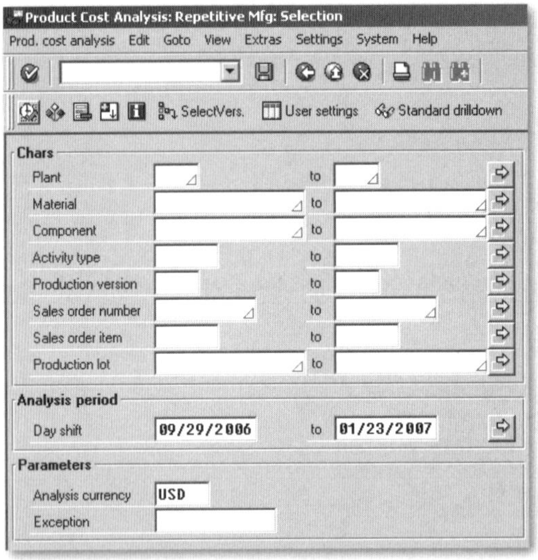

Figure 15.24 Selection Screen for Product Costs Analysis for Repetitive Manufacturing, Transaction MCRK

When this analysis is run for a range of plants, it is advisable to enter an **Analysis currency**, as shown in Figure 15.24. If no analysis currency is entered in the selection screen, then the resulting data for the plants will be in their local currency, for example, USD, GBP, EUR, etc., thus making comparison meaningless. If an **Analysis currency** is entered, then the data is converted from the local currency to the analysis currency. In this case, the analysis currency is **USD**. The returned data for the plants is shown, in Figure 15.25, as USD.

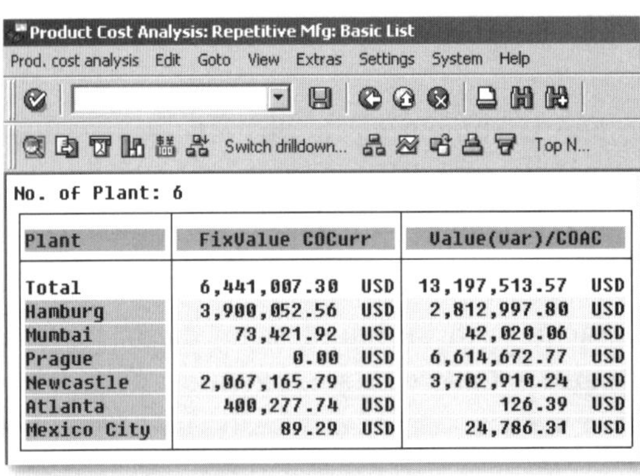

Figure 15.25 Product Costs Analysis for Repetitive Manufacturing in USD, Transaction MCRK

15.4 Kanban

An important concept in manufacturing is that of push and pull systems. Traditional manufacturing uses push systems, where the goal is to ensure all people and equipment are used to best effect. A result of this is that, where there is a sequence of operations, if an earlier operation is faster than a later operation, then semi-finished inventory will build up at a piece of equipment in the routing in a later operation. The semi-finished product takes up floor space, consumes working capital, and is liable to damage and devaluation. The principle of a pull system is that control is transferred from the beginning of the sequence of operations to the end of the sequence.

The pull system used is Kanban, which is Japanese and literally means *visible record*, but is used to mean a kind of signal. It is a method of signaling to an upstream work center that the downstream work center is ready for the upstream to produce another batch of parts. There are two types of Kanban used in manufacturing, single card and dual card.

15.4.1 Single-Card Kanban

In a single-card Kanban system, parts are produced and bought according to a daily schedule, and deliveries to the work center are controlled by a conveyance or withdrawal Kanban, sometimes called C-Kanban. Single-card Kanban controls deliveries so that the work center never has more than a container of semi-finished material. Single-card systems work well in companies with a relatively small range of end products or products that are not subject to unexpected changes in demand levels.

15.4.2 Dual-Card Kanban

Dual-card Kanban, also known as the Toyota system after the car company, employs two Kanban cards. One card is for the supplier process, also known as the production Kanban or P-Kanban. The other card is for the customer process, called the conveyance Kanban or C-Kanban, as mentioned previously.

Dual-card Kanban is more useful in large-scale, high-variety manufacturing operations. Each semi-finished material has its own container designed to hold a precise quantity of that part. The P-Kanban serves the supplier work center and the C-Kanban serves the customer work center. Each container cycles from the supplier work center to its stock point to the customer workstation and its stock point and back, while one Kanban is exchanged for another. No parts are produced unless a P-Kanban authorizes it. There is only one C-Kanban and one P-Kanban for each container, which holds an exact quantity.

15.4.3 Kanban Analysis

The standard analysis for Kanban can be executed using transaction code MCQ, which can be found using the navigation path: **SAP Menu • Logistics • Logistics Controlling • Logistics Information System • Shop Floor Information System • Standard Analyses • Kanban**. The selection screen for the transaction is shown in Figure 15.26.

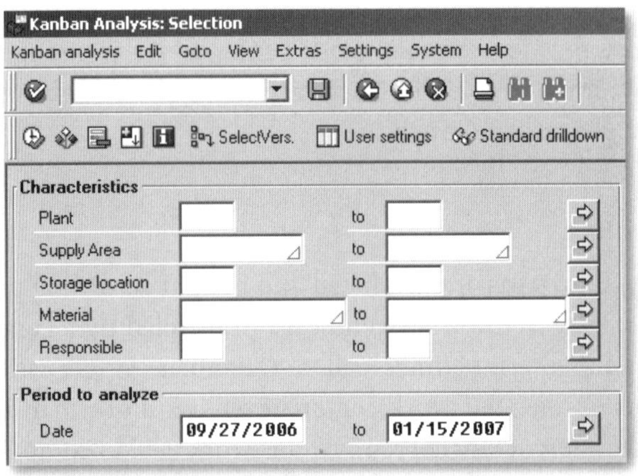

Figure 15.26 Selection Criteria for Kanban Standard Analysis, Transaction MCQ

The data returned for the Kanban analysis is used to monitor the Kanban process in the plant. The resulting fields are as follows:

- Average total replenishment lead time in days
- Average wait time in days
- Sum of the material quantities that have actually been replenished using Kanban for which a goods receipt has been posted
- Sum of the material quantities that would be replenished, i.e., target quantity, using Kanban
- Number of errors occurred when processing Kanban

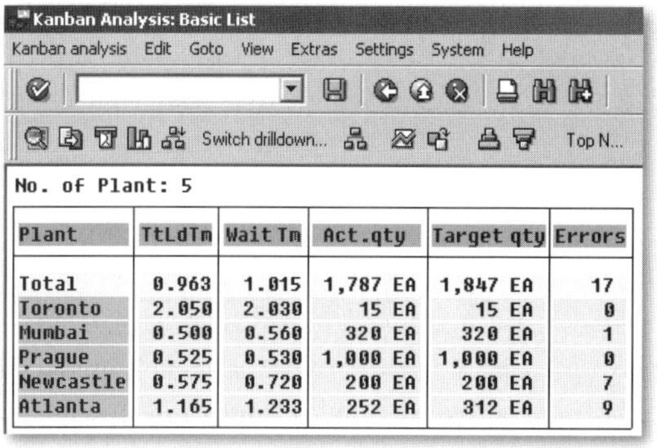

Plant	TtLdTm	Wait Tm	Act.qty	Target qty	Errors
Total	0.963	1.015	1,787 EA	1,847 EA	17
Toronto	2.050	2.030	15 EA	15 EA	0
Mumbai	0.500	0.560	320 EA	320 EA	1
Prague	0.525	0.530	1,000 EA	1,000 EA	0
Newcastle	0.575	0.720	200 EA	200 EA	7
Atlanta	1.165	1.233	252 EA	312 EA	9

Figure 15.27 Results of Kanban Standard Analysis for Monitoring Kanban Processes in the Plant, Transaction MCQ

The analyst can review the Kanban standard analysis, as shown in Figure 15.27, to determine whether the Kanban process is working efficiently and whether any modifications need to be implemented. The number of errors can imply that something is faulty in the Kanban process at that plant and may require further analysis using the drilldown function in the Kanban analysis transaction.

15.5 Summary

In this chapter, I have discussed the Shop Floor Information System and worked through a number of examples from the standard analyses. The production analyst has a number of standard analyses to monitor production facilities and the production process. For the supply chain, this is an area where a lot of time and money can be saved. The shop floor analyses will help the production management see where issues exist when you can produce reports that show actual and target lead times. The production management is under pressure to deliver finished goods to the warehouse on time.

In Chapter 16, I will discuss the Plant Maintenance Information system. Plant maintenance is an important part of the supply chain, as it is a key support function for production. If the equipment has not been maintained, breakdowns can cause production to miss dates and ultimately cause a delay in getting product to customer.

The Plant Maintenance Information System allows reporting and monitoring of the Plant Maintenance (PM) functionality. Without optimum functioning of equipment, production order throughput would suffer and cause delays of shipping finished goods to the customer.

16 Plant Maintenance Information System

Plant Maintenance is about taking specific steps to extend the life of the equipment and to detect issues that may cause equipment failure. This procedure is also known as proactive maintenance. In most companies, proactive means a plant maintenance orientation toward tasks performed that detect or delay future breakdown. Companies have to learn how to develop maintenance programs so that the company experiences fewer and fewer breakdowns.

Equipment lasts longer with a schedule of preventative maintenance, but this scenario requires management leadership in the supply chain and a significant level of financing. Many companies prefer not to commit the financing to plant maintenance. However, as more companies implement world-class supply chain processes, plant maintenance is becoming integral to developing an efficient supply chain.

The reports that are available in the Plant Maintenance Information System allow analysts to review the data collected from plant maintenance transactions. This data is key in monitoring the situation within the production facility and putting resources where they are required.

16.1 Information Structures

The Plant Maintenance Information System uses eight information structures as seen below:

- **Location and Planner Group (S061)**
  Contains the key figures processing days, activities, damage, and downtime

- **Object Class and Manufacturer (S062)**
  Contains the key figures processing days, activities, and breakdown
- **Single Object—Damage Analysis (S063)**
  Contains damage and causes of damage
- **Object Statistics (S065)**
  Contains costing information
- **Breakdown Analysis (S070)**
  Contains time to repair and time between repairs
- **Vehicle Consumption (S114)**
  Contains vehicle consumption data, costs per route, operating hours and costs per hour
- **Cost Analysis (S115)**
  Contains planned and unplanned costs
- **Customer Analysis (S116)**
  Contains processing days, damage, and causes of damages

16.2 Standard Analyses

There are a number of standard analyses that are used for reviewing data in the Plant Maintenance Information System. The standard analyses review the data in the information structures related to Equipment, Functional Location etc. The relevant information structures are identified in Section 16.1.

16.2.1 Object Class

The standard analysis for object class is Transaction MCI1, and it can also be found using the navigation path: **SAP Menu • Logistics • Logistics Controlling • Logistics Information System • Plant Maintenance Information System • Standard Analyses • Object Class**.

The standard analysis for object class allows the plant maintenance user to enter a classification class for an object. The selection, as shown in Figure 16.1, allows a class, as used in classification, to be entered that can be a class for a piece of equipment or a functional location.

The analyst can enter a specific class for a group of equipment or functional locations that will return data for the objects in those classes. Entering other selection criteria can further restrict the resulting data.

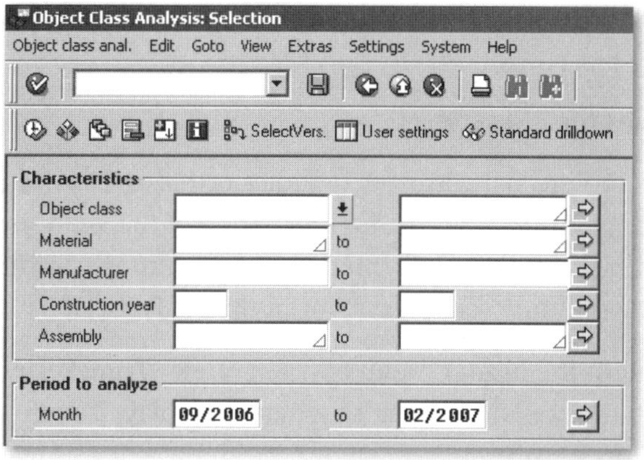

Figure 16.1 Selection Screen for Object Class Analysis, Transaction MCI1

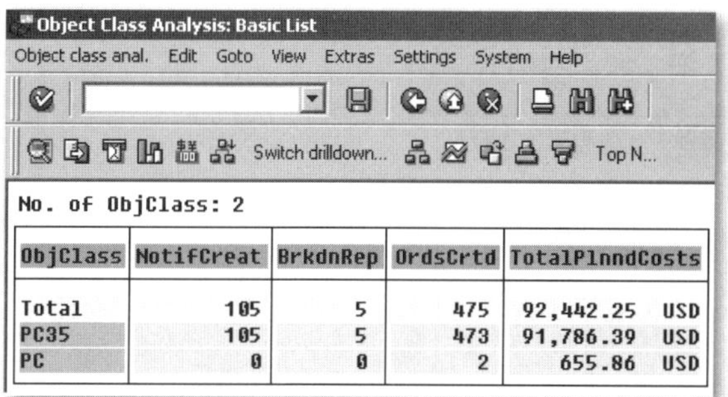

Figure 16.2 Extract from Object Class Standard Analysis, Transaction MCI1

The key figures shown in Figure 16.2 are only four of the 12 key figures that are returned for the object class analysis. A full list of the key figures is given below:

- Number of recorded notifications
- Number of recorded breakdowns that occur with an object
- Number of recorded maintenance orders
- Sum of the planned costs for maintenance orders
- Total actual costs of the maintenance services
- Total PM costs for internal personnel
- Total PM costs for external personnel
- Total PM costs for internal material
- Total PM costs for external material

- Sum of PM costs that result from services
- Total of all miscellaneous PM costs
- Sum of the actual revenues for PM services

The results of the data, as shown in Figure 16.2, indicate that there is an abnormal number of recorded notifications during the period of the analysis. The PM analysis can obtain more specific information on when those notifications were issued by using the time series function in the analysis.

The time series can be found in the header menu by using **View • Time Series** or by using the **Ctrl + Shift + F4** keys. The resulting data is displayed in Figure 16.3.

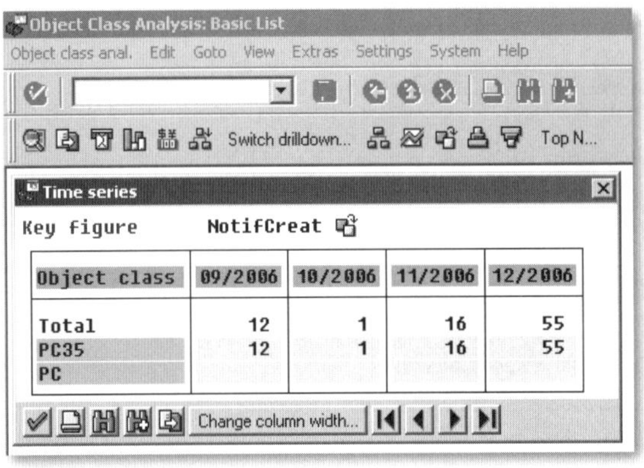

Figure 16.3 Notifications Created for Object Class PC35 Over Selected Period, Transaction MCI1

16.2.2 Manufacturer

The standard analysis for the manufacturer is Transaction MCI2, and it can also be found using the navigation path: **SAP Menu • Logistics • Logistics Controlling • Logistics Information System • Plant Maintenance Information System • Standard Analyses • Manufacturer**.

The standard analysis for manufacturer allows the analyst to enter a manufacturer of equipment (see Figure 16.4). The analysis would include only objects that have that manufacturer's name entered into the master record, for example, functional location, equipment, etc. The analyst can also leave the manufacturer name blank to see all manufacturers where notifications have been entered for an object.

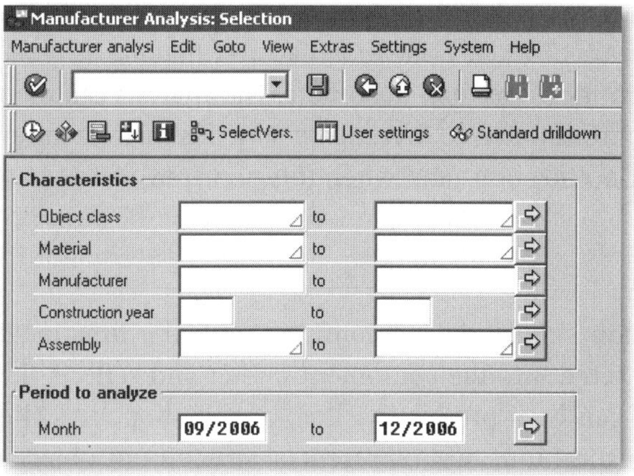

Figure 16.4 Selection Screen for Manufacturer Standard Analysis, Transaction MCI2

By leaving the **Manufacturer** field blank, the resulting data will show all manufacturers. Those with recorded notifications can be sorted in a descending list to see which manufacturers have the greatest number. The manufacturers are shown in Figure 16.5, in descending order, in terms of the number of notifications created (**NotifCreat**).

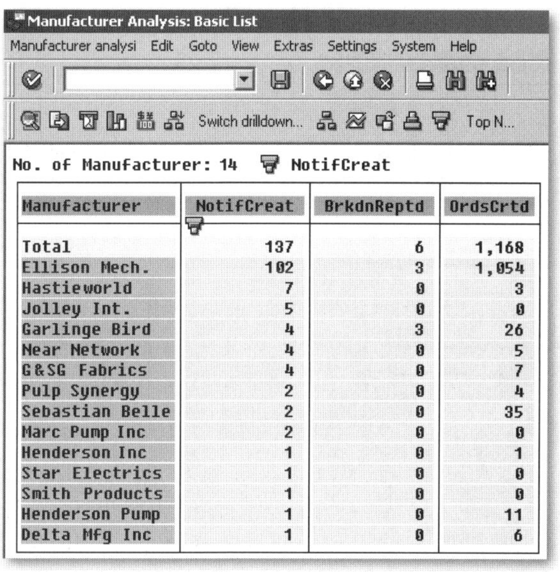

Figure 16.5 List of Manufacturers with Notifications Created in Descending Order, Transaction MCI2

The resulting screen, Figure 16.5, shows the manufacturers with notifications and breakdowns. There is obviously one manufacturer that has a significantly greater number of notifications than the others. The analysts can then drill down further into the information to investigate why this manufacturer has such a large number of notifications and when this occurred.

16.2.3 Location

In this example, the location should not be confused with the functional location. The location is entered into the equipment master and reflects the location of the asset. This can be a production line, a workshop, etc. The functional location is a logistical unit that represents a structure of objects. The location standard analysis allows the analyst to review the data by the location of the objects. The analysis by location can provide the analyst with data to indicate whether issues are grouped in specific areas or limited to specific objects.

The standard analysis for location is Transaction MCI3, and it can also be found using the navigation path: **SAP Menu • Logistics • Logistics Controlling • Logistics Information System • Plant Maintenance Information System • Standard Analyses • Location**.

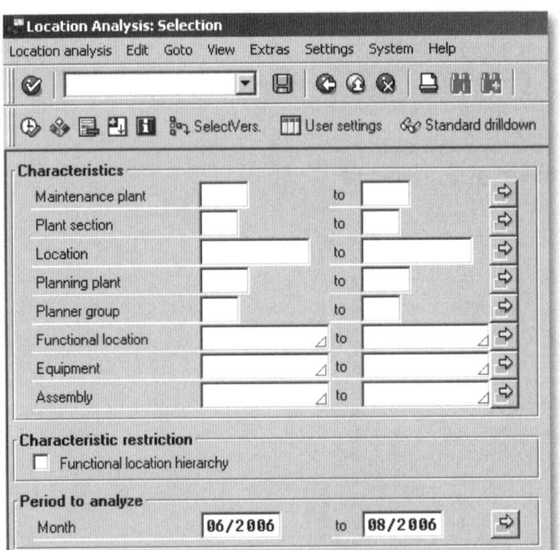

Figure 16.6 Selection Screen for Location Standard Analysis, Transaction MCI3

The selection screen, as shown in Figure 16.6, allows the entry of a specific location if that is required, or a specific maintenance plant. The drilldown provides the results to be viewed initially at the maintenance plant level, and then at the plant section and asset location.

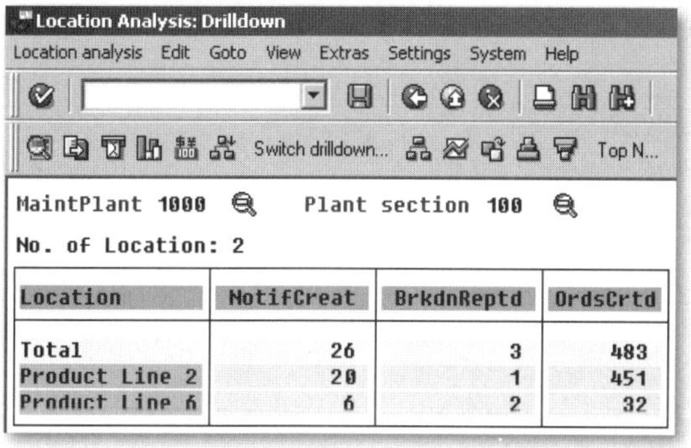

Figure 16.7 Results for Location Standard Analysis, Transaction MCI3

The data in Figure 16.7 shows that two locations (**Product Line 2** and **Product Line 6**) have experienced notifications (**NotifCreat**) and breakdowns (**BrkdnReptd**). The Plant Maintenance management can investigate whether the issues have to do with the location, or are specific to the equipment in that location. The location standard analysis helps analysts to pinpoint issues in the production process.

16.2.4 Planner Group

The planner group is defined as groups that plan maintenance tasks in an organization. The standard analysis for planner groups helps the management analyze the performance of the planner groups.

The standard analysis for location is Transaction MCI4, and it can be found using the navigation path: **SAP Menu • Logistics • Logistics Controlling • Logistics Information System • Plant Maintenance Information System • Standard Analyses • Planner Group**.

The selection screen for MCI4, as shown in Figure 16.8, lets the analyst select by planning plant or maintenance plant, rather than across the organization. The resulting data shows the notifications (**NotifCreat**) and breakdowns (**BrkdnReptd**) per **planner group** and also the mean time for the repairs (**Mn TmToRepair**), as displayed in Figure 16.9.

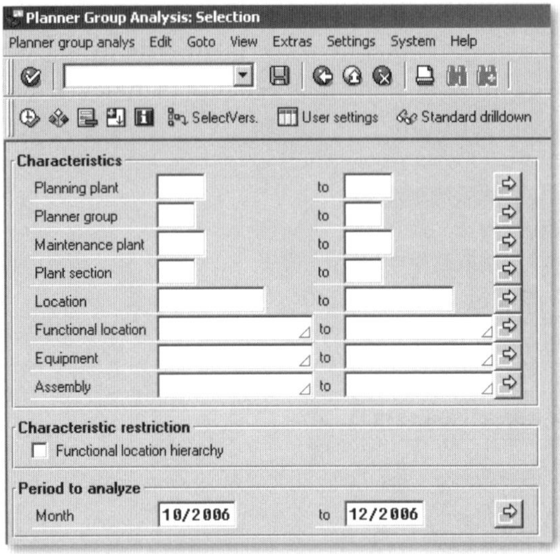

Figure 16.8 Selection Screen for Planner Group Standard Analysis, Transaction MCI4

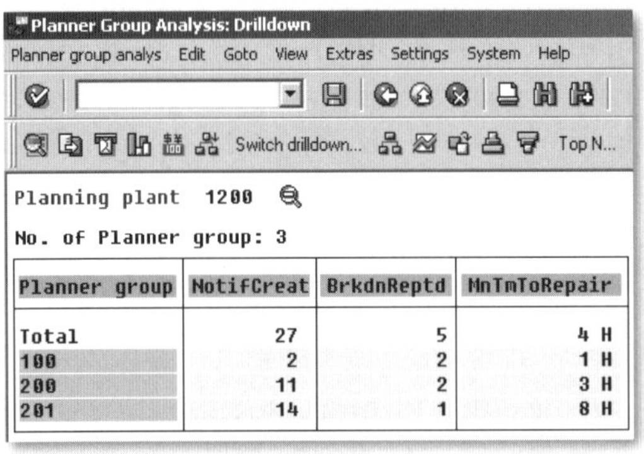

Figure 16.9 Partial Results for Planner Group Standard Analysis, Transaction MCI4

16.2.5 Damage Analysis

The damage analysis has a selection criteria, as shown in Figure 16.10, that allows the analyst to pinpoint data for a specific notification type, cause of damage, or code group. This is useful to investigate when and where certain types of damage occur.

The standard analysis for damage is Transaction MCI5, and it can be found using the navigation path: **SAP Menu • Logistics • Logistics Controlling • Logistics Information System • Plant Maintenance Information System • Standard Analyses • Damage Analysis**.

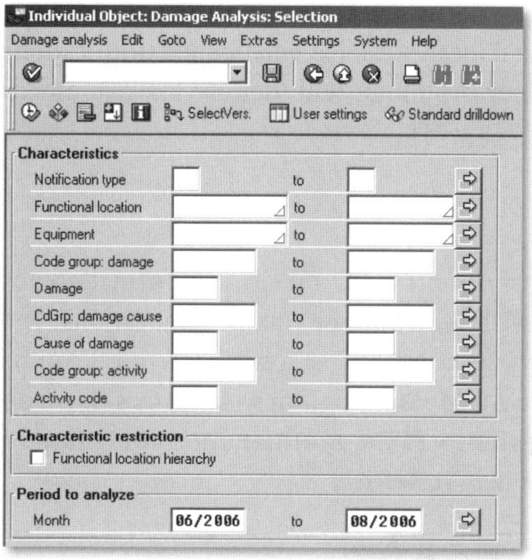

Figure 16.10 Selection Criteria for Damage Analysis, Transaction MCI5

The resulting data for this transaction, displayed in Figure 16.11, for this transaction shows three columns for each functional location:

- **Damage**
  Number of times damage occurred and was entered in the notification
- **Damage Causes (DmgeCause)**
  Code number of the cause of damage that is recorded for an object in the notification
- **Activities**
  Number of activity codes that describe the executed activities recorded in the notification

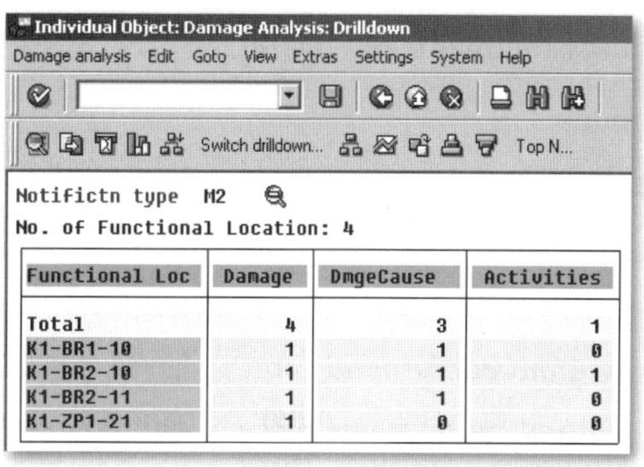

Figure 16.11 Resulting Data for Malfunction Notification Type in the Damage Analysis, Transaction MCI5

The drilldown shown in Figure 16.11 is for the malfunction notification type, and shows that four functional locations have been issued notifications during the period analyzed. Further drilldown will identify the equipment and the causes of damage.

16.2.6 Object Statistics

The object statistics standard analysis provides the basic information for Plant Maintenance management with regard to the functional locations. The standard analysis for the object statistics is Transaction MCI6, and it can be found using the navigation path: **SAP Menu • Logistics • Logistics Controlling • Logistics Information System • Plant Maintenance Information System • Standard Analyses • Object Statistics**.

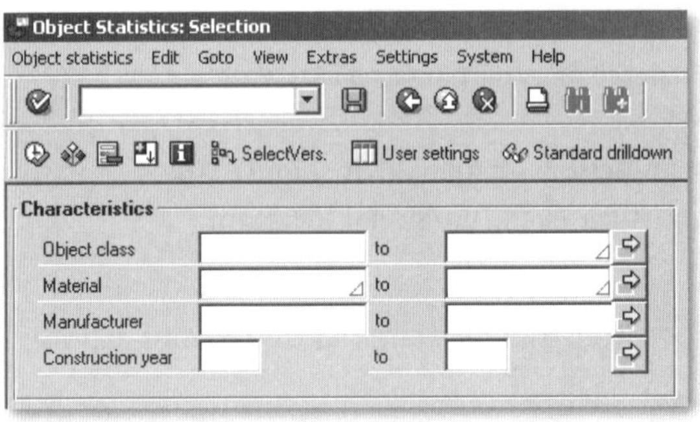

Figure 16.12 Selection Criteria for Object Statistics, Transaction MCI6

The selection criteria, as shown in Figure 16.12, allow the analyst to enter a specific manufacturer number if the total number of objects from that manufacturer is required. Otherwise, by leaving the selection blank, a total inventory of objects can be obtained. The data produced from the analysis, as shown in Figure 16.13, contains the following key figures:

- Total number of functional locations
- Total number of pieces of equipment
- Total acquisition value
- Number of functional locations containing a single piece of equipment
- Number of functional locations without equipment
- Number of functional locations with more than one piece of equipment

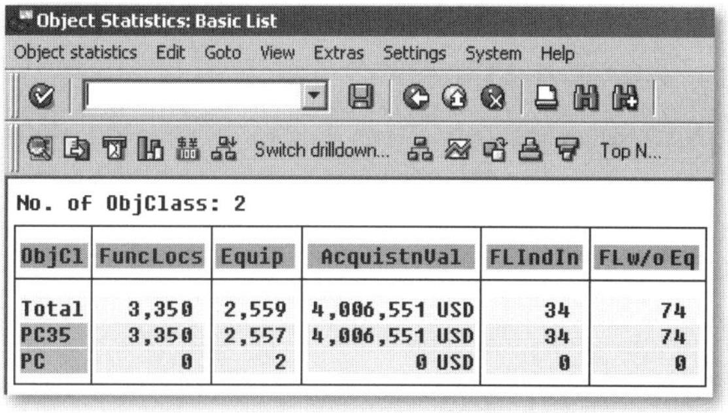

Figure 16.13 Results of Object Statistics Standard Analysis, Transaction MCI6

16.2.7 Breakdown Analysis

The breakdown analysis is available to Plant Maintenance management to review the breakdown figures for the maintenance functional locations and equipment. The standard breakdown analysis is Transaction MCI7, and it can be found using the navigation path: **SAP Menu • Logistics • Logistics Controlling • Logistics Information System • Plant Maintenance Information System • Standard Analyses • Breakdown Analysis**.

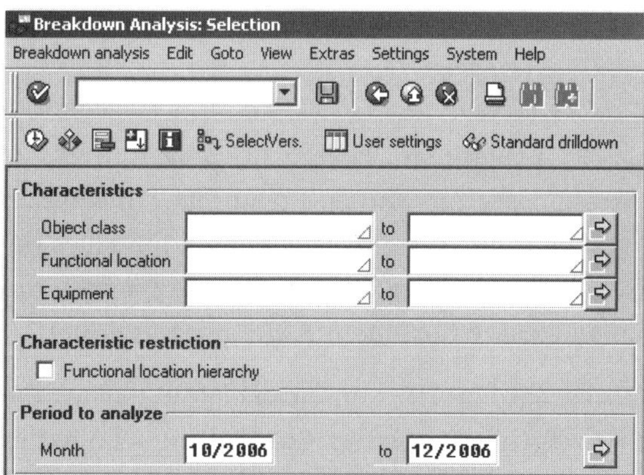

Figure 16.14 Selection Screen for Breakdown Analysis, Transaction MCI7

The selection screen, as shown in Figure 16.14, allows the analyst to enter the specific object, functional location, or equipment. This is appropriate if the analyst is investigating an issue. For general information on breakdown analysis, the options can be left blank. The resulting data, as shown in Figure 16.15, displays the following information for each functional location:

- Actual number of breakdowns (**ActBrkdn**)
- Mean time to complete a repair (**MnTmToRepair**)
- Time in between repairs (**MnTmBetRepair**)

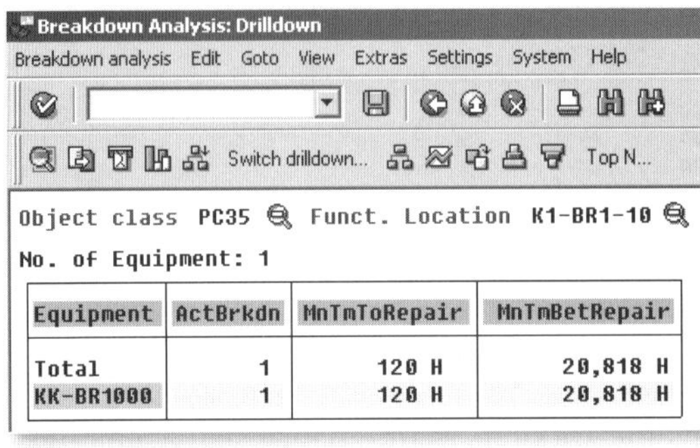

Figure 16.15 Results of Breakdown Analysis, Transaction MCI7

The drilldown function allows the analyst to investigate the breakdown figures with more specificity. Figure 16.15 shows the resulting data for a single piece of equipment after drilling down from the object and functional location.

16.2.8 Cost Analysis

The cost analysis standard analysis is slightly misleading, because it produces information not only on estimated costs, but also on the number of planned and unplanned maintenance orders in the system. This transaction gives the analyst a rapid method of finding the number of planned, unplanned, and completed maintenance orders without resorting to ABAP programming.

The standard cost analysis is Transaction MCI8, and it can be found using the navigation path: **SAP Menu • Logistics • Logistics Controlling • Logistics Information System • Plant Maintenance Information System • Standard Analyses • Cost Analysis**.

The selection screen in Figure 16.16 shows that the analyst can request the data by the particular order type. This is very useful if the client is using different order types for different types of maintenance orders. The resulting data, shown in Figure 16.17, includes the following key figures:

- Number of maintenance orders
- Number of maintenance orders that are performed immediately

- Number of planned maintenance orders
- Number of unplanned maintenance orders
- Number of maintenance orders that are completed
- Estimated planned costs for a single maintenance order

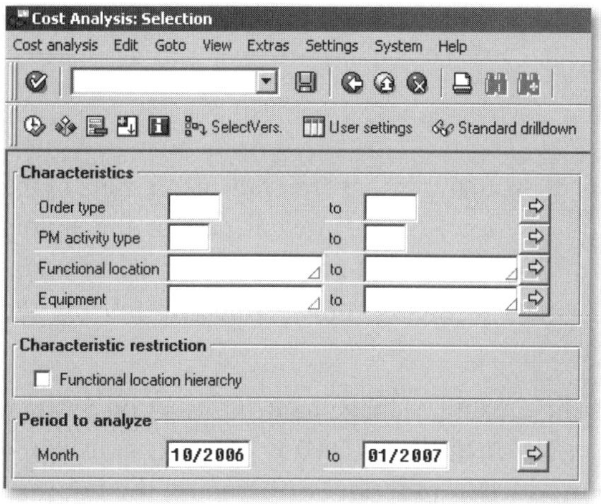

Figure 16.16 Selection Screen for Cost Analysis, Transaction MCI8

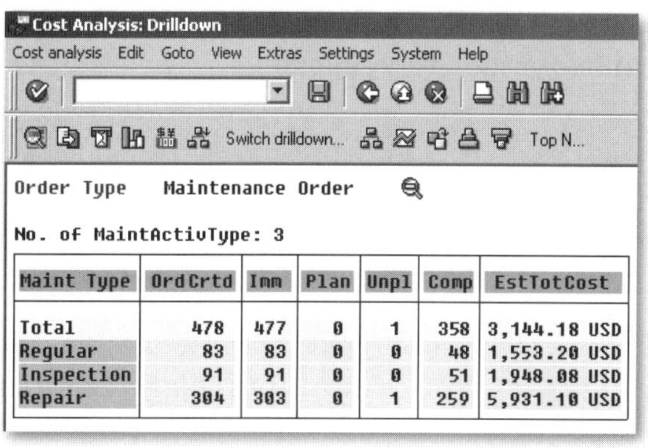

Figure 16.17 Resulting Data for Maintenance Order Type PM01 in the Standard Cost Analysis, Transaction MCI8

The result of this analysis, shown in Figure 16.17, displays the data for the order type PM01. There are three maintenance activity types shown, and each of these has an estimate of the cost of each maintenance order. This is of great importance to Plant Maintenance management, as it is an area where management can see how much the maintenance of equipment costs and it is also a good indicator of how other cost-saving measures affect the cost of maintenance orders. The standard analyses in the Plant Maintenance Information System provide the analyst and supply chain management with a large array of reports to analyze. Nevertheless, there will always be the need to create flexible analyses to produce some reports for Plant Maintenance (PM) that combine elements of Materials Management (MM) or Production Planning (PP).

16.3 Summary

In this chapter, I discussed the main analyses that are available to users of the Plant Maintenance Information System. As an integral part of the supply chain process, maintenance of production equipment is essential to maintaining the flow of finished goods to the customer, while optimizing the assets used in that production.

In Chapter 17, I will discuss the Quality Management Information System. Like Plant Maintenance, Quality Management (QM) is generally considered to be of key support for the production process. Furthermore, the information in QM is vital for the production management team and the procurement team. Quality, along with customer service, is a key influencing factor for the customer when it comes to decision-making, and therefore, supply chain management takes QM information very seriously.

The Quality Management Information System (QMIS) is the tool for management to review the quality procedures within the supply chain. The quality procedures are an important factor in producing a product that meets or exceeds a customer's satisfaction level.

17 Quality Management Information System

In his book *Quality Management for Projects and Programs*, Lewis R. Ireland describes quality as "the totality of features and characteristics of a product or service that bear on its ability to satisfy stated or implied needs." The QMIS allows management to review those features and characteristics through the predefined analyses in the system.

To supply chain management, the cost of quality is always a concern. It is defined as the total of the costs of all of the efforts involved in providing quality processes. In the past, QM has been viewed as a function that costs money rather than a function that can save money. Manufacturers assumed that there will always be errors in the manufacturing of product and the cost of using QM to check for errors was an inevitable part of the cost of doing business.

In today's business environment, companies realize that the cost of not providing a comprehensive quality management solution is far higher than the cost of actually developing a quality plan. The costs of not providing quality are clear if you consider the following:

- Additional material required in each production operation
- Scrap or rework of non-compliant materials
- Lost labor and equipment resources
- Delays in the production process
- Increased warranty repairs
- Reduced customer satisfaction

Many manufacturing companies have now implemented the Toyota principle of customer first, where the customer is not only the ultimate purchaser of the finished product, but also the next person in the value adding process, that is, the next work center. Therefore, nothing should leave a work center unless it has been checked for quality control. This quality process can minimize the costs of quality for supply chain management. There are a number of quality analyses that are available to the analyst in the QMIS, which we'll discuss in this chapter.

17.1 Information Structures

The Quality Management Information System has three information structures for inspection lots, three for quality notifications, and three for QM problems and errors. Let's look at these information structures in more detail.

Inspection Lot Information Structures

The *inspection lot* is a request to inspect a quantity of material, a piece of equipment, or functional location. The inspection lot is documented by an inspection lot record. Let's look at these lot information structures now:

- Vendor (S068), which contains aggregated data from the inspection lot and usage decision
- Material (S069)
- Customer (S104)

Quality Notification Information Structures

The *quality notification* is a request to take action when there is a nonconformance with a quality procedure. This could be internal to the plant, or a complaint against a vendor or its material, or a customer complaint about finished goods. These are:

- Vendor (S098), which contains the aggregated data from the quality notifications
- Material (S097)
- Customer (S099)

QM Problem/Errors Information Structures

These three information structures form the data repository for the standard analyses used to report on quality management data:

- Vendor (S102), which contains the aggregated data from the quality notifications at the problem level
- Material (S100)
- Customer (S103)

17.2 Standard Analyses for Materials

A number of standard analyses can be executed with regard to materials in the Quality Management process:

- **Lots**
  Transaction MCV3
- **Results (General)**
  Transaction MCXB
- **Results (Quantitative)**
  Transaction MCXD
- **Defects**
  Transaction MCXX
- **Notification Overview**
  Transaction MCXV
- **Notification Problems**
  Transaction MCXP

17.2.1 Lots

Figure 17.1 shows the selection criteria for Transaction MCV3, which is the review of lots with relation to materials. This can be found using the navigation path: **SAP Menu • Logistics • Logistics Controlling • QM Information System • Standard Analyses • Material • Lots.**

For this particular selection in Figure 17.1, the analyst has chosen to enter **01 in the Inspection type** field, which is for Goods Receipt Inspection. The results will then be only for that inspection type. The fields that are displayed for each material on the results screen, Figure 17.2, are explained here:

- **Mean Value Quality Score (MeanQScore)**
  Mean of the number of inspection lots whose quality scores lie within the class range
- **Rejection Rate (Reject rate)**
  Total number of rejected inspection lots where the usage decision is not okay
- **Rejected Quantity Rate (Reject qty)**
  Total lot quantities of all rejected inspection lots where the usage decision is not okay
- **Skipped Lots Rate (Skip rate)**
  Total number of skipped inspection lots

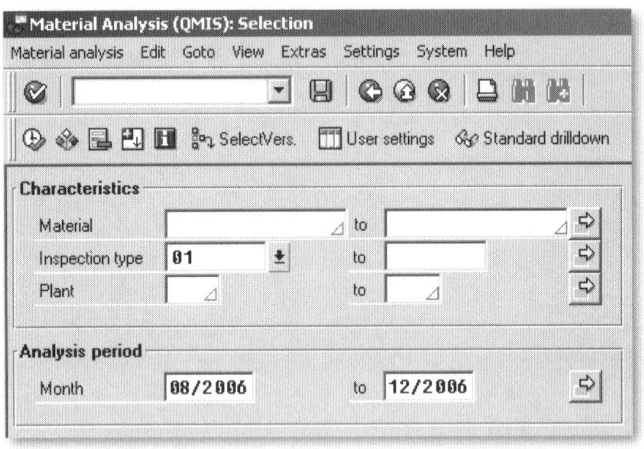

Figure 17.1 Selection Screen for Material Analysis of Lots, Transaction MCV3

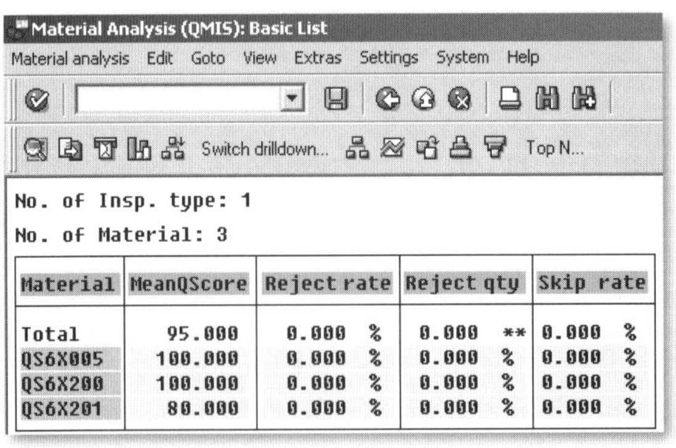

Figure 17.2 Partial View of Results Screen, Transaction MCV3

The following fields are not shown in Figure 17.2, but can be displayed by the transaction.

- **Skipped Quantity Rate**
  Total lot quantities of all skipped inspection lots
- **Sample Quantity Rate**
  Indicates the cumulative inspected amount
- **Defective Quantity Rate**
  This is the sum of the defective quantity for all inspection lots
- **Mean Lead Time**
  Mean of the total lead times of all of the inspection lots that have not been cancelled

The analysis, shown in Figure 17.2, is useful to the analyst in reviewing the quality analysis of each of the materials that proceed through Goods Receipt Inspection. This is significant if there is an issue with a material from a vendor, and the rejection rate and quantity would be of particular importance.

17.2.2 General Results

The general results analysis lets the analyst review the quality data for a variety of characteristics. Figure 17.3 shows the selection criteria for Transaction MCXB, which is the review of general results for materials. This can be found using the navigation path: **SAP Menu • Logistics • Logistics Controlling • QM Information System • Standard Analyses • Material • Results (general)**. The general results analysis provides data for the following key figures:

- Number of inspected and closed samples
- Number of samples that were accepted
- Number of rejected samples
- Number of defects found
- Number of nonconforming units: Total number of units that had one or more defects when inspected
- Number of values below lower tolerance: Total number of recorded values that are below the lower tolerance limit
- Number of values above upper tolerance: Total number of recorded values that are above the upper tolerance limit
- Sample size: Number of valid values in sample

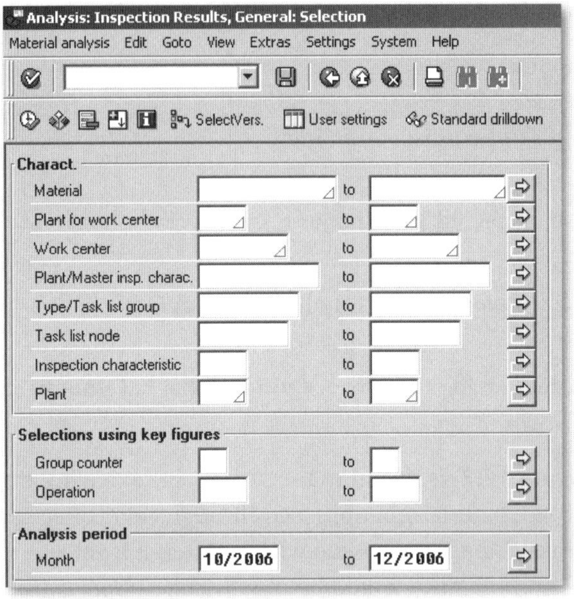

Figure 17.3 Selection Screen for General Results, Transaction MCXB

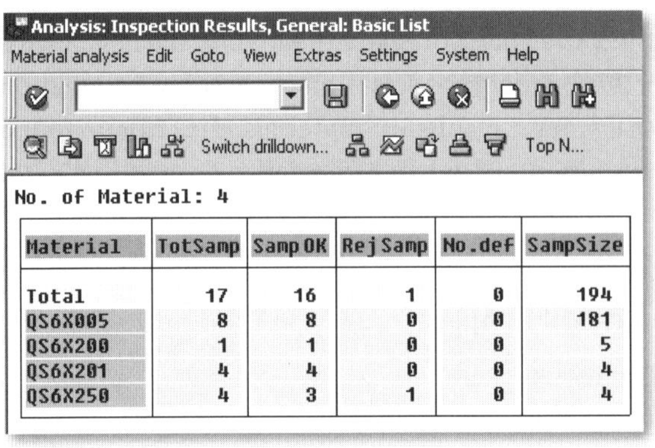

Figure 17.4 Partial View of Data from General Results, Transaction MCXB

The data from the general results analysis is shown in Figure 17.4; it displays the key figures for the materials. More detailed information can be found when the drilldown has been used. The drilldown for this transaction is shown in Figure 17.5.

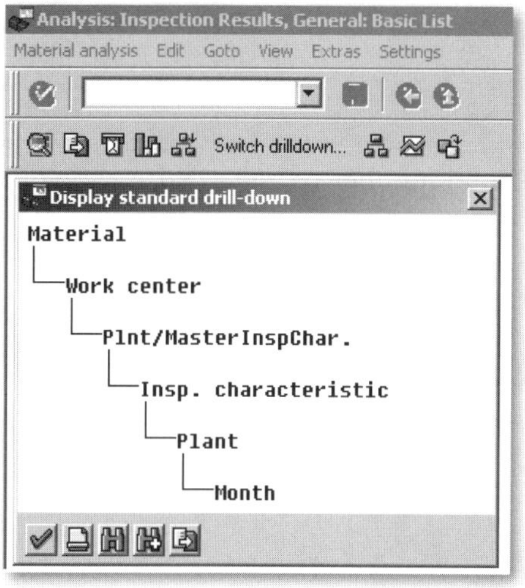

Figure 17.5 Available Drilldown for General Results Analysis, Transaction MCXB

17.2.3 Quantitative Results

Similar to the general results analysis, the quantitative results analysis has more key figures available for each characteristic. Figure 17.6 on the next page shows the selection criteria for Transaction MCXD, which is the review of quantitative results for materials. This can be found using the navigation path: **SAP Menu • Logistics • Logistics Controlling • QM Information System • Standard Analyses • Material • Results (Quantitative)**. The quantitative results analysis, as shown in Figure 17.7 (see next page), provides data for the following key figures:

- Number of inspected and closed samples
- Mean value of the valid measured values in the QMIS.
- Standard deviation of the valid measured values in the QMIS
- Process capability (**Cp Value**): A measurement of the smallest possible fraction of nonconforming units
- Process capability index (**Cpk Value**): A measurement for the expected share of nonconforming units in the process (the larger the value, the smaller the share)
- Number of values below lower tolerance—Total number of recorded values that are below the lower tolerance limit
- Number of values above upper tolerance: Total number of recorded values that are above the upper tolerance limit

- Sample Size: Number of valid values in sample
- Number of rejected samples
- Number of defects found
- Number of nonconforming units—Total number of units that had one or more defects when inspected

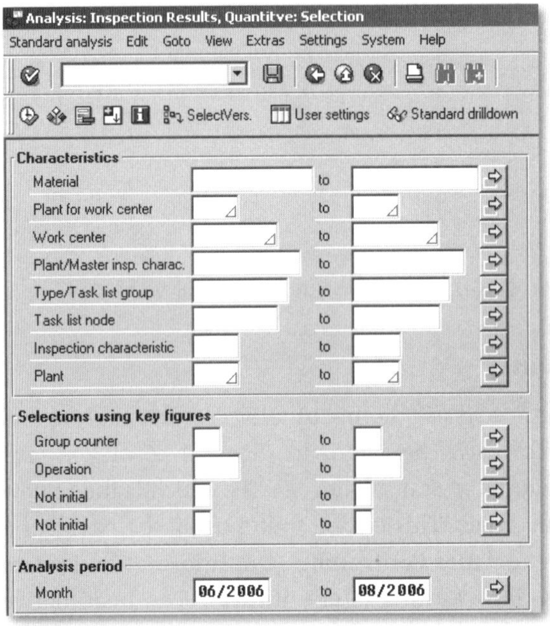

Figure 17.6 Selection Screen for Quantitative Results Analysis, Transaction MCXD

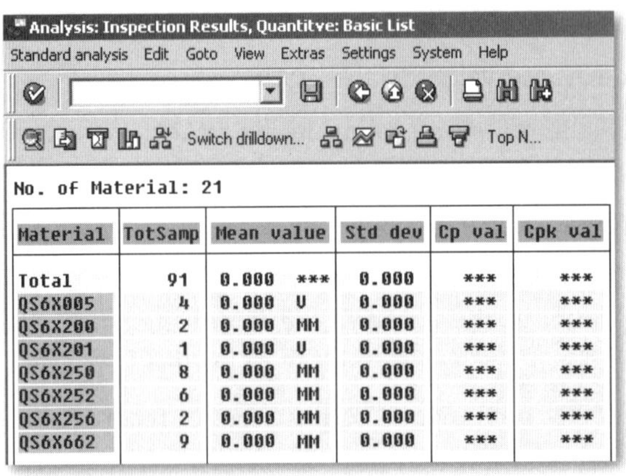

Figure 17.7 Partial View of Data from Quantitative Results, Transaction MCXD

More detailed information from the quantitative analysis can be found when the drilldown is performed. The defects analysis for materials allows the analyst to review the defect statistics for materials for a selected period. Figure 17.8 shows the selection criteria for the Transaction MCXX, which is the review of defect results for materials. This can be found using the navigation path: **SAP Menu • Logistics • Logistics Controlling • QM Information System • Standard Analyses • Material • Defects.**

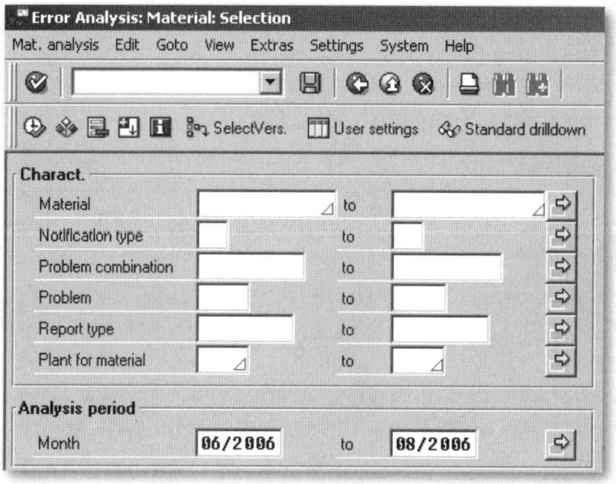

Figure 17.8 Selection Screen for Defect Analysis, Transaction MCXX

The defect analysis allows the analyst to review the material and see what the statistics are with regard to defects. The results screen, as shown in Figure 17.9, displays the following key figures:

- **Problem Frequency (Problem)**
  Frequency with which a code is used in the defect items
- **Mean Value for Defects Valuation (Mean def. Val)**
  Valuation calculated as a function of the number of defect items
- **Total of Defect Valuations (Tot def.val)**
  Contains the total of the defect valuations for all defect positions
- **Problem Items (Prob.items)**
  Displays the number of defect items that contain defect codes

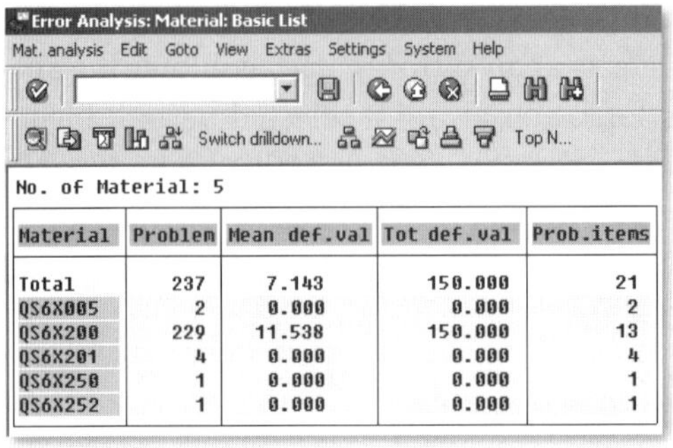

Material	Problem	Mean def.val	Tot def.val	Prob.items
Total	237	7.143	150.000	21
QS6X005	2	0.000	0.000	2
QS6X200	229	11.538	150.000	13
QS6X201	4	0.000	0.000	4
QS6X250	1	0.000	0.000	1
QS6X252	1	0.000	0.000	1

Figure 17.9 Results Screen for Defects Analysis for Materials, Transaction MCXX

17.2.4 Notification Overview

The notification overview shows the analyst information regarding the quality notifications that have been issued. The selection screen, as shown in Figure 17.10, shows that the analyst can choose to highlight a single material or a notification type, or show quality notifications for a plant.

The notification overview analysis for materials can be executed using Transaction MCXV. This can be found using the navigation path: **SAP Menu • Logistics • Logistics Controlling • QM Information System • Standard Analyses • Material • Notification Overview**.

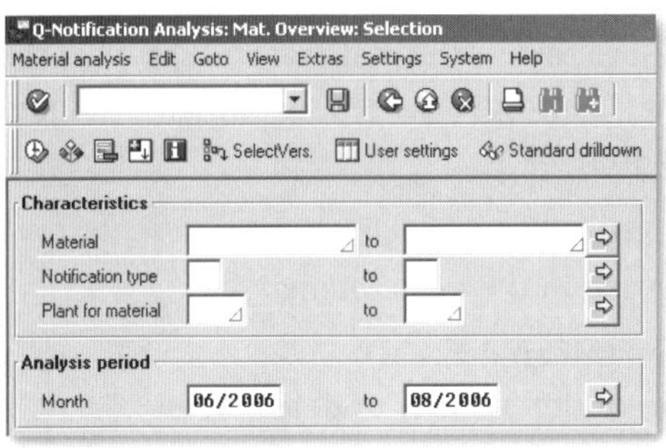

Figure 17.10 Selection Screen for Notification Overview, Transaction MCXV

The notification overview analysis, as shown in Figure 17.11, returns a number of key figures for characteristics such as material and notification type, as seen below:

- Total number of notifications (**Tot Not**): Of any status
- Number of notifications with status outstanding (**Not Out**): Which are not processed yet

- Number of notifications with status being processed (**Not Pro**)
- Number of notifications with status completed (**Not Cmp**)
- Number of notifications with status reset (**Not Res**): Which are to be processed at a later date
- Total number of tasks (**Tot Tks**): Of any status

The following fields do not appear in Figure 17.11, but can be displayed using the notification overview transaction.

- Number of tasks with status Outstanding or Released: Number of tasks, which are yet to be carried out
- Number of tasks with status successful
- Number of tasks with status completed

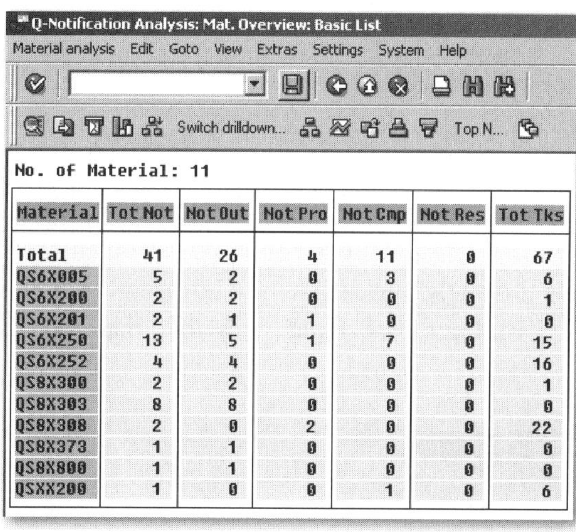

Material	Tot Not	Not Out	Not Pro	Not Cmp	Not Res	Tot Tks
Total	41	26	4	11	0	67
QS6X005	5	2	0	3	0	6
QS6X200	2	2	0	0	0	1
QS6X201	2	1	1	0	0	0
QS6X250	13	5	1	7	0	15
QS6X252	4	4	0	0	0	16
QS8X300	2	2	0	0	0	1
QS8X303	8	8	0	0	0	0
QS8X308	2	0	2	0	0	22
QS8X373	1	1	0	0	0	0
QS8X800	1	1	0	0	0	0
QSXX200	1	0	0	1	0	6

Figure 17.11 Partial List of Key Figures for Notification Analysis, Transaction MCXV

17.2.5 Notification Problems

A problem code can be affixed to the notification that allows the quality department to specifically catalog all of the problems that can occur. The problems are cataloged hierarchically, and the drilldown in the analysis lets the analyst review the notification problem data using that hierarchy.

The selection screen, shown in Figure 17.12, allows the analyst to enter a problem code or problem code combination for specific issues. The analyst may be looking at specific issues with a material and enter a single material or group of materials to analyze the associated problem codes.

The notification problems analysis for materials can be executed using Transaction MCXP. This can be found using the navigation path: **SAP Menu • Logistics • Logistics Controlling • QM Information System • Standard Analyses • Material • Notification Problems.**

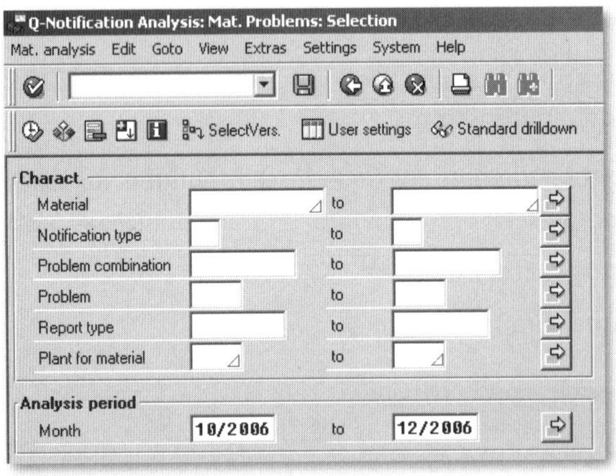

Figure 17.12 Selection Screen for Notification Problems Analysis, Transaction MCXP

The resulting data provides a single quantity value of the number of problems associated with quality notifications during the analysis period entered. The drill-down function allows the analyst to review the information down to the material and then the problems associated with that material, as shown in Figure 17.13.

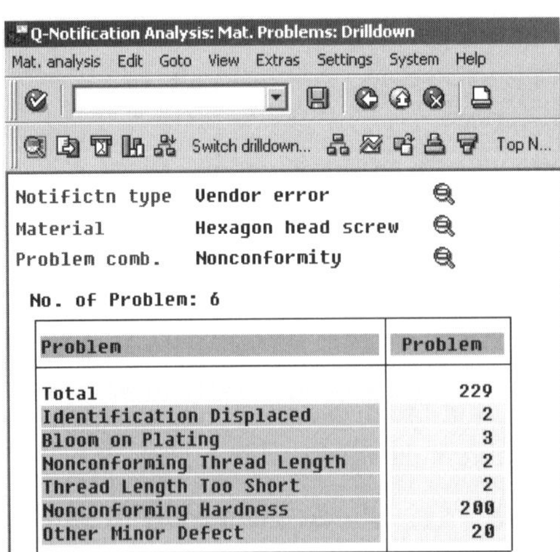

Figure 17.13 Results for Notification Problems Analysis, Transaction MCXP

This analysis is very useful to the analyst and the purchasing department when a notification type, such as vendor error, has been entered. The resulting data shows the problems associated with the material the vendor supplied. This key information gives the purchasing department leverage to reduce the cost of the item or to help find another vendor.

17.3 Standard Analyses for Vendors

Similar to the standard analyses for materials, there are a number of standard analyses that can be executed with regard to vendors in the quality management process. These are:

- **Lots**
  Transaction MCV1
- **Results (General)**
  Transaction MCVB
- **Results (Quantitative)**
  Transaction MCVD
- **Defects**
  Transaction MCVX
- **Notification Overview**
  Transaction MCVZ
- **Notification Problems**
  Transaction MCVP

17.4 Standard Analyses for Customers

Similar to the standard analyses for materials and vendors, there are a number of standard analyses that can be executed with regard to customers in the quality management process. These are:

- **Lots**
  Transaction MCOO
- **Results (General)**
  Transaction MCOB
- **Results (Quantitative)**
  Transaction MCOD

- **Defects**
  Transaction MCOX
- **Notification Overview**
  Transaction MCOV
- **Notification Problems**
  Transaction MCOP

17.5 Summary

In this chapter, I discussed the importance of the quality management standard analysis as it relates to the overall supply chain. The quality management processes are critical; without them, the risk of not producing a satisfactory product for the customer becomes very great. As companies move toward making quality a key differential in their sales marketing, ensuring the highest quality of their products will be a continuous process. The QMIS is a useful tool in that process.

In Chapter 18, I will discuss the Early Warning System (EWS). This functionality combines all the aspects of the Logistics Information System (LIS) that we have discussed so far and provides clients with a tool that can have a powerful effect.

The Logistics Early Warning System (EWS) provides a process whereby an exception can be searched for and then corrected. The EWS also provides a forum where amendments to logistical data and decisions can be tested to ensure that no future exceptions will occur.

18 Early Warning System

The Early Warning System (EWS) is based on all of the key figures in the LIS. The functionality is available in each of the individual areas of the LIS. The EWS is based on the theory of exception. The exception can be defined in an area, for example, Plant Maintenance, Shop Floor etc., and the analysis can be executed to determine whether the exception will occur. This is particularly useful to analysts when they execute an analysis for future requirements; they can see immediately whether an exception will occur. If it is predicted that an exception will occur, then the analyst knows that the company must make amendments to other variables in order to avoid the exception.

The key to the EWS is that if a company wants to use the functionality, it has to be proactive by working methodically with an exception analysis to test every scenario. A procedural methodology should be employed to ensure total coverage as far as testing exceptions.

18.1 Creating an Exception

The first step in creating a valid early warning system is to create a number of exceptions that can be run to test for exceptions. The exception can be created using Transaction MCY1, or by using the navigation path: **SAP Menu • Logistics • Logistics Controlling • Logistics Information System • Early Warning System • Exception • Create.**

The initial screen for the transaction, as shown in Figure 18.1, requires that a name and description be entered, as well as the name of the information structure for which the exception is required. The exception name can be 12-characters long. Because the name of the exception may need to be in a specific format, you might have to check with your data administration team. The exception description can be up to 40 characters long.

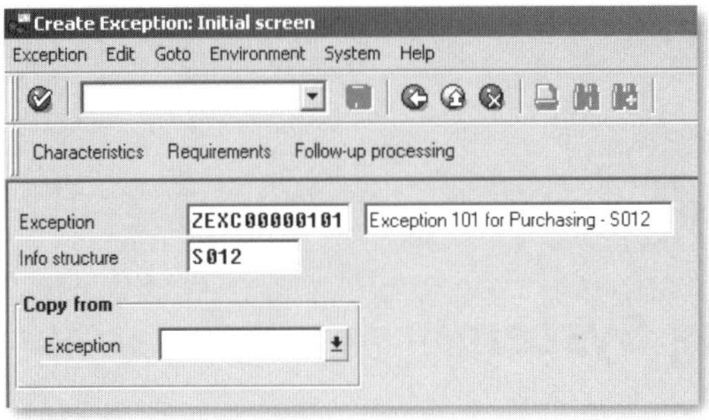

Figure 18.1 Initial Screen for Exception Creation, Transaction MCY1

Once the initial data has been entered, the next part of exception creation is choosing the characteristics from the information structure that you want to incorporate in your exception. The characteristics can be chosen from the information structure as shown in Figure 18.2. You can select all characteristics or just a subset.

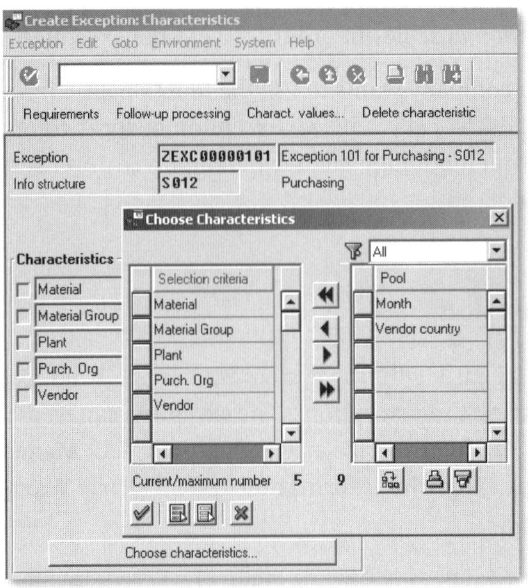

Figure 18.2 Characteristic Selection for Exception Creation, Transaction MCY1

18.1.1 Requirement

After the characteristics have been selected, you can choose the requirement for the exception. The requirements screen can be chosen from the header menu, **Goto • Requirements**, or by using the **Shift + F7** function keys.

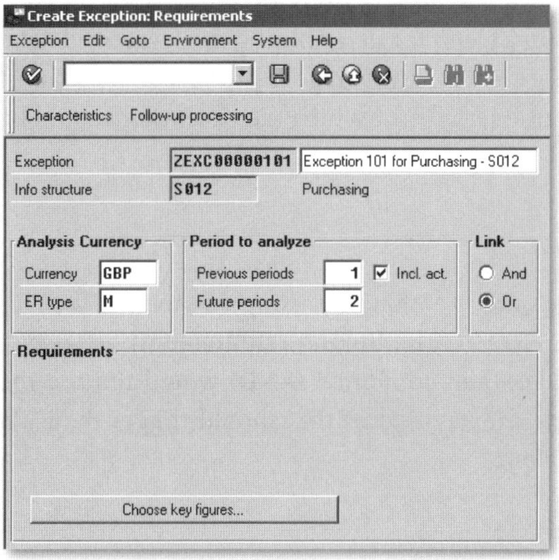

Figure 18.3 Requirements Screen from Which Key Figures Can Be Selected

The requirements screen, as shown in Figure 18.3, has a number of initial fields in which information can be entered. We will discuss these initial fields in the following subsections.

Analysis Currency

There is an option for entering the currency that should be used for the exception. It is important to enter this particular currency if many different currencies will be part of the data selected. Entering an analysis currency ensures that the results can be compared, since all results will be converted to the single currency.

The Exchange Rate Type (ER Type) determines how the currency conversion occurs. There are often many types of conversion that the analyst can choose from, such as Local Daily Rate or Current Bank Rate. A financial analyst would be able to provide more information on the correct exchange rate type to use for your exception.

Periods to Analyze

The analyst can choose a number of previous periods to use for the exception. There is also an indicator that can be set to include or exclude the current period in the analysis.

It is important to note that if more than four periods are selected, the LIS will execute a statistical test based on a trend for determining the forecasted data. If four or fewer periods are chosen, then an average is produced. The analyst can also enter a number of future periods for which the exception should be run.

Linking Requirements

There is an option to link two requirements by using an AND or an OR, which can be selected on this screen. The linking requirements are useful when there are key figures that when combined (**AND**) would require the EWS to be triggered, or if there are key figures that should trigger the EWS if either (**OR**) met the requirement.

18.1.2 Key Figures

You can select the key figures for the requirement by choosing the option from the header menu, **Edit • Choose Key Figures**, or by using the function key **F5**.

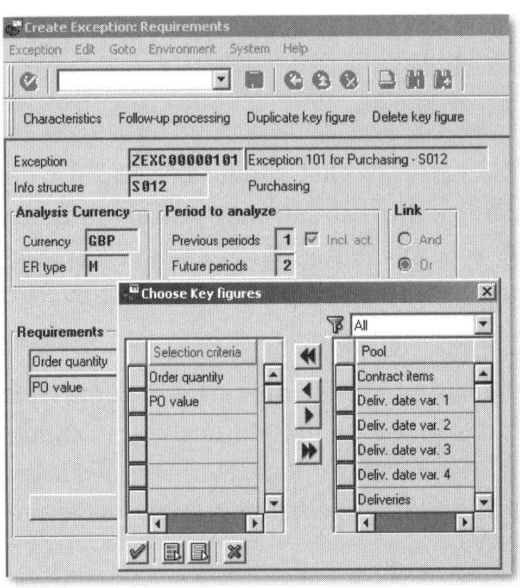

Figure 18.4 Selection of Key Figures for Requirements Section of Exception Analysis

The selection of the key figures should reflect the exception analysis that is required. In this case, the order quantity and the purchase order value have been selected (see Figure 18.4). After the key figures have been selected, the analyst can determine the requirements for each.

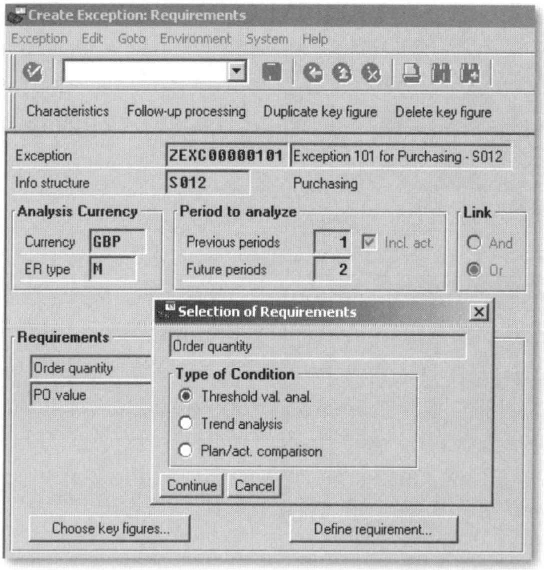

Figure 18.5 Condition Selection for Exception Based on Order Quantity Key Figure

18.1.3 Threshold Value Analysis

The analyst can select the type of condition for the exception. In Figure 18.5, the analyst has selected the threshold value analysis (**Threshold val. Anal.**) for the key figure order quantity. The analyst can then enter the threshold value that should trigger the exception.

The analyst can define the threshold using operators, for example, greater than (>), less than (<), etc., as shown in Figure 18.6. For example, if the analyst required the exception to be triggered when a value of more than 200 is found for the order quantity, then the entry would be **>200**.

The analyst also can enter a number of periods for which a forecast is produced. The forecast data is then compared against the threshold value entered.

The **Check per period** indicator is important, because it determines how the analysis is carried out. If the indicator is checked, the threshold requirement is checked against each period individually. If it is not checked, the accumulated totals of the periods selected are checked against the threshold requirement. This indicator can make a big difference in the results of the threshold analysis.

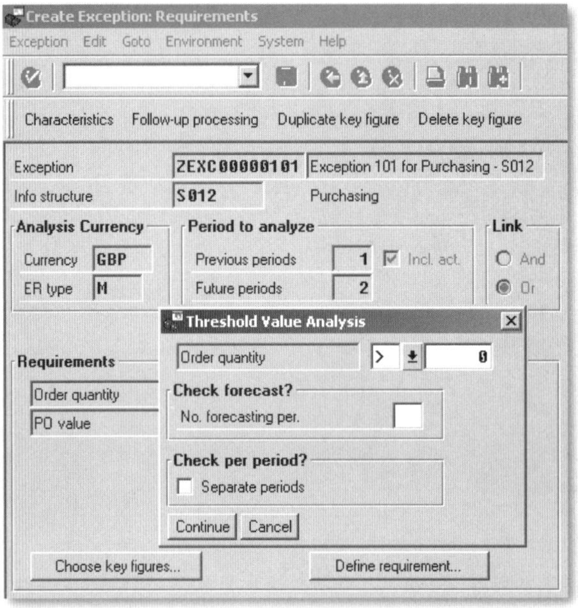

Figure 18.6 Data Entry of Threshold Value Analysis for Key Figure Order Quantity

18.1.4 Plan/Actual Comparison

Instead of the threshold value analysis, the analyst can choose another type of condition for the exception. For a key figure for an exception analysis, the analyst can choose the plan/actual comparison (**Plan/act.comparison**). Here the analyst will check whether there is a deviation from the plan when the actual is compared.

For the plan/actual comparison, the analyst has to enter a planning version of the information structure that he or she is working with. The plan realization is based on the formula where the realization is calculated as the actual divided by the plan value multiplied by one hundred. Therefore, in the example in Figure 18.7, the exception will occur if fewer than 70% of the Purchase Order Values are below the planned value.

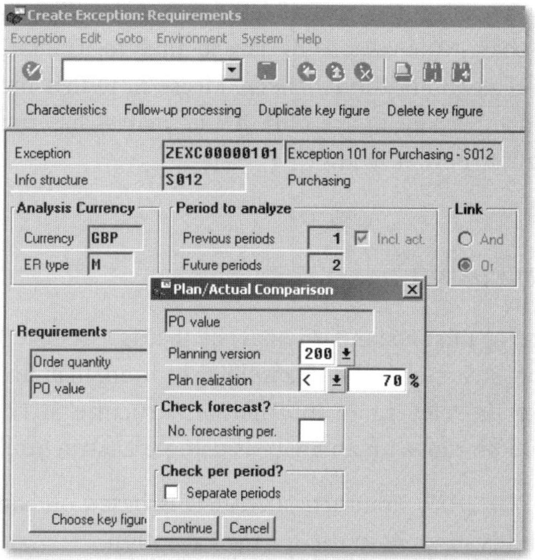

Figure 18.7 Plan/Actual Comparison for Key Figure PO Value in Exception Analysis

18.1.5 Trend Analysis

The third type of condition that can be selected for the key figure is trend analysis. The key figure condition checks for either a positive or negative trend to the data.

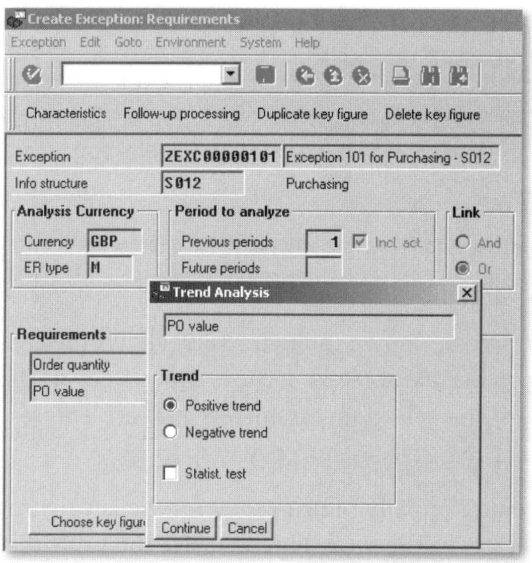

Figure 18.8 Trend Analysis Condition for Exception, Transaction MCY1

There is the ability to add a check for a statistical test for a trend. This is appropriate if there are more than three periods of data to analyze. The statistical test for a trend is useful as an additional check. Please note that the trend analysis can be selected for a key figure only if the analyst has not entered any quantity in the future period field.

18.2 Executing the Exception

The exception can be executed against a standard analysis that is associated with the relevant information structure. The example exception that has been described in this chapter is relevant to information structure S012; therefore, the exception should be run with an analysis using that structure.

The material analysis in the PURCHIS, Transaction MCE7, is based on the S012 information structure and is suitable to use for the exception.

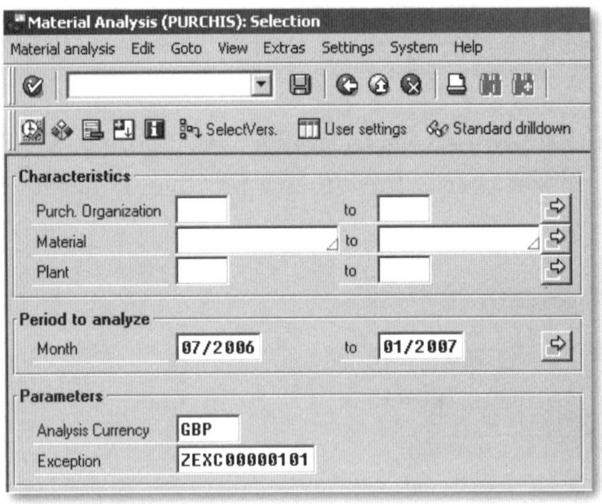

Figure 18.9 Material Analysis Transaction with Exception Entered in Parameters Section, Transaction MCE7

The material analysis selection screen, shown in Figure 18.9, allows the analyst to enter the exception into the **Parameters** section. The values in the **Exception** will overwrite any of the selection parameters that are entered, such as the periods to analyze or the analysis currency.

When the analysis is run, it would normally return values for the key figures for the period entered. In this case, as shown in Figure 18.10, the value that has caused an exception has been highlighted. This indicates that it was outside of the value entered into the exception.

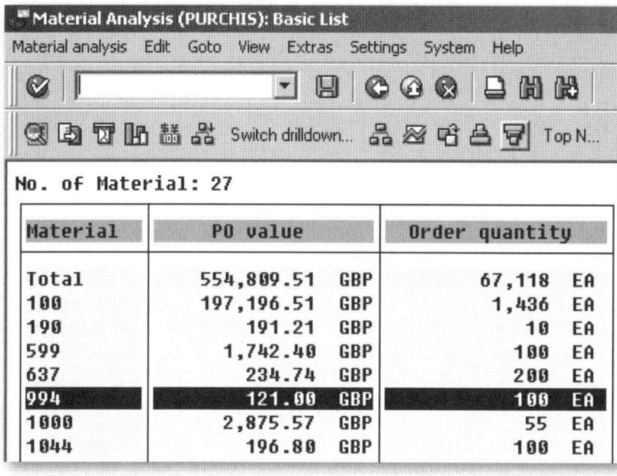

Material	PO value		Order quantity	
Total	554,809.51	GBP	67,118	EA
100	197,196.51	GBP	1,436	EA
190	191.21	GBP	10	EA
599	1,742.40	GBP	100	EA
637	234.74	GBP	200	EA
994	121.00	GBP	100	EA
1000	2,875.57	GBP	55	EA
1044	196.80	GBP	100	EA

Figure 18.10 Exception Value Highlighted in Material Analysis, Transaction MCE7

The analyst can then review these exceptions to determine whether more amendments are needed to stop exceptions from happening or to make management aware of these anomalies.

18.3 Exception Groups

The EWS can group exceptions together. The analyst may require this if two or more exceptions have already been created and if combining existing ones can create a third.

18.3.1 Create an Exception Group

An exception group can be created using Transaction MCY4, or by using the navigation path: **SAP Menu • Logistics • Logistics Controlling • Logistics Information System • Early Warning System • Grouping • Create**. The exception group is created by entering the name of the group, the description, and the information structure, as you would if you were creating a normal exception.

The analyst can then add the exceptions created for that information structure that he or she would want to group together, as shown in Figure 18.11.

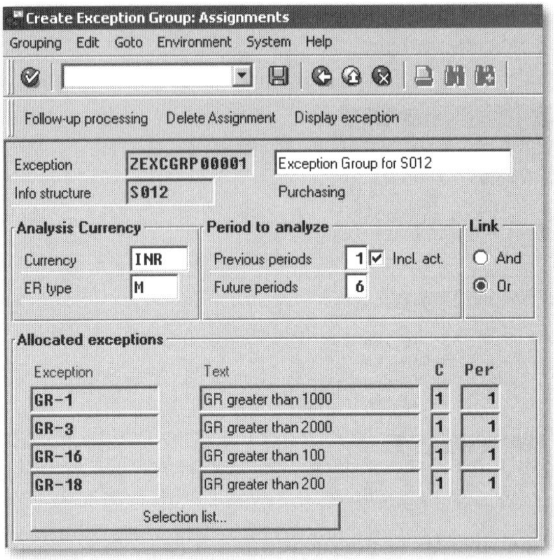

Figure 18.11 Allocated Exceptions Added to Exception Group, Transaction MCY4

18.3.2 Executing the Exception Group

The exception group can be executed in an analysis in the same way as an exception in an analysis. The exception group can be entered into the **Parameters** section of the initial screen of the transaction as shown in Figure 18.12.

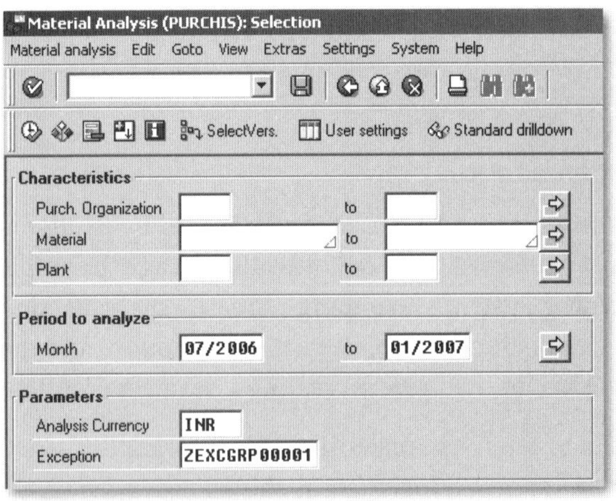

Figure 18.12 Material Analysis Transaction with Exception Group Entered into Parameters Section

18.4 Periodic Analysis

Periodic analysis provides the analyst with ongoing monitoring of data and will provide notification when an exception has occurred. The analysis checks on specific data at a given period that is defined by the analyst.

18.4.1 Creating a Periodic Analysis

The periodic analysis can be created using Transaction MCY7, or by using the navigation path: **SAP Menu • Logistics • Logistics Controlling • Logistics Information System • Early Warning System • Periodic Analysis • Area to Analyze • Create**.

The periodic analysis is based on the analysis of an exception using a specific period defined by the analyst. In creating a periodic analysis, the first screen requires the analyst to enter the exception that will be used for the analysis, as shown in Figure 18.13.

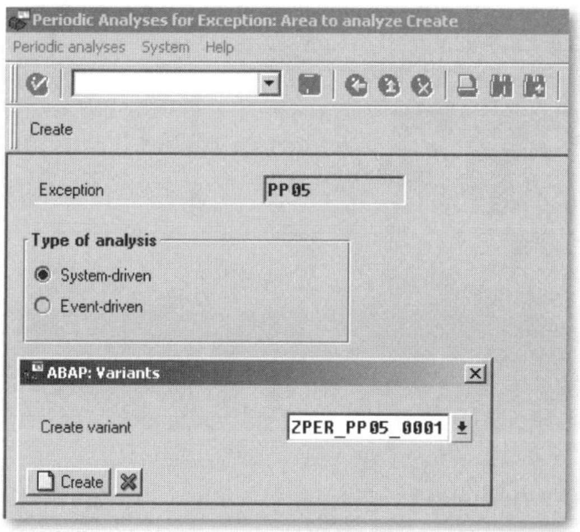

Figure 18.13 Exception and Variant Used in Creating a Periodic Analysis

In this example, exception **PP05** has been used, which is to analyze unplanned scrap in the production process. The analyst then has to choose between a *system-driven* analysis and an *event-driven* one.

System-Driven Analysis

In a system-driven analysis, all of the data is reviewed to check that an exception has occurred. The system will monitor the exception using the whole dataset that has been selected. For example, if the exception were triggered after a vendor supplied more than 100,000 materials, then the exception analysis would use the whole dataset each time it was executed. The exception analysis can be run at regular intervals decided on by the analyst.

Event-Driven Analysis

In an event-driven analysis, the exceptions are searched for only when an event changes. For this example using exception **PP05**, a change in a production order would then provide the trigger for the exception analysis to review the data for exceptions.

Variant

There can be only one variant for each exception. The variant name should comply with your company's naming conventions for programs and variants. Once the variant name has been entered, the next screen in creating the variant will show the exception analysis and the variant selection screen will be displayed, as shown in Figure 18.14.

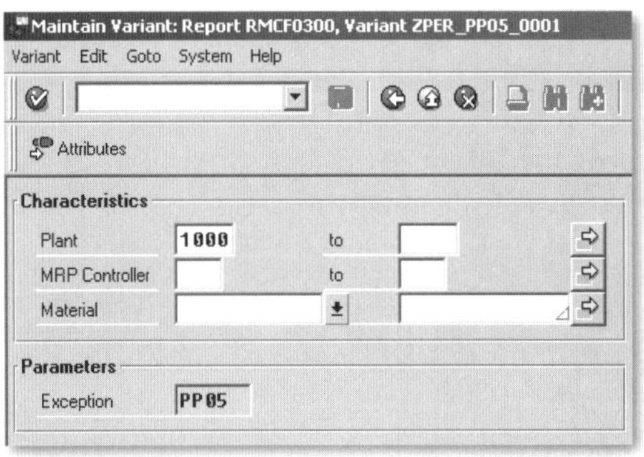

Figure 18.14 Maintaining Variant for Exception, Transaction MCY7

If any attributes need to be entered for the periodic analysis, they can be entered as shown in Figure 18.14 Otherwise, the analyst can review the attributes of the variant (see Figure 18.15). In this screen, the variant name has to be entered. The analyst can set the fields for the variant, such as making fields required, hiding the field, protecting the field, etc. After finalizing any changes, the analyst can save the variant for the exception.

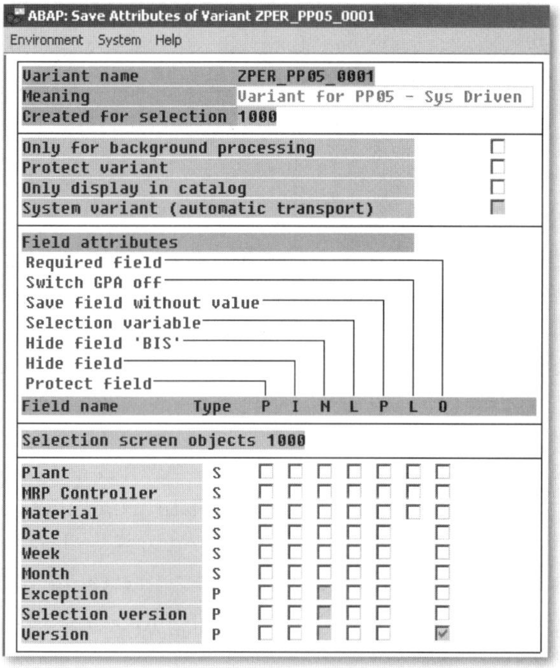

Figure 18.15 Attributes That Can Define Variant for Exception Analysis

18.4.2 Schedule the Periodic Analysis

Once periodic analysis has been defined, it needs to be scheduled to run at specific times based on the analyst's requirements. The periodic analysis can be scheduled by using Transaction MCYB, or by using the navigation path: **SAP Menu • Logistics • Logistics Controlling • Logistics Information System • Early Warning System • Periodic Analysis • Schedule.**

The initial screen requires the exception to be entered. The schedule screen, as shown in Figure 18.16, requires the analyst to enter the date and time that the exception should be first run. Then, by clicking on the **Period values** button, the analyst can choose from a variety of periodic values to schedule the frequency of execution.

After the analyst has selected a frequency to run the analysis, the transaction can be saved. The screen will return to the initial scheduling screen. At this point, the analyst can click on the **Restrictions** button. The analyst may have requirements to allow or not allow the periodic exception analysis to run on certain days. The restrictions screen provides a selection of options for the analyst, as shown in Figure 18.17.

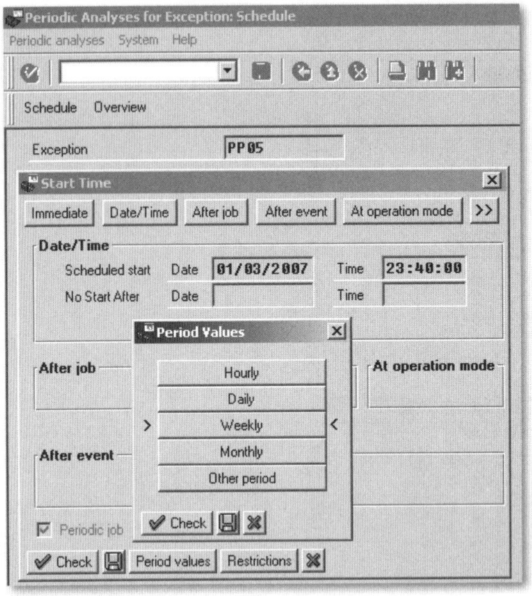

Figure 18.16 Schedule Screen for Periodic Exception Analysis, Transaction MCYB

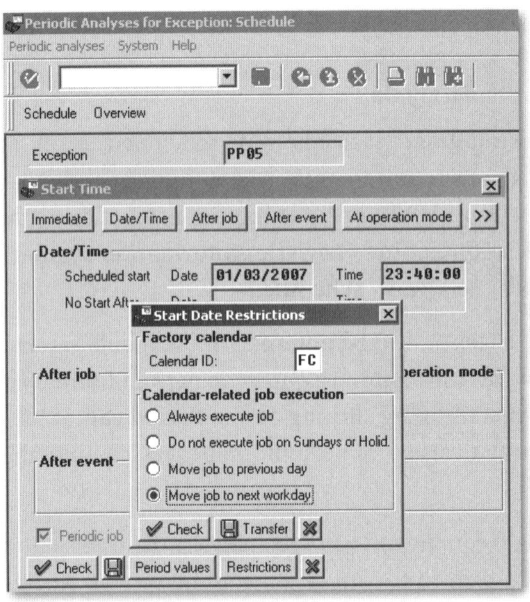

Figure 18.17 Available Options for Date Restrictions on Exception Analysis, Transaction MCYB

18.5 Executing the Exception

Often the analyst will want to test the exception or run the exception on an ad-hoc basis. The exception can be run manually by the analyst rather than in a scheduled job using Transaction MCYN. The transaction can also be found using the navigation path: **SAP Menu • Logistics • Logistics Controlling • Logistics Information System • Early Warning System • Exception Analysis.**

You can run the exception by using the values that are entered into the analysis. The analyst can also change some of the selections and the manual selection indicator must be set, as shown in Figure 18.18.

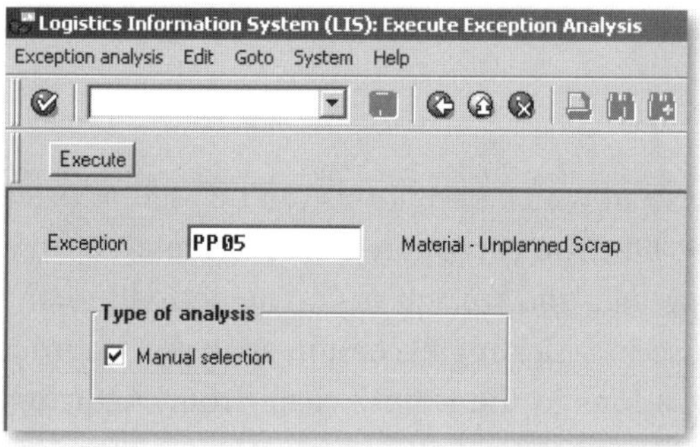

Figure 18.18 Exception Analysis with Manual Selection Indicator Set On, Transaction MCYN

If the manual selection indicator is set to on, then the analyst will be taken to the normal selection screen where he can override any of the selections from the exception. If the indicator is not set, then the transaction is executed with the predefined selections.

The results screen will show the exceptions that have been found in the data. Figure 18.19 shows the exceptions for the example we have been working with, i.e., scrap material.

The results display, seen in Figure 18.19 on the next page, shows the exceptions where the actual scrap total for the period defined was greater than the planned scrap total. Running the exception on an ad-hoc basis is a great way to quickly show the client the EWS and how powerful the exception analysis can be.

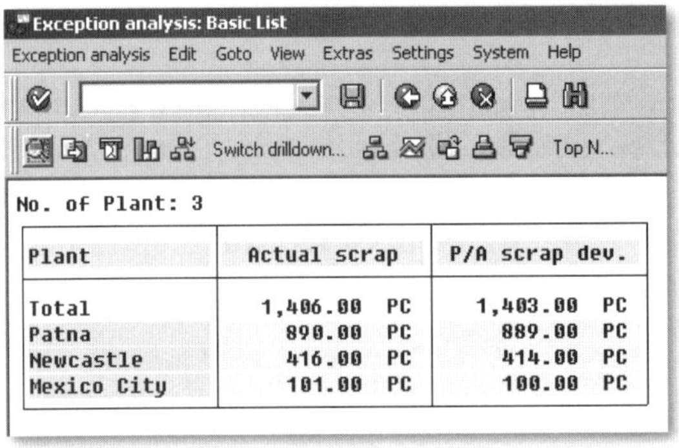

Figure 18.19 Exceptions that are the Result of Exception Analysis, Transaction MCYN

18.6 Summary

In this chapter, I discussed the way in which exceptions can be used to drive the Early Warning System in the LIS. The exception is instrumental in finding potential issues with planning data and current data. The periodic analysis is a key tool for analysts to use in repeating exception analyses, in order to prevent potentially costly situations in the supply chain from occurring. Companies often fail to identify issues before they happen, and are therefore reactive rather than proactive in their approach to supply chain issues. The more you become experienced in the LIS and the EWS, the more you can help your company or your clients leverage existing SAP functionality by developing supply chain monitoring using the EWS.

In Chapter 19, I will examine the elements that make up the Logistics Information Library (LIL), which is the repository for all the key figures of every component.

The Logistics Information Library (LIL) is the area that contains the key figures for each of the LIS components. It is available to the analyst who needs to perform cross-application analysis or work with key figures that are specific to the company.

19 Logistics Information Library

The LIL is found in each of the modular information systems, such as the PURCHIS and the SIS. It is a collection of all of the key figures within the LIS and is available for the analyst to retrieve information from the key figures directly with the data. The LIL also allows analysts to create info sets, which are a combination of key figures.

19.1 Retrieving Key Figures

The LIL allows non-technical team members to retrieve data without any specific technical information. Not all team members will have knowledge of the LIS, and creating evaluations, exceptions, etc., will not be possible for them. However, the LIL contains all the information they require to perform some data retrieval and reporting. The novice LIL user can retrieve data for the key figures via one of the following three methods:

- Retrieval by text string
- Retrieval using classification
- Retrieval using info sets

Now we can look at these in more detail.

19.1.1 Retrieval by Text String

The simplest retrieval method is to search by text string. The transaction allows searches of a number of text strings. The strings can be joined together in a search by using the operators **AND**, **OR**.

You can retrieve the text string by using Transaction MC02, or by using the navigation path: **SAP Menu • Logistics • Logistics Controlling • Logistics Information System • Info Library • Key Figure Retrieval • Using Text Strings.**

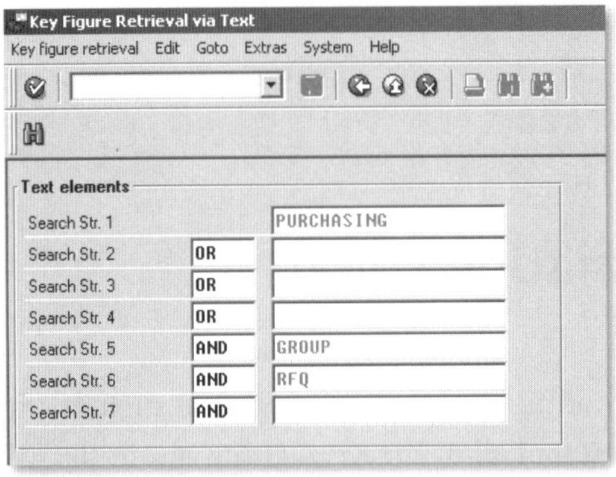

Figure 19.1 Example Key Figure Retrieval by Text String Search, Transaction MC02

In Figure 19.1, the example shows where an LIL user has entered the text "Purchasing" and also the text strings "Group" and "RFQ". The LIL user is therefore trying to find key figures that contain the words Purchasing AND Group AND RFQ.

Figure 19.2 Results of Key Figure Retrieval, Transaction MC02

The resulting screen, as shown in Figure 19.2, shows that there are three key figures that have the text strings that were entered in the initial screen. From this screen, there are a number of functions that can be carried out, which we will now address.

Call Up the Key Figure

The key figure can be called up by using the **F2** function key or from the menu: **Edit • Call Up Key Figure**. The system will link to the purchasing group analysis transaction where it can be executed and the results for the analysis displayed, as shown in Figure 19.3.

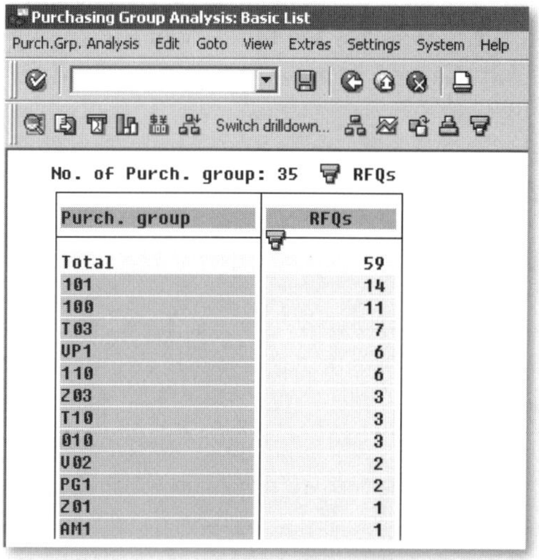

Figure 19.3 Basic List of Purchasing Group Analysis Transaction

Display Technical Information

The technical information of the key figure can be displayed, as seen in Figure 19.4, by using the menu, **Extras • Technical Info**, or by using the **Shift + F6** function keys.

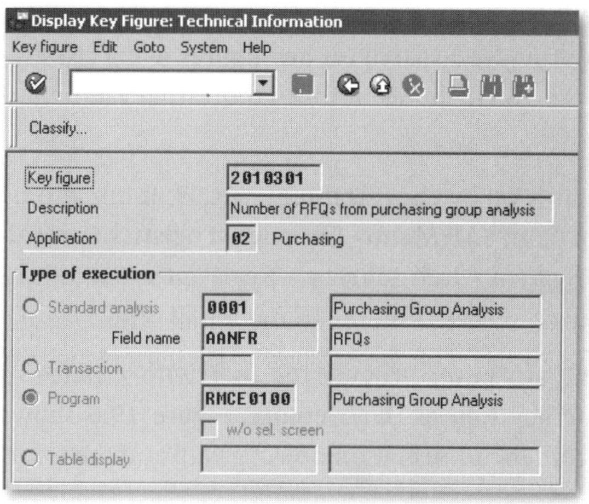

Figure 19.4 Display of Technical Information for Key Figure, Transaction MC02

Display the Retrieval Path

The retrieval path is a log of what was entered to find the key figures using the text search. The retrieval path can also be used with a classification search. The log, as shown in Figure 19.5, displays the number of the key figures shown on the results screen and the text strings that were entered initially.

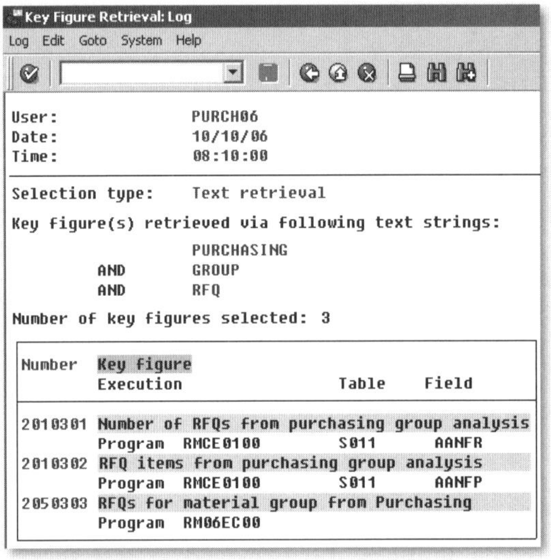

Figure 19.5 Retrieval Path, Transaction MC02

19.1.2 Retrieval by Classification

The retrieval by classification provides a search for key figures using classifying attributes. In total, there are 36 attributes in four groups that can be utilized.

The transaction code for the retrieval by classification is MC03; it can also be found by using the navigation path: **SAP Menu • Logistics • Logistics Controlling • Logistics Information System • Info Library • Key Figure Retrieval • Using Classification**.

The four groups of classifying attributes provide the user with a range of selections to help retrieve the key figures they require. Figure 19.6 shows the first screen of attributes from the information object group and the information category group.

The user can select as many classifying attributes as he or she wants to provide a narrow search. For this example, the attributes **Customer** and **Number** were selected. Figure 19.7 shows the key figure retrieval results for the search by classification from the Customer and Number attributes.

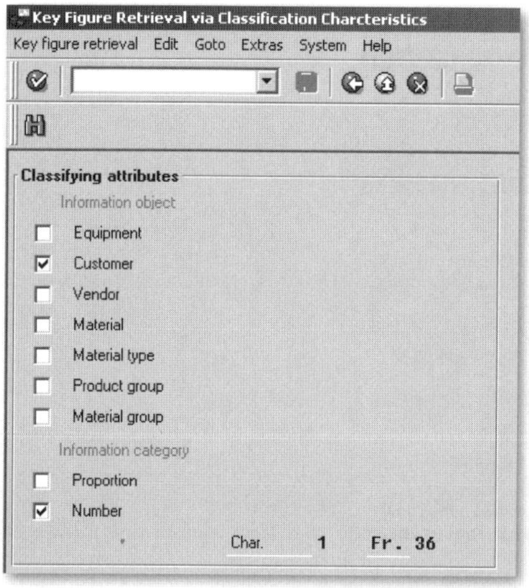

Figure 19.6 Key Figure Retrieval by Classification, Transaction MC03

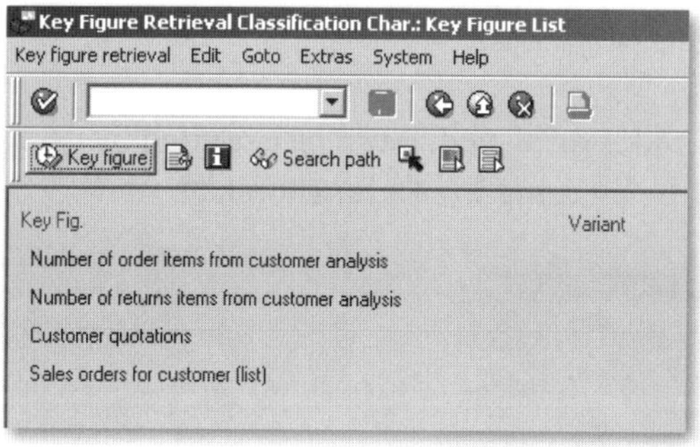

Figure 19.7 Key Figures Retrieved, Transaction MC03

19.1.3 Retrieval by Info Set

Info sets will be described in more detail in Section 19.3, but put simply; they are groups of key figures that are combined as they have common elements.

To retrieve key figures by info set, use Transaction MC01. The transaction can also be found by using the navigation path: **SAP Menu • Logistics • Logistics Controlling • Logistics Information System • Info Library • Key Figure Retrieval • Using Info Sets**.

The transaction displays the screen, shown in Figure 19.8, where the hierarchy is shown, and by selecting the info set, the next layer or the actual key figure is displayed.

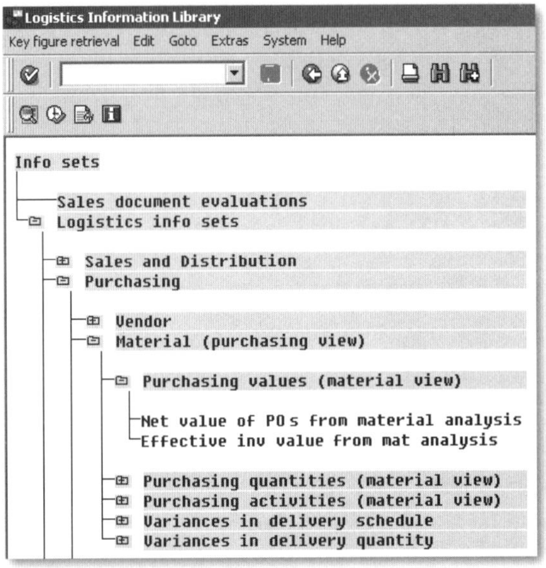

Figure 19.8 Key Retrieval by Info Set, Transaction MC01

When the key figure that is required is displayed, it can be executed by using the header menu, **Edit • Execute**, or by using the **F8** function key.

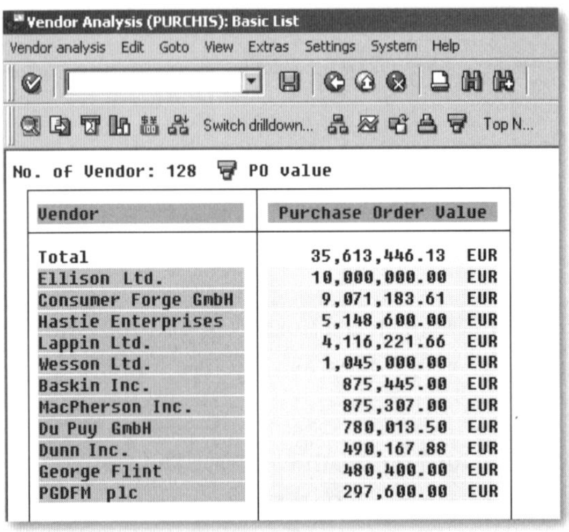

Figure 19.9 Results for Key Figures from Retrieval Using Info Sets, Transaction MC01

The results for the key figures, shown in Figure 19.9, are retrieved when the analysis is executed.

19.2 Adding Key Figures to the LIL

You can add to the LIL so that it includes key figures, which may be part of some additional functionality that has been extended to the base system, or part of another system linked to SAP. Either way, you can add key figures to the LIL to use them in the functionality.

19.2.1 Configure Key Figure Number Range

Before adding any key figures to the LIL, the number ranges for the key figures should be configured. The transaction for this configuration is MCOA, and it can be found in the configuration menu: **IMG • Logistics—General • Logistics Information System • Logistics Information Library • Number Ranges • Define Number Range Intervals for Key Figures**.

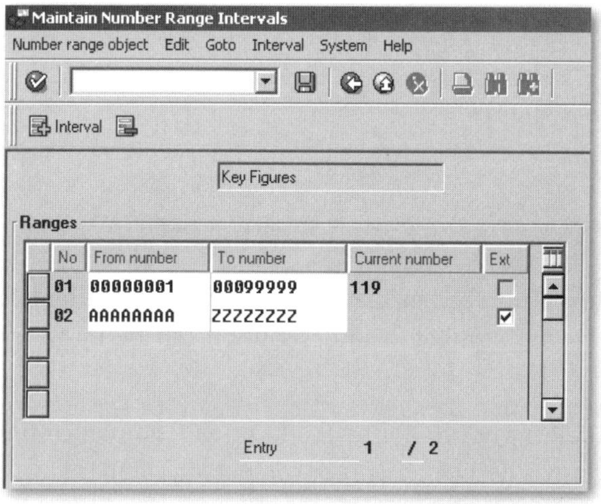

Figure 19.10 Configuration for Internal and External Number Ranges for LIL Info Sets, Transaction MCOA

The transaction allows you to configure the internal and external number ranges, as seen in Figure 19.10. The configured number ranges should conform to your company's data policies and procedures.

There is one caveat, however, when configuring the key figure number ranges. SAP uses the number range 90000000–99999999 for key figures. If the number range that you configure conflicts with SAP's internal numbering, there is the possibility that any key figures will be overwritten during a system upgrade.

19.2.2 Adding a Key Figure

To add a key figure, use Transaction MC07 or use the navigation path: **SAP Menu • Logistics • Logistics Controlling • Logistics Information System • Info Library • Key Figure • Create**.

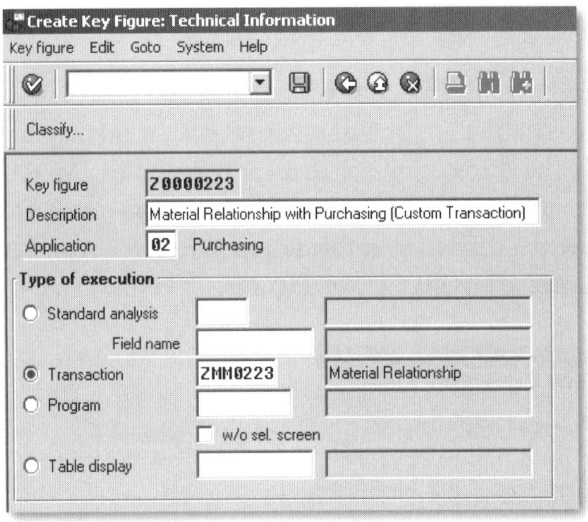

Figure 19.11 Entry Screen for Entering a New Key Figure in the LIL, Transaction MC07

The new key figure requires a number in the external range or can be left blank for an internally assigned number. The description can be up to 60 characters long.

Figure 19.11 shows that the user has to define the location from which the information for the key figure is derived. The user can enter a standard analysis, transaction, program, or table display, which will determine how the key figure is displayed.

After entering the relevant information, the user can enter the details on classifying the key figure, as shown in Figure 19.12. This information allows the retrieval of the key figure using classification.

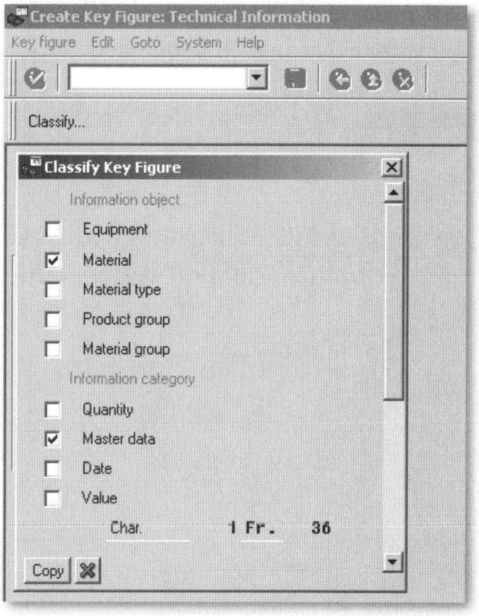

Figure 19.12 Classification Information Entered in Key Figure Creation, Transaction MC07

19.3 Adding Info Sets to the LIL

An info set is a group of key figures combined due to similar common elements. The SAP system is delivered with a hierarchy of info sets, but it is possible to add custom info sets for new key figures that are entered.

19.3.1 Types of Info Sets

There are two types of info sets: single level and multi-level. The initial screen for info set creation allows the user to determine which type of info set is being created. These are:

- Single-level info sets are where the key figures are attached to an info set
- Multi-level info sets are where the info sets are linked to another info set, thus creating a hierarchy

19.3.2 Configure Info Set Number Range

Before adding any info sets to the LIL, the number ranges for the info sets should be configured. The transaction for this configuration is MCOC, and the transaction can be found in the configuration menu: **IMG • Logistics—**

General • Logistics Information System • Logistics Information Library • Number Ranges • Define Number Range Intervals for Info Sets.

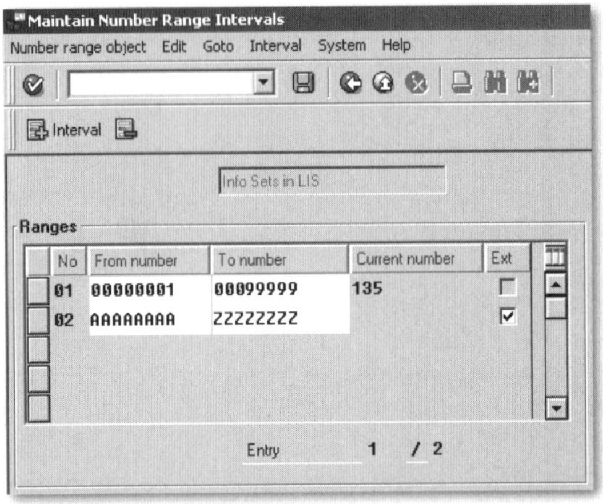

Figure 19.13 Number Range Configuration for Info Sets, Transaction MC0C

The configuration for the external number range, as shown in Figure 19.13, should not interfere with the predefined SAP number range for info sets, which is between 01000000–99999999.

19.3.3 Adding a Single-Level Info Set

The transaction to create an info set is MC04, which can be found using the navigation path: **SAP Menu • Logistics • Logistics Controlling • Logistics Information System • Info Library • Info Set • Create.**

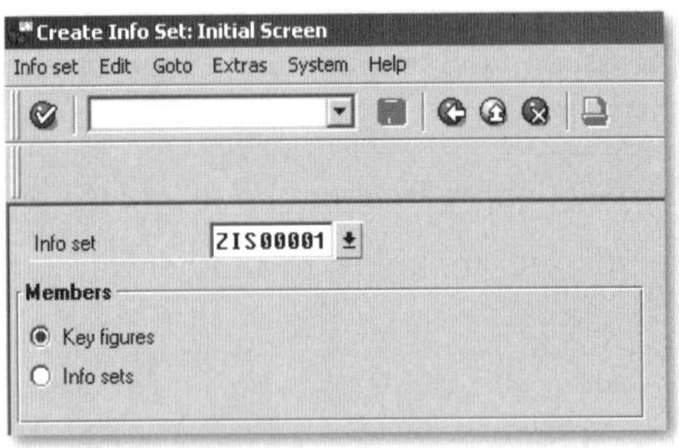

Figure 19.14 Initial Screen for Creating an Info Set, Transaction MC04

The choice can be made on the initial screen, seen in Figure 19.14, as to whether the info set is a single-level or multi-level. The user can create a single-level info set by highlighting the option in the **Members** section, which says **Key figures**.

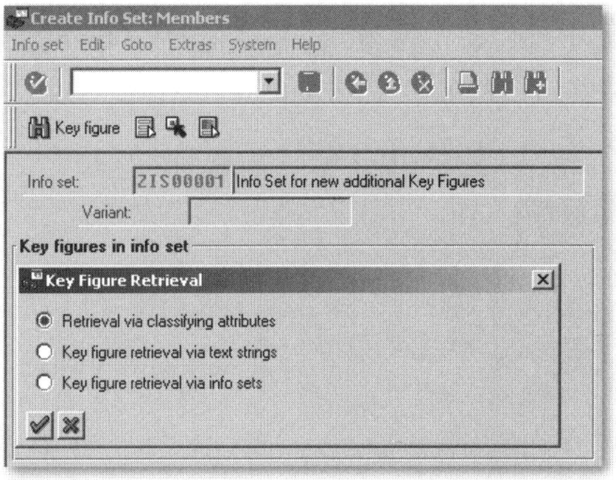

Figure 19.15 Detail Screen, Transaction MC04

The detail screen will require the addition of key figures. The key figures can be found by using one of the retrieval methods shown in Figure 19.15. We already discussed the retrieving key figures earlier in this chapter. Using one of the three retrieval methods, you can add the key figures to the info set.

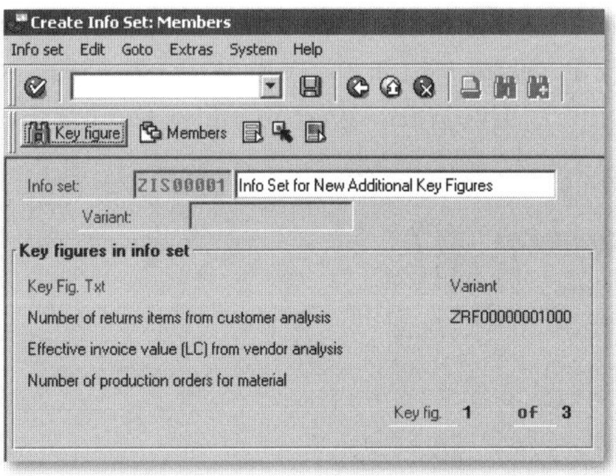

Figure 19.16 Key Figures Added to Single-Level Info Set

A number of key figures are added to the single-level info set, as shown in Figure 19.16. There is also the ability to create a variant for the key figure, which can aid in the selection of that key figure. To create a variant, use the header menu with selection, **Edit • Members Variant**, or use the **F2** function key. A pop-up dialog screen will appear asking for the variant name. From there, the variant can be created.

19.3.4 Adding a Multi-Level Info Set

The multi-level info set is created by the same transaction as the single-level, MC04. The choice is made on the initial screen as to whether the info set is single-level or multi-level. The user can create a multi-level info set by highlighting the option in the **Members** section, seen in Figure 19.17, which is **Info sets**.

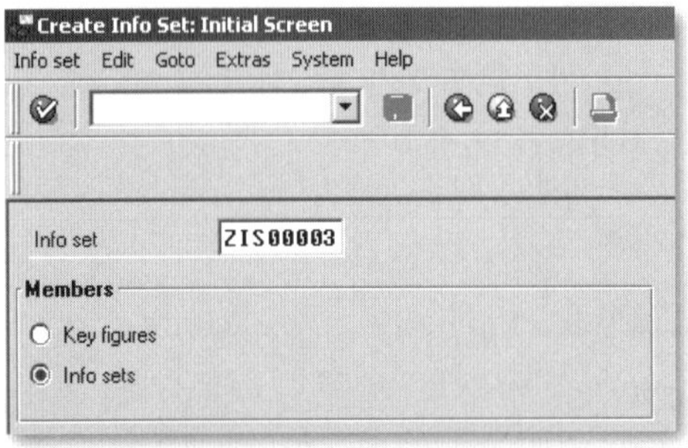

Figure 19.17 Initial Screen for Creating a Multi-Level Info Set, Transaction MC04

The multi-level info set is created by assigning other info sets to it. These info sets may be single-level or multi-level info sets. Figure 19.18 shows the assignment of the info sets to the info set you are creating. The info sets can be directly entered into the transaction, or the info sets can be searched for by using the Info set icon, which is seen in Figure 19.18, as the binoculars graphic next to it. The info set hierarchy is displayed to allow the user to search for the info set to assign.

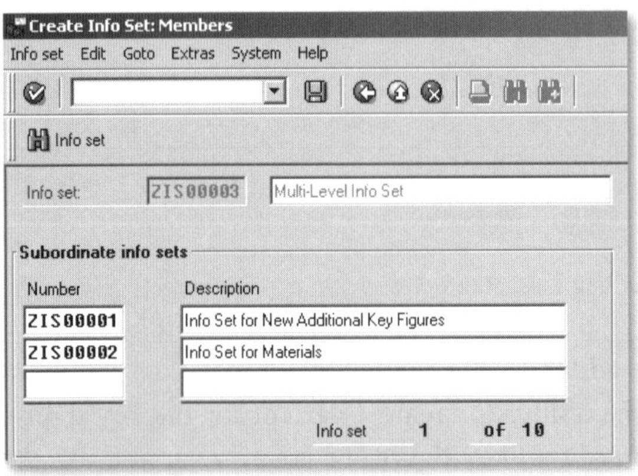

Figure 19.18 Entry Screen for Creating a Multi-Level Info Set, Transaction MC04

19.4 Summary

In this chapter, I discussed how the Logistics Information Library can be used to find information on key figures. The search facility using text, classification, or info set is quite straightforward to use. Creating key figures is important if the information is outside the norm of standard LIS functionality and needs to be retrieved by users. The creation of single-level and multi-level info sets aids users in finding key figures that were not included in the default info sets.

19.5 Book Conclusion

In this book, I examined the LIS in depth. Hopefully, you have discovered that the LIS is a powerful but flexible tool, enabling various users to perform simple tasks such as executing a standard analysis, and complex tasks such as creating exceptions in the Early Warning System, thereby preventing major catastrophes in the supply chain.

The functionality of the LIS is not well understood by clients, who have this powerful tool sitting on their systems, sometimes untouched and unused for many years, while they spend time and money on ABAP programming to perform the same tasks. You can advise your clients on the functionality of the LIS that you have learned from reading this book. I recommend that you practice what you have read here. For example, you could try creating evaluation structures, running evaluations, and performing exception analyses. Don't expect perfection in one day. Like any other module in SAP, the more you practice, the more you will hone your skills, and ultimately the LIS will become invaluable to you as a consultant and to your client who will benefit from your newfound skills.

Appendix

A Glossary

ABC Analysis This analysis is performed to classify objects according to specific criteria or performance measures. As well as being used in the Logistics Information System (LIS), ABC analysis is used in Materials Management, Plant Maintenance, Cost Accounting, and ABAP Query.

Analysis Currency This is the key for the currency in which the analysis is carried out.

Application Number The application number is the logical subdivision of the LIS into the individual business areas such as, 01 for Sales and Distribution, 02 for Purchasing, 03 for Inventory Controlling, etc.

Characteristic A characteristic is a component of an information structure. Key figures can be summarized by period for these characteristics. Each characteristic has a characteristic value.

Characteristic Drilldown A characteristic value is shown in detail with regard to a characteristic.

Classification A classification is a function that divides characteristic values into classes with reference to one key figure. This gives you a quick overview of all characteristic values for this key figure and allows you to identify trends and relationships.

Drilldown A drilldown is a function to vary the level of detail in which the information is displayed.

Dual Classification A dual classification is a function that divides characteristic values into classes with reference to two key figures. This gives you a quick matrix overview of all characteristic values for both key figures and allows you to identify trends and relationships.

Evaluation Structure Structure on which data analysis is based in the LIS. It provides the data for flexible analyses in the information systems, which consists of characteristics and key figures.

Exception An exception consists of specified characteristics or characteristic values and requirements. Requirements can be the threshold value or a trend.

Exception Group To check complex material, you can combine individual exceptions into one exception group.

Field Catalog A table that contains all defined fields with their respective attributes from all aspects. Depending on its use, a field can be a characteristic, a basic key figure, or a fixed field of the aspect's data structure.

Flexible Analyses Flexible analyses enable you to tailor the way data is combined and consolidated in order to meet individual client requirements.

Hierarchy Drilldown A characteristic value is shown in detail in an existing hierarchy.

Information Structure The area in which data is collected in the LIS. It defines a group of fields and is used for collecting and reducing data from an

SAP application. It forms the basis for analyses and evaluation.

Info Set An info set can be single-level or multilevel. The items of a single-level info set are key figures. The items of a multilevel info set are one or more subordinate info sets.

Key Figure A key figure is a criterion for evaluating the performance of a logistical activity in the past or forecasting the performance of a logistical activity in the future. Key figures can be a number or a percentage and are expressed in a currency or unit of measure.

Period Unit A period unit is assigned to every information structure. It can be a day, a week, a month, or a posting period.

Planning Scenario A planning scenario is used to determine the control parameters for long-term planning. This includes the plant where long-term planning is to be carried out, the planning period, and the independent requirements versions to be planned.

Planning Type A planning type describes a customized planning table. It is used to create and store important data from any information structure.

Selection Version Selection versions in LIS enable you to save the data of a standard analysis, or to predefine a view of the data.

Subnodes The subnodes are objects or characteristic values that exist in the system.

B Bibliography

- Arabe, Katrina C.: *Solutions for Common Purchasing Challenges*. ThomasNet Industrial NewsRoom. February 23, 2001.
- Bock, Geoffrey E.: *Business Benefits of Supply Chain Connectivity.* Patricia Seybold Group. 2001.
- Evans, James R, & Lindsay, William M.: *The Management and Control of Quality (6th Edition).* South-Western College Publications. 2004.
- Ireland, Lewis R: *Quality Management for Projects and Programs.* Project Management Institute. 1991.
- Levitt, Joel: *Complete Guide to Predictive and Preventive Maintenance.* Industrial Prcss. Ncw York, NY. 2003.
- Liker, Jeffrey: *The Toyota Way.* McGraw Hill. New York, NY. 2004.
- Monden, Yasuhiro: *Toyota Production System: An Integrated Approach to Just-In Time. Second edition.* Industrial Engineering and Management Press, Institute of Industrial Engineers. Norcross, GA. 1993.
- Roper, Matthew: *Why Shouldn't Your Business Benefit from Best Practice Buying?* Buying Support Agency, Cheltenham, United Kingdom. 2005.
- Rubrich, L. & Watson, M.: *Implementing World Class Manufacturing.* WCM Associates. Fort Wayne, IN. 1998.
- Schonberger, R.J.: *Japanese Manufacturing Techniques: Nine Hidden Lessons in Simplicity.* Free Press. New York, NY. 1982.
- Tague, Nancy: *The Quality Toolbox.* ASQ Quality Press. Milwaukee, WI. 2005.

C The Author

Born and raised in London, England Martin Murray graduated from Middlesex University in 1986, after which he entered the computer industry. In 1991 he began working with SAP R/2 in Materials Management (MM) for a London-based, multi-national beverage company.

In February 1994, Martin moved to the United States to work as a SAP R/3 MM consultant. He has implemented MM and Warehouse Management (WM) projects throughout the world. Currently employed by IBM Martin lives with his wife in Orange County, California. He is also the author of the successful 2006 SAP PRESS title, *SAP MM—Functionality and Technical Configuration*.

Acknowledgments

The author would like to specially thank Jawahara Saidullah of SAP Press for her faith in the author and her tireless efforts in getting this book completed.

Index

N

O

P

Q

R

S

T

U

V

W